Cryptocurrencies and Beyond

Cryptocurrencies and Beyond

Adapting Portfolio Theories for the Digital Era

Dr. Chenjiazi Zhong

BEP

BUSINESS EXPERT PRESS

Leader in applied, concise business books

Cryptocurrencies and Beyond: Adapting Portfolio Theories for the Digital Era

First published in 2025 by
Business Expert Press, LLC
222 East 46th Street, New York, NY 10017
www.businessexpertpress.com

ISBN-13: 978-1-63742-810-8 (paperback)
ISBN-13: 978-1-63742-811-5 (e-book)

Business Expert Press Finance and Financial Management Collection

First edition: 2025

10 9 8 7 6 5 4 3 2 1

EU SAFETY REPRESENTATIVE
Mare Nostrum Group B.V.
Mauritskade 21D
1091 GC Amsterdam
The Netherlands
gpsr@mare-nostrum.co.uk

This book, Cryptocurrencies and Beyond: Adapting Portfolio Theories for the Digital Era, *is dedicated with love and gratitude to the two most important people in my life, who have been my unwavering support and joy throughout this journey.*

To my husband, Yu Zhuang: your steadfast support, patience, and encouragement have guided me through every step of this process. Thank you for walking this path alongside me, for helping to balance the demands of work and family, and for always believing in me.

And to our son, Aiden Zhong Zhuang: your laughter, innocence, and boundless energy have brightened my days and inspired me to keep going. You are my sweetest reminder of what truly matters, and your happiness has fueled my motivation to pursue this project with heart and purpose.

To Yu and Aiden—thank you for being my foundation and my greatest joy. This book is not just a dedication to my work; it is for you, with all my love.

Description

In just over a decade, cryptocurrencies have evolved from niche interests into key players reshaping global finance. Meanwhile, central bank digital currencies combine blockchain's benefits with central bank oversight. These assets, with their high growth potential and volatility, demand new approaches to investing.

This book revisits modern portfolio theory and examines how traditional principles can be adapted for portfolios that include digital assets. Taxation and evolving compliance requirements are explored. Institutional adoption and emerging trends such as sustainable investing and AI's role in digital assets are also examined.

One of the key strengths of this book is its focus on real-world application. Each concept is illustrated with examples from actual market scenarios. This approach aims to explain not only the "why" but also the "how" of integrating digital assets, highlighting the tangible impact of various strategies on portfolio performance. **This book is a roadmap that empowers readers to seize opportunities while maintaining a disciplined and informed approach.**

Contents

Preface

In just over a decade, digital assets have transformed from a niche interest into a significant force reshaping global finance. Cryptocurrencies such as Bitcoin and Ethereum have become household names, recognized not only as innovative technologies but also as viable investments that attract both institutional players and retail investors. Central bank digital currencies (CBDCs) are pushing boundaries by combining the benefits of blockchain technology with the security and oversight of central banking, signaling the digital evolution of national currencies.

These new assets, characterized by their potential for remarkable growth and unprecedented volatility, necessitate a shift in how we approach investing and portfolio management. This book, *Cryptocurrencies and Beyond: Adapting Portfolio Theories for the Digital Era*, aims to bridge the gap between traditional investment wisdom and the rapidly evolving world of digital assets. It provides readers with the tools and insights needed to navigate this exciting yet complex landscape.

In writing this book, my goal was to create a resource that goes beyond basic explanations of digital assets. This text fills an existing gap by guiding readers through the integration of modern portfolio theory (MPT) and digital assets. Rather than relying on speculation or hype, it is grounded in rigorous research and evidence-based strategies, incorporating meta-studies from leading academics and industry experts. This approach offers a science-based perspective on digital assets, empowering readers to make well-informed decisions rather than speculative guesses.

Each chapter builds logically, offering both theoretical insights and practical applications for investors seeking to understand and leverage digital assets in their portfolios. The book begins with a thorough overview of cryptocurrencies and CBDCs, exploring the origins, structure, and future potential of each asset class. These chapters lay the groundwork for understanding digital assets as unique yet interconnected components of the financial landscape. Following this, the book revisits MPT and examines how traditional principles of diversification, risk management, and return optimization can be adapted for portfolios that include digital assets. By merging foundational concepts with new applications, these chapters establish a framework for building a resilient investment strategy that can withstand the dynamic nature of digital assets.

One of the key strengths of this book is its focus on real-world application. Each concept is illustrated with examples from actual market scenarios, including institutional investment cases and diversified digital portfolios. This approach aims to explain not only the "why" but also the "how" of integrating digital assets, highlighting the tangible impact of various strategies on portfolio performance. In the chapters "Asset Allocation Strategies" and "Assessing Digital Asset Investments," readers will discover actionable methods for balancing growth potential and risk across multiple asset classes. These sections cover strategies such as including stablecoins for stability, determining allocation percentages for cryptocurrencies based on risk tolerance, and implementing advanced diversification techniques to optimize the integration of digital assets within a traditional portfolio.

Risk management is another essential theme throughout the book. Digital assets present a unique risk profile characterized by high volatility, regulatory uncertainty, and rapid innovation cycles. Chapter 7, titled "Risk and Portfolio Management," addresses these challenges by exploring both traditional risk management principles and new approaches tailored to digital assets, such as position sizing, hedging with stablecoins, and dynamic rebalancing. These tools are designed to empower investors to leverage the upside potential of digital assets while protecting against significant drawdowns. Furthermore, the chapter discusses strategies for navigating liquidity risks, coping with extreme market volatility, and using technology to gain deeper insights into asset behavior, providing a comprehensive and adaptable framework.

No investment strategy is complete without considering the taxation and regulatory environment, particularly in the intricate world of digital assets. Chapter 8, "Taxation and Regulatory Compliance," offers a thorough overview of how various jurisdictions treat digital assets from a tax perspective, along with the implications for investors. It covers topics such as capital gains on cryptocurrency transactions and the taxation of income generated from staking and yield farming, preparing readers to meet their tax obligations and avoid costly mistakes. Additionally, the chapter addresses the evolving regulatory landscape, discussing everything from anti money laundering (AML) requirements to global trends in digital asset regulation, helping readers understand the rules and restrictions that could impact their portfolios.

The closing chapters of the book explore the institutional adoption of digital assets and provide final insights and recommendations. Chapter 9, "Institutional Adoption of Digital Assets," examines how major financial institutions, hedge funds, and asset managers are increasingly integrating cryptocurrencies, nonfungible tokens (NFTs), and other digital assets into their offerings. This shift not only underscores the growing legitimacy of digital assets but also signals to individual investors that these assets are here to stay. Through case studies and industry examples, this chapter investigates the various ways institutions approach digital asset integration and its implications for everyday investors. Finally, Chapter 10, "Final Thoughts," provides a forward-looking perspective, addressing emerging trends such as environmental, social, and governance (ESG) considerations, the role of artificial intelligence (AI) in digital asset investing, and best practices for building a sustainable digital asset strategy.

At its core, this book serves as more than just a guide to digital assets; it is a roadmap for adapting traditional investment frameworks to the new digital economy. Through a balanced blend of theoretical foundations, empirical research, and practical insights, *Cryptocurrencies and Beyond* offers a holistic view of digital asset integration, empowering readers to seize new opportunities while maintaining a disciplined and informed approach. As you engage with these chapters, I hope you find the tools and confidence needed to explore this new frontier with clarity and purpose.

In today's fast-paced financial landscape, staying ahead of trends while honoring timeless investment principles is crucial. This book is dedicated to those seeking that balance. Whether you are an asset owner, asset manager, financial intermediary, technologist, policy maker, regulator, scholar, or simply curious about the digital revolution, this book offers insights that will illuminate the path forward. Welcome to the future of investing.

PART 1

The Digital Currency Revolution

From Bitcoin to Central Bank Digital Currencies

CHAPTER 1

Cryptocurrencies

The emergence of cryptocurrencies has transformed our understanding of money, financial systems, and decentralized technologies. It all started in 2009 with the creation of Bitcoin, a digital currency designed to function independently of central banks and governments, providing a peer-to-peer (P2P) alternative to traditional financial systems. Bitcoin's innovative use of blockchain technology established the groundwork for a new era of digital assets.

As Bitcoin gained popularity, a wave of new cryptocurrencies, known as altcoins, emerged, each offering unique innovations and value propositions. This chapter explores the birth of Bitcoin, the rise of altcoins as alternatives, and the transformative role cryptocurrencies are playing in the broader financial ecosystem, reshaping industries, and challenging long-established financial norms.

Bitcoin

In the aftermath of the 2008 global financial crisis, which exposed significant vulnerabilities in the centralized banking system, an anonymous entity using the pseudonym Satoshi Nakamoto introduced Bitcoin to the world. On October 31, 2008, Nakamoto published the well-known white paper titled "Bitcoin: A Peer-to-Peer Electronic Cash System." This document outlined the framework for what would become the first decentralized digital currency, fundamentally changing our understanding of money and value.

Nakamoto (2008) proposed a system that allowed for P2P transactions without the necessity of intermediaries such as banks or financial institutions. The concept involved a decentralized network of participants, or *"nodes,"* that would verify transactions and ensure their security through cryptography.

Nakamoto also addressed the issue of double-spending, a significant challenge that had hindered earlier attempts to create digital currencies. By utilizing a *Proof-of-Work* (*PoW*) consensus mechanism that required computational effort to validate transactions, Bitcoin was able to ensure that each unit of currency could only be spent once, effectively solving this problem. Nakamoto's vision carried profound ideological implications—it challenged centralized authorities and offered an alternative to the existing financial system, which many viewed as flawed and vulnerable.

At its core, Bitcoin was designed as a decentralized digital currency, free from the control of governments, central banks, and financial intermediaries. Its creator, Nakamoto, aimed to establish a system that would restore financial sovereignty to individuals, allowing them to transfer value without relying on third parties or being subject to the decisions of central authorities.

One of the main motivations for creating Bitcoin was to address the inherent problems within fiat currency systems, where governments and central banks can manipulate the money supply. Issues such as inflation, changes in monetary policy, and economic crises often erode the purchasing power of traditional currencies, leading to instability and mistrust. Bitcoin, with its fixed supply cap of 21 million coins, offers an alternative: a deflationary currency that cannot be devalued through excessive money printing.

Bitcoin's decentralized nature also enhances transparency. Every transaction is publicly recorded on the blockchain, ensuring accountability without compromising user privacy. Moreover, by eliminating intermediaries, Bitcoin transactions can bypass geographical boundaries and reduce fees, making it particularly appealing for cross-border payments.

Additionally, Bitcoin represents a significant shift in our understanding of money ownership. In traditional banking systems, access to funds is controlled by institutions that can freeze or seize assets. In contrast, Bitcoin allows individuals complete control over their funds, protected by private keys known only to them. Essentially, Bitcoin offers financial autonomy, free from institutional interference or censorship. The birth of Bitcoin marked the beginning of a new era in finance and technology.

Bitcoin's Role as Digital Gold

In its early days, Bitcoin was envisioned primarily as a medium of exchange—a digital currency that could be used for everyday transactions. Nakamoto described it as an "electronic cash system," capable of replacing traditional money for payments (Nakamoto 2008). However, as Bitcoin gained more users and its price began to rise, it increasingly took on a secondary role: that of a store of value, akin to digital gold.

Bitcoin as a Medium of Exchange

Initially, Bitcoin was used for small P2P transactions, with early adopters trading it for goods and services in niche online markets. One of the most famous early transactions occurred on May 22, 2010, when a programmer, Laszlo Hanyecz, paid 10,000 Bitcoin (BTC) for two pizzas—an event now celebrated annually as Bitcoin Pizza Day (Wu and Wu 2023). At that time, Bitcoin was still in its infancy, and its use as a currency was limited to a small circle of enthusiasts.

As Bitcoin gained popularity, an increasing number of merchants started accepting it as a form of payment. However, Bitcoin's volatility made it less practical for everyday transactions. Prices could fluctuate wildly in short periods, which made it challenging for both businesses and consumers to use Bitcoin as a stable medium of exchange.

Bitcoin as a Store of Value

Bitcoin's transformation into digital gold" gained traction as both investors and institutions began to recognize its potential as a hedge against inflation and economic uncertainty. Similar to gold, Bitcoin is scarce, with a finite supply of 21 million coins. It is also durable and easy to store. This scarcity, coupled with its decentralized nature, made

Bitcoin an appealing option for those looking for protection against the inflationary pressures of fiat currencies.

Over time, Bitcoin's reputation as a store of value became more pronounced, making it a popular choice among long-term holders, or "HODLers," who viewed it as a means to preserve wealth. Investors increasingly regarded Bitcoin as a safe-haven asset, especially during times of financial instability or when confidence in traditional markets declined.

Key Milestones in Bitcoin's History

Halving Cycles

One of the key features of Bitcoin is its halving cycles. Approximately every four years, the reward for mining new blocks is halved, which decreases the rate at which new Bitcoins are created. These "halvings" are important because they reduce the supply of new coins, creating scarcity that has historically been followed by significant price increases.

1. First Halving (2012): Bitcoin's first halving occurred in November 2012, reducing the block reward from 50 to 25 BTC. Shortly after, Bitcoin experienced its first major bull run, with the price rising from around US$12 to over US$1,000 in the following year (Han 2024).
2. Second Halving (2016): The second halving in July 2016 reduced the reward to 12.5 BTC per block. This halving was followed by another significant rally, culminating in Bitcoin reaching its then all-time high of nearly US$20,000 in December 2017 (Taskinsoy 2021).
3. Third Halving (2020): In May 2020, the reward was halved again, this time to 6.25 BTC. The period following this halving saw Bitcoin reach new heights, with its price surpassing US$60,000 in 2021, driven by growing institutional interest and macroeconomic factors (Volosovych et al. 2023).

Major Bull Runs

Bitcoin's history has been punctuated by dramatic price increases, or bull runs, often following halving events. These rallies are typically fueled by increasing demand, media attention, and new investors entering the market.

- The 2013 Bull Run: After the first halving, Bitcoin surged from under US$100 to over US$1,000 by late 2013 (Kshetri 2023). Although this was followed by a significant correction, it marked Bitcoin's first entry into mainstream awareness.
- The 2017 Bull Run: The 2017 bull run brought Bitcoin into the spotlight, with its price soaring to nearly US$20,000 (Serres 2023). This run was largely driven by retail investors and the initial coin offering boom, though it was followed by a prolonged bear market in 2018.
- The 2020–2021 Bull Run: The most recent bull run saw Bitcoin reach an all-time high of over US$60,000, driven by institutional adoption, economic stimulus measures, and growing recognition of Bitcoin as digital gold (Humayun et al. 2024).

The Technology Behind Bitcoin

Bitcoin fundamentally combines blockchain technology with cryptographic principles. Its unique features, including decentralization, a consensus mechanism known as PoW, and cryptographic security, truly set it apart from other digital currencies.

Blockchain

At the core of Bitcoin's technology is the blockchain, a decentralized and public ledger that records all transactions made on the Bitcoin network. The blockchain consists of a series of blocks, each containing a list of verified transactions. These blocks are linked together in chronological order, forming a "chain" that extends back to the first block, known as the genesis block.

When a user initiates a Bitcoin transaction, it is broadcast to the network, where it awaits validation by miners. Once validated, the transaction is combined with others into a block. Each block includes a cryptographic hash of the previous block, linking them together and ensuring that no one can alter a past block without invalidating the entire chain. This process guarantees the integrity and immutability of the transaction history, making it resistant to tampering.

Decentralization.   Unlike traditional financial systems, where a central authority like a bank maintains and updates the ledger, Bitcoin's blockchain is managed by a global network of nodes—individual computers that run Bitcoin software. Each node keeps a copy of the blockchain, and together, they verify and share transactions across the network. This decentralized structure enhances Bitcoin's security and resilience, as there is no single point of failure that can disrupt the system or alter transaction records.

Transparency.   All Bitcoin transactions are recorded publicly on the blockchain, which makes the network highly transparent. Anyone can view the transaction history, although the identities of participants are pseudonymous and represented by their Bitcoin addresses. Cryptographic techniques ensure that only the owner of a Bitcoin address can authorize transactions from it, adding an extra layer of security.

Proof-Of-Work Consensus Mechanism

The PoW consensus mechanism is foundational to Bitcoin's security and decentralization. PoW is the consensus mechanism that powers Bitcoin and many other early blockchain networks. Its primary purpose is to secure the network, validate transactions, and ensure the integrity of the blockchain without relying on a central authority. By requiring participants to solve complex mathematical problems, PoW creates a system where verifying transactions is both difficult and energy-intensive, making attacks on the network costly and impractical.

In a PoW system, miners are responsible for validating transactions and adding them to the blockchain. Miners compete to solve a complex cryptographic puzzle that requires significant computational power. This puzzle involves finding a specific number (known as a nonce) that, when combined with the data in the block and hashed using the SHA-256 algorithm, produces a hash that meets a certain condition—typically a hash with a specific number of leading zeros.

- This puzzle is essentially trial and error, and solving it requires miners to perform millions or even billions of calculations per second. The first miner to solve the puzzle gets the right to add the next block of transactions to the blockchain.
- In return for solving the puzzle, the successful miner is rewarded with newly minted Bitcoin (known as the block reward) and the transaction fees from the transactions included in the block.

The PoW system is secured by making the process of solving the cryptographic puzzle extremely difficult and resource-intensive, but verifying the solution is computationally trivial. Once a block is added to the blockchain, other nodes can quickly verify its validity without needing to resolve the puzzle. This high level of difficulty deters malicious actors from trying to alter the blockchain because:

1. Rewriting the blockchain would require more than 50 percent of the network's total computational power, which is incredibly expensive and difficult to achieve. This is known as the 51 percent attack problem (Aponte-Novoa et al. 2021). The energy and hardware costs involved in such an attack make it highly unlikely, ensuring network security.
2. To maintain consistency in the time it takes to find a new block (approximately every 10 minutes for Bitcoin), the network regularly adjusts the difficulty of the puzzles (Kraft 2016). If more miners join the network and block times get faster, the difficulty increases, and if miners leave and block times slow down, the difficulty decreases. This self-adjustment keeps the blockchain stable and secure.

The PoW mechanism promotes decentralization because it allows anyone with the necessary computing power to participate in the mining process. There is no need for trust between participants; the network operates on cryptographic proof rather than human intervention. PoW ensures that the blockchain is maintained by a decentralized network of nodes, removing the need for a central authority. The fact that thousands of miners compete globally adds to the security of the system, as no single entity controls the network.

The sheer computational power required to attack a PoW network makes it incredibly secure. The higher the hash rate (total computational power of the network), the more secure the blockchain. Additionally, PoW is relatively straightforward to understand and implement. It has been proven to work effectively, with Bitcoin running securely on this mechanism since 2009. Miners are incentivized to act honestly because they receive block rewards for mining valid blocks. If they attempt to add fraudulent transactions, the block would be rejected by the network, and they would lose the computational effort and potential reward.

PoW ensures that the blockchain remains immutable, transparent, and trustless by making attacks on the network prohibitively expensive. While it has faced criticism for its environmental impact (Wendl et al. 2023), PoW has proven to be an effective and secure system for blockchain networks, laying the groundwork for the rise of cryptocurrencies and decentralized technologies.

Cryptography

Cryptography is at the heart of how digital assets function, providing the foundation for security, privacy, and trust in blockchain systems. At its core, cryptography is the practice of securing communication through techniques that ensure data privacy, authenticity, and integrity. Public-key cryptography, hash functions, digital signatures, and advanced cryptographic techniques such as elliptic curve cryptography (ECC) and Merkle trees ensure that transactions on blockchain networks are secure, tamper-proof, and efficient.

Public-Key Cryptography. *Public-key cryptography*, also known as asymmetric cryptography, is the core cryptographic system used in digital assets such as Bitcoin. This system uses two keys—a public key and a private key—to secure transactions.

1. The public key is like an address that others can use to send digital assets to you. It is shared openly on the blockchain, and anyone can use it to initiate transactions with you.
2. The private key, however, must be kept secret. It is used to sign transactions and prove ownership of the digital assets associated with a public key. Without the private key, a user cannot access or transfer their digital assets.

When a transaction is made, the sender uses their private key to sign the transaction. This signature is then verified by the network using the sender's public key. The verification process ensures that the transaction was authorized by the correct person (the holder of the private key) and that the transaction has not been altered.

- Example: In a Bitcoin transaction, when someone sends you Bitcoin, they use your public key to send the funds, but only you can access and spend the Bitcoin using your private key. If you want to send Bitcoin, you must use your private key to sign the transaction, which the network can verify using your public key.

Hash Functions. Cryptographic hash functions play a crucial role in securing the blockchain. A hash function takes an input (data of any size) and produces a fixed-length string of characters, typically represented as a hash. The result is a unique output that is mathematically tied to the input but cannot be reversed to discover the original input.

Hash functions ensure the immutability of blockchain transactions. Each block in the blockchain contains a hash of the previous block's data, which links the blocks together in a chain. If a single transaction within a block is changed, the hash of that block will change, breaking the chain and alerting the network to the tampering.

In Bitcoin, the cryptographic hash function used is SHA-256. This algorithm processes data into a 256-bit hash, providing high security for both transactions and block verification. Hash functions are also used to ensure the integrity of transactions. Since any small change in the input data produces a completely different hash, users and nodes can instantly verify whether data has been altered.

- Example: In Bitcoin mining, miners attempt to find a nonce (a number) that, when combined with the data in a block and hashed, produces a hash that meets specific criteria (e.g., starting with a certain number of zeros). The difficulty of finding such a nonce ensures the security of the network.

Digital Signatures. Digital signatures ensure that cryptocurrency transactions are both authentic and tamper-proof. When a user initiates a transaction, their private key is used to create a digital signature, which proves the authenticity of the transaction without revealing the private key itself. Digital signatures verify that the transaction came from the rightful owner of the funds. Since the private key is never shared, the system provides strong authentication while maintaining privacy. Once a digital signature is created, the user cannot deny their involvement in the transaction, as the signature can only be generated with the user's private key. This ensures nonrepudiation, meaning the sender cannot later claim they did not authorize the transaction.

- Example: When Alice sends Bob one Bitcoin, her private key signs the transaction. The digital signature can be verified using her public key, confirming that Alice authorized the transfer without ever exposing her private key to the network.

Elliptic Curve Cryptography.   *ECC* is a type of public-key cryptography used in Bitcoin and other digital assets for efficient encryption. ECC provides the same level of security as traditional cryptographic systems but with smaller key sizes, making it faster and more efficient.

ECC is preferred in cryptocurrency systems because it uses smaller key sizes, which means lower computational overhead while maintaining strong security. This makes ECC well-suited for the resource-constrained environments in blockchain networks where millions of transactions are processed.

- Example: Bitcoin uses the secp256k1 elliptic curve for generating public–private key pairs. This curve allows users to securely generate a small public key from a private key while ensuring that the relationship between the keys remains secure.

Merkle Trees. *Merkle trees* are a cryptographic structure used to efficiently and securely verify large amounts of data. In blockchain technology, Merkle trees ensure the integrity and consistency of transactions in each block.

A Merkle tree works by hashing individual transaction data and pairing the hashes to create a higher level hash, continuing this process until a Merkle root is formed. The Merkle root is a single hash that represents all the transactions in the block. The Merkle tree structure allows for efficient verification of large sets of data, as only a small subset of the data needs to be checked to verify that a specific transaction is part of a block. This is particularly useful for light nodes that do not need to store the entire blockchain but can still verify transactions.

- Example: In Bitcoin, the Merkle root is included in the block header, and miners use it to verify that all transactions within the block are valid and haven't been altered.

Beyond Bitcoin, several cryptocurrencies use advanced cryptographic techniques to enhance privacy and anonymity. As digital assets continue to evolve, cryptographic innovations will remain central to their advancement, enhancing both security and privacy in the digital financial ecosystem.

Altcoins

While Bitcoin's innovation was revolutionary, it had certain limitations that became apparent as the technology evolved. Bitcoin was designed primarily as a store of value and medium of exchange, but its architecture and consensus mechanism—PoW—created hurdles in terms of scalability, transaction speed, and energy consumption. These constraints opened the door for alternative cryptocurrencies, or *altcoins*, to emerge. Altcoins refer to all cryptocurrencies other than Bitcoin. Altcoins provide alternatives with unique features, innovations, and use cases and are designed to improve upon Bitcoin's design or address specific needs in the growing blockchain and cryptocurrency ecosystem.

Altcoins vary widely in their consensus mechanisms, utility, governance models, and underlying technology, providing investors and users with a diverse range of options for participating in the digital asset market. Altcoins are often categorized based on their purpose or underlying technology. The major categories of altcoins include stablecoins, utility tokens, governance tokens, security tokens, meme coins, privacy coins, and platform tokens.

Stablecoins

Stablecoins are designed to reduce the volatility typically associated with cryptocurrencies by pegging their value to a stable asset such as fiat currency (e.g., the U.S. dollar), commodities (e.g., gold), or even other cryptocurrencies.

- Examples: Tether (USDT), USD Coin (USDC), and Dai (DAI).

Stablecoins are often used for payments, trading, or as a hedge against market volatility. They provide stability in decentralized finance (DeFi) ecosystems and are a popular choice for moving money quickly and efficiently within the cryptocurrency space.

Utility Tokens

Utility tokens grant users access to specific products or services within a blockchain network. These tokens are used to power *decentralized applications (dApps)* and protocols, offering various functionalities such as transaction fees, governance voting, and access to platform services.

- Examples: Ethereum (ETH), Chainlink (LINK), and Filecoin (FIL).

Utility tokens are crucial for the functioning of decentralized ecosystems, enabling interactions within DeFi platforms, nonfungible token (NFT) marketplaces, and decentralized data storage networks.

Governance Tokens

Governance tokens give holders the ability to vote on protocol changes and governance decisions within a decentralized organization or network. These tokens allow the community to have a say in the development and direction of a project, aligning with the ethos of decentralization.

- Examples: Uniswap (UNI), Aave (AAVE), and Compound (COMP).

Holders of governance tokens can participate in protocol upgrades, changes to fee structures, and other governance matters, helping to steer the direction of DeFi projects and dApps.

Security Tokens

Security tokens represent ownership in real-world assets such as stocks, bonds, real estate, or other investment products. These tokens are regulated and subject to securities laws, making them different from utility tokens. Security tokens provide liquidity and fractional ownership of traditionally illiquid assets.

- Examples: tZERO and Polymath.

Security tokens enable the tokenization of assets, allowing fractional ownership and greater liquidity for real estate, company shares, or other investment vehicles.

Meme Coins

Meme coins are a subcategory of altcoins that are often created as a joke or based on internet culture and memes. Despite their lighthearted nature, some meme coins have gained significant popularity and market value.

- Examples: Dogecoin (DOGE) and Shiba Inu (SHIB).

While often speculative and lacking in technical innovation, meme coins have garnered large communities and have been used for tipping, charitable donations, and online payments.

Privacy Coins

Privacy coins are cryptocurrencies designed to provide greater anonymity and privacy for users by obscuring transaction details such as sender, receiver, and transaction amount. They use advanced cryptographic techniques to ensure transactions are private.

- Examples: Monero (XMR), Zcash (ZEC), and Dash.

Privacy coins are popular among users who prioritize financial privacy and data security. They are designed to offer untraceable transactions, which can appeal to users in regions with restrictive financial oversight or individuals seeking more discretion.

Platform Tokens

Platform tokens are digital assets that power blockchain networks, typically those designed for creating and hosting dApps and *smart contracts*. These tokens are used to pay transaction fees, execute smart contracts, and reward network participants.

- Examples: Ethereum (ETH), Cardano (ADA), and Polkadot (DOT).

Platform tokens are essential for the operation of blockchain ecosystems that support smart contracts and decentralized applications, enabling developers and users to interact with the blockchain.

As altcoins gained traction, Bitcoin's dominance in the cryptocurrency market has slowly declined over time. Altcoins represent a vibrant and competitive ecosystem, with each new project offering unique innovations that push the boundaries of blockchain technology.

Ethereum

Among all the altcoins that have emerged since Bitcoin, none has had as profound an impact as Ethereum. Launched in 2015 by Vitalik Buterin and a group of developers, Ethereum expanded the potential of blockchain technology beyond simple transactions (Youvan 2024).

Unlike Bitcoin, which primarily serves as a decentralized currency, Ethereum is a general-purpose blockchain that introduced the concept of smart contracts. These are self-executing contracts that automatically enforce the terms of an agreement when certain conditions are met (Parenti et al. 2023).

Ethereum is often described as a Turing-complete blockchain, meaning it can execute complex computations and support a wide range of programming instructions. This flexibility allows Ethereum to serve as a platform for various dApps, including financial services, gaming, supply chain management, and more.

At the heart of Ethereum's technology is the Ethereum Virtual Machine (EVM). This decentralized computational engine enables anyone to deploy and execute smart contracts on the Ethereum network. The EVM ensures that smart contracts run consistently and independently across the network, regardless of where the contract is executed. This programmability makes Ethereum an attractive option for developers aiming to build decentralized applications.

Ether (ETH) is the native cryptocurrency of the Ethereum network. While it can be used for payments such as Bitcoin, its primary purpose is to function as "gas" to pay for the computational resources required to execute smart contracts and transactions. Users must pay gas fees in

ETH to compensate miners (or validators, in Ethereum's Proof-of-Stake [PoS] system) for validating and processing transactions.

Smart Contracts

Ethereum's most significant innovation is the introduction of smart contracts. A smart contract is a piece of code stored on the Ethereum blockchain that defines the terms of an agreement and the conditions under which it will execute.

- Example: In an online marketplace, a smart contract could automatically transfer payment to a seller once the buyer confirms receipt of the goods. Once deployed, smart contracts cannot be altered, ensuring trustless execution and reducing the need for intermediaries such as banks, lawyers, or brokers.

Ethereum has become the backbone of the DeFi movement, which aims to recreate traditional financial services—such as lending, borrowing, trading, and earning interest—on the blockchain without the need for centralized institutions. Platforms such as Aave, Compound, and Uniswap utilize Ethereum's smart contracts to offer users financial services that are accessible, transparent, and secure.

Nonfungible Tokens.   Ethereum is also home to the boom of NFTs, offering a robust infrastructure for the creation, trading, and ownership of unique digital assets such as art, music, collectibles, and virtual real estate. The ERC-721 token standard underpins NFTs on Ethereum, allowing developers to build tokens that represent distinct, noninterchangeable items (Ko et al. 2024). This standard enables each token to hold unique metadata, making it possible for creators to mint one-of-a-kind digital assets.

Platforms such as OpenSea and Rarible, two of the largest NFT marketplaces, rely on Ethereum's blockchain to facilitate decentralized trading of these assets. Despite rising competition, Ethereum remains the dominant platform for NFT innovation due to its well-established ecosystem, extensive developer support, and proven security of its smart contract functionality.

Proof-Of-Stake

One of Ethereum's most significant developments is its transition from a PoW consensus mechanism, similar to Bitcoin's, to a PoS model as part of the Ethereum 2.0 upgrade, also known as "The Merge." This transition addresses some of Ethereum's key challenges, including scalability, energy efficiency, and transaction costs (Kapengut and Mizrach 2023).

Under the original PoW system, miners compete to solve complex cryptographic puzzles to validate transactions and secure the network, consuming large amounts of energy. In contrast, the PoS mechanism replaces miners with validators who are selected to propose and validate new blocks based on the amount of ETH they hold and stake. This shift reduces energy consumption and makes the network more environmentally friendly.

A major motivation for transitioning to PoS was the environmental concerns associated with PoW mining. After "The Merge," which occurred in September 2022, Ethereum reduced its energy consumption by over 99 percent, making it far more sustainable and appealing to climate-conscious investors (Zhong 2024).

With PoS, Ethereum now relies on validators who must stake a minimum amount of ETH to participate in securing the network. Validators are randomly chosen to propose and validate new blocks, receiving rewards in ETH for their efforts. If validators behave dishonestly, they risk losing a portion of their staked ETH, which incentivizes good behavior and helps maintain network security.

Beyond Ethereum

While Ethereum dominates the altcoin space due to its pioneering smart contract platform, a wide range of other altcoins have emerged, each offering unique features, consensus mechanisms, and use cases that address specific challenges or introduce new innovations to the blockchain ecosystem. These altcoins extend beyond just being alternatives to Ethereum, with many playing critical roles in DeFi, interoperability, scalability, and privacy.

Cardano

Cardano (ADA) is a third-generation blockchain that focuses on scalability, sustainability, and interoperability. It uses a unique PoS consensus mechanism called Ouroboros, which is designed to be more energy-efficient than Ethereum's PoW system.

Cardano's development is based on a peer-reviewed research model, with a strong emphasis on formal methods and security. Cardano's Alonzo upgrade introduced smart contract functionality, enabling dApps and DeFi on its network. Cardano allows ADA holders to participate in the governance and future upgrades of the network through its Project Catalyst system.

Cardano aims to provide solutions for real-world problems, especially in areas such as financial inclusion in developing countries, with initiatives in education, identity verification, and supply chain management.

Polkadot

Polkadot (DOT) is a next-generation blockchain that focuses on interoperability between different blockchains, allowing them to operate together and share information seamlessly. Created by Gavin Wood, one of Ethereum's cofounders, Polkadot enables multiple blockchains to interconnect using a shared security model (Arnone 2024).

Polkadot's unique architecture allows individual blockchains (parachains) to run in parallel, enabling higher throughput and scalability. Polkadot's relay chain enables different blockchains to communicate and transfer data securely, solving the issue of blockchain fragmentation. Polkadot uses a more advanced version of PoS to secure its network, ensuring decentralization and efficient block validation.

Polkadot is ideal for developers creating decentralized applications that need to communicate across different blockchains and for those focused on scalable, high-performance platforms.

Solana

Solana (SOL) is a highly scalable blockchain designed for fast, low-cost transactions. It has gained popularity due to its ability to handle thousands of transactions per second (TPS) with very low fees, making it a strong competitor to Ethereum in the dApp and DeFi space.

Solana's unique consensus mechanism combines PoS with Proof of History, which timestamps transactions to increase throughput and enable high-speed transactions. Solana boasts a throughput of more than 50,000 TPS, significantly higher than Ethereum's current capacity, making it suitable for decentralized exchanges, NFTs, and other high-volume applications. Solana's fast processing speeds result in much lower transaction costs compared to Ethereum, making it more attractive for dApps, especially DeFi projects.

Solana is known for its burgeoning DeFi and NFT ecosystems, with popular projects such as Serum (decentralized exchange) and Metaplex (NFT platform) built on its network.

Avalanche

Avalanche (AVAX) is a blockchain platform known for its speed, scalability, and low fees. It aims to offer DeFi solutions and supports smart contracts that are fully compatible with Ethereum, making it easy for developers to migrate their dApps from Ethereum to Avalanche.

Avalanche uses a novel consensus mechanism known as Avalanche consensus, which achieves finality in just a few seconds and allows for thousands of validators to participate in the network's security. Avalanche is compatible with EVM, meaning developers can easily deploy their Ethereum-based applications on Avalanche. Avalanche enables the creation of custom blockchains, called subnets, that can be tailored for specific use cases, industries, or regulations.

Avalanche is growing as a platform for DeFi projects, gaming, and enterprise applications, with major projects such as Aave and Curve Finance expanding to its ecosystem.

Binance Coin

Binance Coin (BNB) is the native cryptocurrency of the Binance Smart Chain (BSC), a blockchain platform launched by the world's largest cryptocurrency exchange, Binance. BSC is known for its fast transaction speeds and low fees, making it a popular alternative to Ethereum, especially for DeFi and NFT projects.

BSC runs in parallel with the Binance Chain, allowing users to move assets between the two blockchains for improved flexibility and performance. BSC offers significantly lower transaction fees compared to Ethereum, making it a popular platform for decentralized exchanges, NFTs, and other dApps. BSC can handle up to 160 TPS, providing faster settlement times for transactions compared to Ethereum's current capabilities.

BNB is used to pay for transactions on the BSC and Binance exchange, and BSC hosts a growing ecosystem of DeFi projects such as PancakeSwap, Venus, and Autofarm.

Chainlink

Chainlink (LINK) is a decentralized oracle network that enables smart contracts to securely interact with real-world data, APIs, and traditional systems. It's essential for bringing off-chain data into blockchain applications, making smart contracts more versatile and useful.

Chainlink connects smart contracts to external data sources, ensuring that the data used in blockchain applications is accurate, secure, and tamper-proof. Chainlink can integrate with any blockchain, enabling cross-chain functionality and expanding the reach of its data services. Chainlink aggregates data from multiple sources, improving the accuracy and reliability of the information used by smart contracts.

Chainlink is critical for DeFi applications, insurance, gaming, and supply chain management that require real-world data to function. DeFi platforms such as Aave, Synthetix, and Yearn Finance rely on Chainlink oracles for price feeds and other essential data.

Tezos

Tezos (XTZ) is a self-amending blockchain known for its focus on governance and upgradability without requiring hard forks. It uses PoS and is designed to evolve over time through an on-chain governance system where token holders vote on protocol upgrades.

Tezos allows its community to vote on changes and upgrades to the network, ensuring that it can adapt to future innovations without splitting into different chains. Tezos's PoS mechanism is more energy-efficient compared to PoW systems, making it attractive for environmentally conscious projects. Tezos supports smart contracts and decentralized applications, with a growing ecosystem in areas such as DeFi and NFTs.

Tezos is increasingly being used for NFT platforms, gaming, and decentralized finance. It is also known for being adopted in enterprise and institutional applications due to its focus on security and governance.

Algorand

Algorand (ALGO) is a blockchain platform that focuses on speed, security, and decentralization. It uses a unique Pure Proof-of-Stake (PPoS) consensus mechanism that promotes inclusivity and decentralization by allowing token holders to participate in block validation.

Algorand is highly scalable, with the ability to process thousands of transactions per second while maintaining low fees and fast finality. Its PPoS mechanism ensures that the network remains environmentally sustainable, with minimal energy consumption. Algorand has been gaining traction in the DeFi space, with projects such as Yieldly and Algofi building on its platform.

Algorand is used for cross-border payments, digital asset issuance, and DeFi, with applications ranging from government-issued digital currencies to enterprise solutions.

Cryptocurrencies in the Broader Financial Ecosystem

Cryptocurrencies, once considered a fringe technology, have steadily gained traction and become integrated into the broader financial ecosystem. Originally introduced as decentralized alternatives to fiat currencies, their role has expanded significantly beyond simple transactions. As of this writing, cryptocurrencies are viewed not only as a medium of exchange but also as a hedge against inflation, speculative investment vehicles, and part of a new financial infrastructure powered by blockchain technology.

As a Hedge Against Inflation or Fiat Currency Devaluation

One of the most compelling narratives surrounding cryptocurrencies, especially Bitcoin, is their potential to act as a hedge against inflation and the devaluation of fiat currencies. This aspect has gained more attention during periods of economic instability and rising inflation, when trust in traditional financial systems diminishes. Bitcoin, for example, has a maximum supply of 21 million coins, meaning that no central authority can inflate its supply by creating more coins. This inherent scarcity sharply contrasts with fiat currencies, which are subject to monetary policy decisions, such as quantitative easing, that can increase the money supply and diminish purchasing power.

In countries facing rapid inflation or hyperinflation—such as Venezuela, Argentina, and Turkey—cryptocurrencies have offered a safe haven for those looking to protect their wealth. As fiat currencies lose value due to central bank policies or political instability, Bitcoin's deflationary design and global accessibility make it a viable alternative for preserving wealth.

- Example: During Venezuela's hyperinflation crisis, the local currency, the bolívar, saw its purchasing power erode dramatically. Many Venezuelans turned to Bitcoin and other cryptocurrencies as a means to safeguard their savings, frequently using peer-to-peer exchanges to convert their devalued fiat currency into digital assets.

Beyond inflation, cryptocurrencies have gained popularity as a hedge against currency devaluation in countries with unstable governments or economies. When national currencies face devaluation due to economic mismanagement or geopolitical risks, cryptocurrencies provide an alternative that is not tied to any specific country's fiscal policies.

- Example: In Turkey, the value of the lira has significantly declined due to rising inflation and central bank interventions. As a result, Turkish citizens increasingly turned to cryptocurrencies to protect their wealth. Bitcoin and Tether (a stablecoin pegged to the US. dollar) experienced notable spikes in trading volume as locals sought to escape their weakening currency.

Adoption in Everyday Transactions Versus Speculative Investment Vehicles

Although Bitcoin was originally envisioned as a peer-to-peer electronic cash system, its purpose has evolved over time. In the cryptocurrency ecosystem, there is a tension between two main roles: using Bitcoin for everyday transactions and treating it as a speculative investment.

- Example: Major companies such as Microsoft, Overstock, and AT&T now accept Bitcoin as a form of payment. Additionally, platforms such as PayPal and Square have integrated features for buying, selling, and using cryptocurrency, enabling millions of users to engage with crypto in their daily transactions.

While some cryptocurrencies are designed to function as a medium of exchange, much of the market activity surrounding Bitcoin and other altcoins has been driven by speculation. In recent years, Bitcoin has gained a reputation as an investment asset, similar to commodities such as gold and oil, and this has primarily fueled its dramatic price increases.

The speculative nature of cryptocurrencies has attracted both retail investors and institutions. Major bull runs in 2017 and again in 2020–2021 saw Bitcoin reach all-time highs, driven by increased institutional adoption, retail fear of missing out, and the introduction of new financial products such as Bitcoin exchange-traded funds (ETFs) and futures contracts.

- Example: The launch of Coinbase's IPO in April 2021 and the introduction of the ProShares Bitcoin Strategy ETF in October 2021 have added legitimacy to the idea of Bitcoin as a speculative asset, appealing to a wider range of investors. However, this has also resulted in increased volatility, as many investors tend to buy and sell cryptocurrencies based on market sentiment rather than underlying fundamentals.

Cryptocurrencies occupy a unique position in the financial landscape, serving both as a medium of exchange and as investment assets. Stablecoins such as Tether (USDT) and USD Coin (USDC), which are pegged to fiat currencies, are increasingly used for payments and cross-border remittances, which helps stabilize their use in commerce. In contrast, more volatile cryptocurrencies such as Bitcoin and Ethereum are often viewed as long-term investments, akin to stocks or commodities.

Summary

The rise of Bitcoin marked the beginning of a financial revolution, introducing a decentralized form of digital currency that operates independently of traditional financial institutions. Its innovative use of blockchain technology paved the way for the emergence of altcoins—various cryptocurrencies that provide alternatives to Bitcoin, each aimed at improving or specializing in different aspects of decentralized finance. From Ethereum's smart contracts to privacy-focused coins, these digital assets have expanded the cryptocurrency ecosystem, fostering innovation and competition. Together, Bitcoin and altcoins are not just reshaping the concept of money; they are challenging the fundamental principles of the global financial system, offering new opportunities for financial inclusion, transparency, and disruption. As cryptocurrencies continue to evolve, their influence in the broader financial world is likely to deepen, affecting how we save, invest, and exchange value in the digital age.

CHAPTER 2

Central Bank Digital Currencies

As the digital revolution transforms the global financial landscape, CBDCs have become a key focus for governments and central banks. Unlike decentralized digital currencies such as Bitcoin, CBDCs are state-backed digital versions of traditional fiat currencies. They are designed to combine the advantages of digital assets while maintaining central authority and control over the monetary system.

This chapter explores the essential differences between CBDCs and cryptocurrencies, emphasizing how central banks aim to modernize payment systems and enhance financial inclusion, all while ensuring security and regulatory oversight. Additionally, we will examine prominent CBDC projects from around the world, including China's digital yuan, The Bahamas's Sand Dollar, the European Central Bank (ECB)'s plans for a digital euro, and the Federal Reserve (Fed)'s potential digital dollar.

Lastly, we will investigate the evolving roles of governments and central banks in the adoption of digital assets, including El Salvador's Bitcoin experiment and the emergence of regulatory sandbox initiatives that foster innovation while addressing the risks associated with this new digital era.

Central Bank Digital Currencies Versus Digital Currencies

Unlike traditional forms of central bank money, such as physical cash or reserves held by commercial banks, CBDCs exist solely in digital form. However, like cash, CBDCs represent a direct claim on the central bank and can be used for everyday transactions, whether in retail payments by the public or in wholesale markets between financial institutions. CBDCs are essentially the digital equivalent of fiat currency, backed by the full faith and credit of the issuing central bank. They are designed to function as legal tender, meaning they are recognized by law as an official medium for exchanging goods, services, and settling debts.

The primary purpose of CBDCs is to provide a secure, efficient, and accessible digital currency that can be seamlessly integrated into the digital economy. As digital payments become increasingly common in many countries, central banks are exploring CBDCs as a way to modernize the monetary system, reduce reliance on cash, and offer a stable, state-backed alternative to private cryptocurrencies.

CBDCs can serve multiple functions in modern economies, including:

1. Enhancing Payment Efficiency: CBDCs can enable faster, cheaper, and more secure payment systems, both domestically and internationally.
2. Fostering Financial Inclusion: In areas where access to traditional banking services is limited, CBDCs could offer a simple, low-cost way for individuals to access digital financial services.
3. Supporting Monetary Policy: CBDCs provide central banks with a new tool for conducting monetary policy, allowing for more precise measures, such as direct transfers to citizens during economic crises.

There are two main types of CBDCs: retail CBDCs and wholesale CBDCs.

1. Retail CBDCs: These are designed for general public use, allowing individuals and businesses to hold digital currency directly with the central bank, similar to how they hold physical cash or commercial bank deposits. Retail CBDCs can be used for everyday transactions, providing a digital alternative to cash.
2. Wholesale CBDCs: Aimed at financial institutions, wholesale CBDCs facilitate interbank settlements and other high-value transactions. They can streamline payment systems, making

settlement processes faster and more efficient, particularly in cross-border transactions.

While CBDCs share some similarities with digital currencies like cryptocurrencies, they differ fundamentally in terms of their structure, purpose, and governance (Allen et al. 2022).

Centralized Versus Decentralized

A key distinction is that CBDCs are centralized; they are issued and fully controlled by a central bank (Allen et al. 2022). The central bank is responsible for regulating, issuing, and ensuring the stability of the currency, all while operating within the framework of the traditional financial system.

In contrast, most cryptocurrencies, such as Bitcoin and Ethereum, are decentralized. They function on public blockchains without a central governing authority. These cryptocurrencies rely on distributed networks and consensus mechanisms, like PoW or PoS, to validate transactions, making them independent of any central bank or government.

Value and Stability

The value of a CBDC is directly linked to the fiat currency of the issuing country, such as the U.S. dollar or the euro. Consequently, CBDCs are expected to maintain a stable value, similar to physical cash or bank deposits. Central banks ensure that CBDCs reflect the same stability as their paper currency counterparts.

Stablecoins, which are digital assets pegged to traditional currencies or other assets, are designed to maintain a stable value but are issued by private entities rather than central banks. Popular stablecoins like Tether (USDT) or USD Coin (USDC) are backed by reserves held by private companies, which introduces a certain level of counterparty risk. In contrast, CBDCs eliminate this risk because they are fully backed and guaranteed by the central bank (Allen et al. 2022).

Cryptocurrencies, on the other hand, are highly volatile, with their value determined by market demand and speculation. For instance, the value of Bitcoin can fluctuate significantly based on changes in investor sentiment, market liquidity, or broader economic factors. This volatility makes cryptocurrencies less suitable as a stable medium of exchange or a reliable store of value compared to CBDCs.

Legal Status and Regulation

CBDCs hold official status as legal tender, meaning they can be used for all transactions within a country, including paying taxes and settling debts (Allen et al. 2022). Central banks oversee the regulation and stability of their CBDCs.

In contrast, cryptocurrencies like Bitcoin and Ethereum are generally not recognized as legal tender and operate outside traditional regulatory frameworks (Irina 2018). While stablecoins may offer more stability than cryptocurrencies, their issuance by private entities subjects them to varying levels of regulatory oversight. Recent regulatory initiatives in the United States and Europe aim to bring stablecoins under stricter supervision to mitigate risks to the broader financial system.

The key difference between CBDCs and cryptocurrencies or stablecoins lies in the element of trust: CBDCs are backed by a central bank and supported by the government, while cryptocurrencies and stablecoins depend on decentralized networks or private organizations.

Leading CBDC Projects Worldwide

As digital currencies become more popular worldwide, several central banks are actively developing and implementing CBDCs. These initiatives are at various stages of progress, with some already fully deployed and others still exploring options.

China's Digital Yuan

China's digital yuan, also known as the eCNY, is the most advanced and prominent CBDC project in the world. Officially launched in 2020 by the People's Bank of China (PBOC), the eCNY marks a significant step in the digitalization of China's financial system (Wang 2023). While the primary goal of the digital yuan is to modernize the domestic payment infrastructure, its global implications are also noteworthy. The eCNY has generated considerable interest and debate, as it represents both financial innovation and a potential geopolitical shift in the global monetary landscape.

The development of the eCNY has progressed through a series of pilot programs in major Chinese cities such as Shenzhen, Suzhou, Chengdu, and Beijing. During these trials, consumers and businesses have been able to use the digital yuan for various everyday transactions, from shopping to paying for public services. The PBOC has distributed eCNY through partnerships with major state-owned banks and payment platforms like Alipay and WeChat Pay, ensuring widespread adoption.

- During key holidays such as the Lunar New Year, the Chinese government has distributed digital red envelopes containing eCNY to citizens in selected cities. This serves both as a promotional tool and a way to test the system's functionality in real-world settings.
- Major ecommerce platforms, including JD.com, have also integrated the eCNY, allowing users to pay for goods and services with the digital currency.

The PBOC continues to expand the scope of its pilot programs, introducing the eCNY to more cities and industries while preparing for a broader national rollout. The 2022 Winter Olympics in Beijing provided a high-profile testing ground for the eCNY, allowing international visitors to use the digital currency during their stay.

The Bahamas' Sand Dollar

While much of the world has focused on the development of CBDCs by major economies, The Bahamas made history by launching the world's first fully deployed CBDC: the Sand Dollar. Introduced in October 2020 by the Central Bank of The Bahamas, the Sand Dollar was created to address specific challenges facing the island nation's economy, such as financial inclusion and the need for a more resilient payment system (Rossi 2024).

The Bahamas, an archipelago of more than 700 islands, faces unique challenges in providing banking services to its population, particularly in remote areas. Many residents have limited access to traditional banking infrastructure, and cash-based transactions remain common in these regions. The Sand Dollar was designed to offer a digital alternative to cash, ensuring that all Bahamians, regardless of their location, have access to a secure and efficient payment method.

The Sand Dollar is pegged to the Bahamian dollar, which is itself tied to the value of the U.S. dollar, ensuring price stability. The Central Bank of The Bahamas manages the issuance and redemption of Sand Dollars through authorized financial institutions and mobile payment platforms, enabling both individuals and businesses to conduct digital transactions using their mobile phones.

The Sand Dollar is accessible via digital wallets on mobile devices. Users can store, send, and receive Sand Dollars with other wallet holders, making it particularly beneficial for people without access to traditional banks. The central bank has also integrated the Sand Dollar with local payment service providers, allowing businesses to accept digital payments through smartphones and other devices.

Additionally, the Sand Dollar addresses the issue of disaster resilience. Given The Bahamas's vulnerability to hurricanes and other natural disasters, the central bank designed the Sand Dollar to provide a more reliable payment system that could continue to function even if physical banking infrastructure were disrupted.

The European Central Bank's Digital Euro

In July 2021, the ECB officially launched a two-year investigation into the development of a *digital euro*. This digital euro would serve as a CBDC for the eurozone, aimed at complementing physical cash and enhancing the efficiency of digital payments across Europe (Thomadakis et al. 2023). The ECB envisions the digital euro as a secure, efficient, and user-friendly digital payment solution accessible to all citizens and businesses in the eurozone. It is designed to work alongside physical cash, offering a public digital payment system that maintains the central bank's role in issuing currency in an increasingly digital economy.

The ECB seeks to ensure that the euro remains stable and widely accepted, even as private digital currencies and alternative payment solutions become more commonplace. The digital euro would facilitate faster, cheaper, and more secure payments throughout the eurozone, including cross-border transactions within the European Union (EU). By creating a digital euro, the ECB aims to preserve Europe's monetary sovereignty in the face of competition from private digital currencies, stablecoins, and foreign CBDCs, such as China's digital yuan.

The investigative phase of the ECB focuses on examining the potential impact of a digital euro on the eurozone's monetary system, financial stability, and banking sector. This phase emphasizes the technological infrastructure required for integrating the digital euro into existing payment systems, such as TARGET2 and TIPS, which facilitate real-time gross settlements and instant payments.

The ECB has already conducted public consultations to gather insights from citizens and stakeholders regarding the digital euro. This feedback has addressed important issues, including privacy, security, and user experience. Although a fully operational digital euro is still several years away, this project represents a significant step toward modernizing Europe's financial system.

While the ECB has articulated a clear vision for the digital euro, several challenges remain. One major concern raised by European citizens during consultations is privacy. The ECB must find a balance between safeguarding privacy in digital euro transactions and adhering to regulatory requirements for AML and counterterrorism financing measures. Additionally, there are concerns about potential bank disintermediation, where citizens may prefer to hold digital euros directly with the central bank rather than keeping deposits in commercial banks. This shift could disrupt traditional banking models, particularly if significant amounts of money are moved from bank deposits into digital euros.

Federal Reserve's Stance on a Digital Dollar

The Fed has taken a cautious approach toward the development of a digital dollar, unlike some other central banks. While interest in a CBDC is growing within the U.S. government and financial sector, the Fed emphasizes the importance of careful research and analysis before making any decisions.

The Fed has been actively researching the potential benefits and risks of a digital dollar. In 2022, the Federal Reserve Bank of Boston, in collaboration with the Massachusetts Institute of Technology (MIT), released initial findings from Project Hamilton. This exploratory project examined the technological foundations of a CBDC.

Project Hamilton showed that a digital dollar system could process 1.7 million transactions per second, indicating its technological feasibility for supporting a high-volume, real-time payment system. The research also underscored the necessity of incorporating strong privacy protections into any potential digital dollar, alongside ensuring that the system remains secure and resistant to cyberattacks.

Despite ongoing research, the Fed has emphasized that it has not yet decided whether to proceed with a digital dollar. Fed Chair Jerome Powell stated that any decision would require support from both Congress and the executive branch, highlighting the complex and politically sensitive nature of introducing a CBDC in the United States.

Similar to the ECB, the Fed is concerned about the potential for bank disintermediation. A digital dollar could reduce the role of commercial banks in the economy by encouraging people to hold digital currency directly with the Fed. As the issuer of the world's leading reserve currency, the United States must carefully consider how a digital dollar would impact the global financial system and the U.S. dollar's position as the dominant currency in international trade and finance.

The Fed released a discussion paper titled "Money and Payments: The U.S. Dollar in the Age of Digital Transformation," which outlines potential benefits and challenges of a digital dollar and invites public feedback (Hemphill 2024). The Fed continues to gather input from stakeholders and experts.

The Role of Governments and Central Banks

As digital assets gain significance, governments and central banks worldwide are increasingly developing their policies and attitudes toward this transformative technology. A notable example is El Salvador, which made headlines by becoming the first country to adopt Bitcoin as legal tender. This bold move underscores both the potential benefits and challenges of integrating digital assets into national economies. Simultaneously, many governments and central banks are implementing regulatory "sandbox" initiatives. These initiatives aim to foster innovation while maintaining oversight by providing a controlled environment for testing new financial technologies.

Governments' Attitudes Toward Digital Assets

As the market for digital assets has matured, governments have shifted their approach, moving from skepticism to cautious integration. Initially, many governments adopted a restrictive stance on cryptocurrencies due to concerns about their potential use in money laundering, terrorism financing, and tax evasion. Cryptocurrencies, especially Bitcoin, were often associated with illicit activities on the dark web and were viewed as threats to the stability of traditional financial systems.

China was one of the first major economies to take a hostile approach to cryptocurrencies. In 2017, it banned cryptocurrency exchanges and initial coin offerings, and later, in 2021, it intensified its crackdown on cryptocurrency mining. The Chinese government cited concerns about financial stability, capital outflows, and energy consumption as key reasons for these stringent regulations (Kavaloski 2024).

Similarly, India introduced regulatory restrictions on cryptocurrency trading and on banking services for crypto companies (Thakur et al. 2022). However, recent developments indicate a possible softening of this stance, as policy makers search for ways to effectively regulate and integrate digital assets into the economy.

Despite initial resistance, it increasingly became clear that banning or ignoring digital assets would not stop their growth or adoption. Over time, governments and central banks began to recognize the potential benefits of digital assets, such as the efficiency and security offered by blockchain technology, the expansion of digital finance, and the rising interest from institutional investors.

As a result, governments started exploring ways to integrate cryptocurrencies into their financial systems while also addressing the associated risks. This shift from skepticism to integration highlights the growing acknowledgment that digital assets are here to stay, making thoughtful regulation essential for managing the opportunities and risks they present.

El Salvador's Bitcoin Adoption

In 2021, El Salvador made global headlines by becoming the first country to adopt Bitcoin as legal tender, marking a significant milestone in the history of digital assets. President Nayib Bukele's administration presented this move as a means to improve financial inclusion, attract foreign investment, and reduce the cost of remittances, which are a vital source of income for many Salvadorans (Yuliana and Muhammad 2024).

Several key factors drove El Salvador's decision to adopt Bitcoin:

1. Unbanked Population: An estimated 70 percent of El Salvador's population is unbanked and lacks access to traditional financial services (Alvarez et al. 2023). By adopting Bitcoin and promoting the use of digital wallets like the government-backed Chivo Wallet, El Salvador aimed to provide its citizens with access to financial services, enabling them to save money and make payments without needing a traditional bank account.

2. Remittance Costs: Remittances from Salvadorans working abroad account for nearly 20 percent of the country's Gross Domestic Product. However, traditional remittance services, such as Western Union, charge high fees—sometimes as much as 10 percent of the amount sent (Parada 2022). By using Bitcoin, the Salvadoran government sought to lower these costs and ensure that more money reaches families in need.

3. Monetary Independence: Since 2001, El Salvador has relied on the U.S. dollar as its official currency (Vázquez 2022). Adopting Bitcoin was seen as a way to diversify the economy and reduce dependence on the dollar, providing the country with greater monetary independence.

4. Attracting Investment: By positioning itself as a crypto-friendly nation, El Salvador aimed to attract foreign investment in Bitcoin and blockchain technologies. The government introduced several incentives for crypto entrepreneurs, including tax exemptions on Bitcoin gains.

El Salvador's Bitcoin Law embodies a bold vision, but its implementation has encountered several challenges. Many Salvadorans remain skeptical about the volatility and practicality of Bitcoin. Although the government launched the Chivo Wallet and offered a US$30 Bitcoin bonus to every citizen, adoption has been slow, particularly in rural areas where access to smartphones and internet connectivity is limited.

Bitcoin's notorious price fluctuations have also raised concerns regarding its reliability as a medium of exchange. Critics, such as Černý (2023), Jaatinen (2022), and Angwald (2023), argued that the potential for loss made Bitcoin unsuitable for everyday transactions, especially in a country with high poverty levels. Additionally, El Salvador's decision to adopt Bitcoin has attracted criticism from international organizations, such as the International Monetary Fund and the World Bank, which have voiced concerns about its impact on financial stability and regulatory compliance.

Despite these challenges, El Salvador's initiative represents a bold experiment in the use of cryptocurrency at a national level, and marks a historic moment in the integration of cryptocurrencies into national economic policies.

Regulatory "Sandbox" Initiatives

As governments and central banks strive to balance the potential benefits of digital assets with the risks they present, several countries have created regulatory sandboxes. These sandboxes foster innovation in a controlled environment, allowing businesses to test new financial technologies under the supervision of regulators. This approach helps ensure compliance with existing laws while exploring new applications for blockchain and cryptocurrencies.

Singapore

Singapore is widely recognized as one of the most innovative and crypto-friendly regulatory environments globally. The Monetary Authority of Singapore (MAS), which is the country's central bank and financial regulatory authority, introduced a regulatory sandbox in 2016 to foster the growth of FinTech companies, including those involved with blockchain and cryptocurrencies (Jenweeranon 2023).

This regulatory sandbox allows companies to test innovative financial products and services in a controlled environment, with the MAS offering regulatory support and flexibility (Jenweeranon 2023). As a result, the sandbox has stimulated the development of blockchain-based solutions for payments, remittances, and digital identity verification, helping establish Singapore as a FinTech hub.

Additionally, Singapore's Payment Services Act provides a comprehensive regulatory framework for cryptocurrencies, clarifying licensing requirements for crypto exchanges and wallet providers. By balancing regulation with flexibility, Singapore has successfully attracted major cryptocurrency companies, such as Crypto.com, to set up their operations in the city-state.

United Arab Emirates

The United Arab Emirates (UAE) has emerged as a leader in promoting blockchain innovation through regulatory sandboxes. The Abu Dhabi Global Market (ADGM) and the Dubai International Financial Centre (DIFC) have established themselves as crypto-friendly jurisdictions, providing legal frameworks and regulatory sandboxes to support the growth of digital asset businesses (Grossman 2022).

The ADGM's RegLab is the first regulatory sandbox in the Middle East specifically designed for FinTech companies. This sandbox allows startups to test blockchain and cryptocurrency solutions—including digital wallets, smart contracts, and security tokens—in a controlled environment before introducing them to the broader market.

Dubai aims to become a global leader in blockchain technology through its Dubai Blockchain Strategy and the creation of free zones where crypto companies can operate with regulatory support. The Dubai government has also launched DubaiCoin, a blockchain-based digital currency intended to facilitate government and commercial transactions.

Regulatory sandboxes provide a safe testing ground for innovation, offering numerous benefits for both businesses and regulators. By allowing FinTech companies to experiment with new technologies, sandboxes foster the development of advanced blockchain and cryptocurrency solutions that can be scaled once they meet regulatory requirements. Additionally, these sandboxes help regulators understand and manage risks associated with digital assets, such as fraud, cyberattacks, and money laundering. By closely monitoring participants in the sandbox, regulators can identify potential risks early and ensure that businesses develop secure and compliant solutions. Furthermore, countries with supportive regulatory environments like Singapore and the UAE attract foreign investment and crypto start-ups, driving economic growth and positioning themselves as global hubs for digital finance.

Summary

As CBDCs move from theoretical concepts to practical implementations, their potential to transform the global financial system is becoming increasingly apparent. In contrast to decentralized digital currencies, CBDCs offer governments a way to modernize payments, enhance financial inclusion, and maintain control over monetary policy in a rapidly digitizing world. The leading projects discussed in this chapter—China's digital yuan, The Bahamas's Sand Dollar, the ECB's plans for a digital euro, and the Fed's exploration of a digital dollar—illustrate the diverse approaches that countries are taking to address their unique economic and regulatory needs. Additionally, governments are playing a crucial role in shaping the future of digital assets, from El Salvador's Bitcoin adoption to the development of regulatory sandbox initiatives aimed at fostering innovation while safeguarding stability. As we look ahead, it is clear that CBDCs will play an increasingly prominent role in the global economy, with the potential to redefine how individuals and businesses engage with money.

PART 2

From Theory to Innovation

Modern Portfolio Theory and Digital Assets

CHAPTER 3

Modern Portfolio Theory Revisited

MPT, developed by Harry Markowitz in 1952, transformed how investors approach portfolio construction and risk management by formalizing the connection between risk and return. MPT introduced a mathematical framework that helps investors create optimal portfolios, aiming to maximize expected returns for a given level of risk or minimize risk for a desired level of return.

This chapter revisits the origins and core principles of MPT, including key concepts such as the efficient frontier and mean-variance optimization. We will also explore the theory's underlying assumptions, such as rational investor behavior and efficient markets. Furthermore, we will address the criticisms and limitations of MPT in today's evolving financial landscape, where real-world complexities—such as market inefficiencies, behavioral biases, and changing volatility—challenge some of its fundamental ideas.

By examining both the strengths and weaknesses of MPT, this chapter aims to provide a nuanced understanding of its enduring relevance and how it has adapted to modern investment strategies.

Origins and Core Principles

The origins of MPT can be traced back to Harry Markowitz's influential paper, "Portfolio Selection," which was published in the *Journal of Finance* in 1952. Before this work, the common investment approach was to focus on selecting individual securities based mainly on their expected returns. Markowitz introduced a groundbreaking concept: investors should look at the portfolio as a whole, considering how different assets interact to influence overall risk and return.

Markowitz's key insight was that the risk of a portfolio is not simply the sum of the individual risks of its assets; instead, it depends on the correlations between those assets. By diversifying investments across assets that do not move in perfect sync with one another, investors can reduce the overall risk of their portfolios. This principle, known as diversification, is a fundamental aspect of modern investment strategy.

Risk-Return Trade-Off

MPT formalizes the relationship between risk and return by offering a framework for constructing portfolios that optimize performance based on these two factors. MPT assumes that investors are rational and aim to maximize returns for a given level of risk or, conversely, minimize risk for a desired level of expected return. This trade-off between risk and return serves as the foundation for portfolio construction.

Risk is quantified through variance or standard deviation of portfolio returns, which measures the volatility or uncertainty of returns over time. In contrast, return is typically measured as the expected return of a portfolio, reflecting the average outcome weighted by the probabilities of different scenarios.

Efficient Frontier

One of the most significant contributions of MPT is the concept of the efficient frontier. The efficient frontier is a graphical representation of the set of optimal portfolios that offer the highest expected return for a given level of risk (Markowitz 1952). In a two-dimensional plot, risk (measured by standard deviation) is represented on the x-axis, while expected return is plotted on the y-axis. The curve that forms the efficient frontier is upward-sloping, indicating that higher returns generally come with increased risk. Conversely, it also displays the portfolios that incur the least amount of risk for a desired level of return. This curve visually represents the balance between risk and return that investors seek to achieve.

Each portfolio on the efficient frontier is well-diversified, maximizing the benefits of diversification by combining assets with varying levels of risk and different correlations. Portfolios that lie below the efficient frontier are considered suboptimal, as they either generate lower returns for a given level of risk or expose investors to unnecessary risks for the same expected return. The objective for investors is to position their portfolios along this frontier in order to achieve maximum efficiency.

When a risk-free asset (such as Treasury bills) is introduced, the efficient frontier is adjusted by the addition of the capital market line (CML). The CML represents the combination of a risk-free asset with a portfolio on the efficient frontier and often leads to the identification of the tangency portfolio—the optimal portfolio of risky assets (Abdul et al. 2024). This portfolio is particularly relevant for determining the market portfolio in capital asset pricing models.

Mean-Variance Optimization

Through mean-variance optimization, investors can maximize expected returns based on their tolerance for risk or minimize risk while still achieving a predefined return objective (Markowitz 1952).

In this context, the "mean" refers to the expected return of the portfolio, representing the average return the investor can anticipate based on historical or forecasted performance. Conversely, "variance" reflects the portfolio's risk, measured by the variability of returns over time.

MPT also introduces the concept of correlation between assets, emphasizing that risk is not solely about the volatility of individual assets but also about how assets behave in relation to one another.

Mean-variance optimization employs statistical techniques to assess how each asset's expected return, variance, and correlation with other assets contribute to the portfolio's overall risk and return. The objective is to determine the ideal asset mix.

Assumptions

MPT is based on several key assumptions that underlie how investors approach portfolio optimization, risk management, and returns

(Zhong 2013). These assumptions simplify the complexities of the real world to create a mathematical framework for constructing investment portfolios.

Investors Are Rational and Risk-Averse

MPT assumes that all investors act rationally, aiming to maximize expected returns for a given level of risk. They utilize all available information and are consistently focused on optimizing their portfolios.

Additionally, investors are considered risk-averse, meaning they prefer less risky investments over riskier ones, provided that the expected returns are the same. This implies that when faced with two portfolios that offer identical expected returns, a rational investor will choose the one with lower risk.

Efficient Markets

MPT assumes that markets are efficient, meaning all available information is fully reflected in asset prices. Consequently, investors cannot consistently achieve returns above the market average without taking on additional risk.

In an efficient market, there are no opportunities for arbitrage or "free lunch" trades, as any mispricings are quickly corrected.

Investors Have Homogeneous Expectations

MPT assumes that all investors share the same expectations regarding market returns, risk (measured as standard deviation), and asset correlations. In this framework, every investor views future market conditions identically, leading them to calculate the same optimal portfolios.

This assumption means that differences in portfolios stem solely from variations in risk tolerance, rather than differing perceptions of potential returns or asset behaviors.

Risk Is Measured by Variance or Standard Deviation

MPT assumes that risk can be fully captured by the variance or standard deviation of returns. In this framework, higher variance (or higher standard deviation) means higher risk because it indicates greater uncertainty in an asset's returns.

Investors are assumed to be primarily concerned with minimizing risk and maximizing return, and thus they seek portfolios that offer the highest expected return for a given level of risk.

Investors Consider Portfolios, Not Individual Assets

According to MPT, investors do not focus on individual assets when constructing their portfolios. Instead, they consider the portfolio as a whole, taking into account how different assets interact with one another in terms of correlation.

The theory suggests that investors should diversify their portfolios by combining assets that are not perfectly correlated. By doing this, they can reduce unsystematic risk and improve their risk-return trade-off.

No Transaction Costs or Taxes

Additionally, MPT assumes that there are no transaction costs or taxes when buying or selling assets. This assumption simplifies the model by eliminating factors that could impact portfolio returns and rebalancing strategies.

In the real world, transaction fees and taxes can significantly influence an investor's decision making, but MPT treats these costs as negligible.

Assets Are Infinitely Divisible

Another simplifying assumption is that assets can be divided into infinitely small units, allowing investors to buy or sell any fraction of a security. This flexibility enhances portfolio construction, enabling investors to create precise allocations that align with their desired risk-return profile.

Criticisms and Limitations

Changing Dynamics in Volatility and Correlation

One of the foundational principles of MPT is the diversification benefit gained from combining assets that have low or negative correlations. However, during times of market stress, the correlations between asset classes can increase dramatically, diminishing the advantages of diversification (Ilmanen and Jared 2012). This phenomenon, often referred to as "correlation breakdown," was especially evident during financial crises such as the 2008 Global Financial Crisis.

Market Efficiency Questioned

The assumption of efficient markets has been widely debated, particularly in light of research from behavioral finance. Investors do not always act rationally; instead, markets can be influenced by emotions, herd behavior, and other psychological factors that lead to bubbles, crashes, and market anomalies such as momentum or value effects (Bhanu 2023). This challenges the assumption that all information is perfectly reflected in asset prices.

Liquidity Concerns

MPT does not account for liquidity risk—the risk that an investor may not be able to sell an asset quickly without significantly impacting its price (Beyhaghi and Hawley 2013). In periods of low liquidity, investors may face sharp declines in asset prices, a factor that the standard MPT framework fails to address.

Focus on Historical Data

MPT relies heavily on historical returns and covariances to forecast future portfolio behavior. Critics, including Sheth and Shah (2023) and Che et al. (2024), argued that past performance might not provide an accurate prediction of future risk and return, especially in rapidly changing markets. This has led to the development of more advanced models that incorporate forward-looking data and macroeconomic factors.

Risk-Aversion Assumption

While MPT assumes that all investors are risk-averse, some investors might be willing to take on more risk in pursuit of higher returns—especially in contemporary markets where speculative behavior can be prevalent. Additionally, MPT posits that risk is inherently negative; however, some investors may perceive volatility as an opportunity rather than a threat.

In their study, Rodríguez et al. (2021) analyzed the performance of 20 S&P 500 stocks from January 2013 to December 2017. They found that diversified behavioral portfolios outperformed the mean-variance portfolio. Rodríguez et al. proposed a portfolio choice model that incorporates various distributional characteristics of returns into the decision-making process. This model accounts for investors' preferences, which are represented as nonstatistical uncertainties through fuzzy theory. This methodological approach can serve as a valuable managerial tool for making investment portfolio decisions.

Summary

In summary, MPT is a foundational concept in contemporary investment strategy, providing a structured approach to balancing risk and return through diversification and optimization. By examining its origins, core principles, and assumptions, we can see how MPT has influenced traditional portfolio management, helping investors aim for efficient portfolios that maximize returns for a given level of risk.

However, as financial markets have evolved, MPT has faced various criticisms and limitations. Factors such as market inefficiencies, behavioral biases, and the ever-changing nature of risk highlight the necessity for more adaptive approaches. While MPT still offers valuable insights, recognizing its limitations enables investors to better navigate today's complex financial landscape and encourages the adoption of more flexible and comprehensive investment strategies.

CHAPTER 4

Reimagining Portfolio Theory for the Digital Age

As digital assets—such as cryptocurrencies, stablecoins, and tokenized assets—become more integrated into financial markets, their role in portfolio management is evolving. MPT, which emphasizes balancing risk and return through diversification, faces both opportunities and challenges when applied to these new asset classes.

Digital assets can offer investors benefits, including diversification and the potential for significant returns (Holovatiuk 2020). However, the extreme volatility and speculative nature of digital assets such as Bitcoin and altcoins introduce risks that deviate from traditional MPT assumptions. To achieve long-term sustainability, it is essential to go beyond conventional portfolios and develop innovative strategies that adapt to ongoing financial and technological changes (Ma et al. 2020).

In this chapter, we will explore how MPT can be adapted to accommodate digital assets, highlighting areas where they align with, as well as diverge from, classical portfolio theory. Additionally, we will examine the diversification advantages offered by stablecoins and tokenized assets.

Modern Portfolio Theory in the Context of Digital Assets

As digital assets such as Bitcoin, Ethereum, and other altcoins become increasingly prominent in global financial markets, MPT encounters both new challenges and opportunities. To effectively apply MPT principles to these emerging asset classes, it is essential to gain a deeper understanding of their unique characteristics. This includes their high volatility, their correlation with traditional assets, and their role within a decentralized financial ecosystem.

Applying Modern Portfolio Theory to Digital Assets

Digital assets can be classified as a distinct asset class. Holovatiuk (2020) used six indexes, including the cryptocurrency index CRIX, as proxies for major asset classes to examine all cryptographic assets. Cryptocurrencies met seven key requirements for being classified as an asset class, which include stable aggregation, investability, internal homogeneity, external heterogeneity, expected utility, selection skill, and cost-effective access.

Volatility

Digital assets, particularly cryptocurrencies, are well-known for their extreme volatility. For example, Bitcoin has experienced sharp price swings over short periods, with daily fluctuations often exceeding 10 percent. Historically, its annualized volatility has ranged from 60 to 100 percent, which is significantly higher than that of traditional asset classes such as equities and bonds (Conlon et al. 2024). Other altcoins, especially smaller and emerging tokens, can be even more volatile, occasionally seeing gains of several hundred percent in just a few weeks or months, only to face rapid corrections and crashes shortly thereafter (Santos-Alborna 2021).

Sarmini et al. (2024) analyzed the daily volatility and Generalized Autoregressive Conditional Heteroskedasticity(GARCH) volatility of six major cryptocurrencies: Bitcoin, Ethereum, Litecoin, USD Coin, Tether, and Ripple over specific time periods. Their analysis shows that Bitcoin has an average daily percentage change of 0.366 percent, while Ethereum has a daily change of 0.376 percent. Litecoin (LTC) displays a daily change of 0.166 percent, whereas USD Coin and Tether have very low daily percentage changes, approaching zero.

In terms of GARCH volatility, Sarmini et al. found that Ethereum stands out with a volatility of 0.198, followed by Bitcoin at 0.121. These findings indicate that cryptocurrencies are susceptible to extreme price fluctuations, as evidenced by their asymmetric distribution and kurtosis. This volatility correlation analysis reveals significant relationships that are important for risk management and portfolio diversification.

Building on insights from post-MPT, Holovatiuk (2020) noted a significant deterioration in downside risk and the Sortino ratio when cryptocurrencies were included in investment portfolios. Aggarwal (2022) applied the pairwise bivariate Baba-Engle-Kraft-Kroner (BEKK)-GARCH (1,1) model to analyze the short- and long-term volatility relationships among Litecoin, Stellar, and Ripple from August 2015 to June 2020, discovering that Litecoin is the most influential sender of volatility among these three cryptocurrencies.

Using a time-varying parameter vector autoregression (TVP-VAR) approach, Goodell et al. (2023) examined the interconnectedness among traditional assets, digital assets, and renewable energy, analyzing data from December 31, 2019 to January 2, 2023. Their findings revealed that Chainlink, a DeFi asset, is the highest receiver of shocks, while Bitcoin is the primary transmitter of shocks within the network.

Unlike traditional markets, digital assets are still in the early stages of adoption and are influenced by several unique factors that increase volatility:

1. Technological Innovation: New developments, such as blockchain upgrades, DeFi protocols, or NFT projects, can lead to sudden price surges, especially if they promise enhanced utility or adoption. Conversely, technical issues or project failures can result in sharp declines.

2. Regulatory Announcements: Changes in regulation—such as bans on cryptocurrency trading, tax policies, or governmental support for digital assets—can cause significant price movements, both upward and downward. Markets often react strongly to announcements from key regulators, including the U.S. *Securities and Exchange Commission (SEC) or the ECB.*

3. Macroeconomic Factors: Cryptocurrencies, especially Bitcoin, are increasingly viewed as hedges against inflation and uncertainties related to monetary policy. Announcements regarding

interest rate hikes or quantitative easing can lead to sudden inflows or outflows of capital in cryptocurrency markets.

4. Speculative Behavior and Market Sentiment: Digital assets are particularly prone to speculative trading, often driven by Fear Of Mission Out (FOMO), social media hype, or news cycles. The dominance of retail investors, combined with limited liquidity in some markets, can amplify price movements, resulting in sudden surges or flash crashes.

Within the MPT framework, volatility is generally viewed as a risk factor. Higher volatility signifies a broader range of potential outcomes, increasing the uncertainty of returns. However, for some investors—especially those with a higher risk tolerance—the volatility of digital assets can present opportunities for significant returns.

Jeribi and Fakhfekh (2021) explored the relationship between five cryptocurrencies, oil prices, and U.S. indexes. Using daily data from January 4, 2016 to November 29, 2019, they employed the FIE-GARCH-EVT-Copula model and conducted hedge ratio analyses. Their findings indicated that the WTI and U.S. index returns exhibit a persistent negative and significant leverage effect, while the cryptocurrency markets show a positive asymmetric volatility effect.

One of the biggest challenges for investors is managing the volatility of digital assets within a broader, diversified portfolio. Although MPT promotes diversification to reduce unsystematic risk, the correlations between digital assets and traditional asset classes can be inconsistent, complicating allocation strategies.

Returns

Despite their volatility, digital assets have provided substantial returns over the past decade, making them appealing to investors seeking high-growth opportunities. For instance, Bitcoin's annualized return has consistently exceeded that of many traditional assets, including equities, real estate, and commodities. This trend has established Bitcoin's status as both a speculative investment and a potential store of value (Chu et al. 2021). These impressive returns, coupled with increasing mainstream adoption, have attracted both institutional and retail investors who aim to enhance their portfolio performance.

When assessed through the lens of MPT, the high potential returns offered by digital assets can justify their inclusion in a portfolio, especially for investors with a higher risk tolerance. For these investors, the favorable risk-return trade-off means that extreme price fluctuations may be outweighed by a positive long-term trend in returns. Furthermore, when added strategically to a diversified portfolio, digital assets can improve risk-adjusted returns, provided their low or inconsistent correlations with traditional investments are managed carefully. This characteristic makes cryptocurrencies particularly attractive for those looking to boost portfolio performance without being overly exposed to a single asset class.

Correlation With Traditional Assets

The correlation between digital assets and traditional assets, such as stocks, bonds, and commodities, can vary significantly based on market conditions, particularly during bull markets and times of market stress.

Correlation During Bull Markets.   In bull markets, Bitcoin and other major cryptocurrencies often show a lower correlation with traditional assets such as stocks and bonds (Rashid et al. 2023). During periods of strong economic growth and rising equity markets, digital assets frequently enter their own bullish cycles, driven by technological advancements, institutional adoption, and increased speculative interest.

DeFi tokens—associated with platforms that offer decentralized lending, borrowing, or trading—can also exhibit low correlations with traditional asset classes. The growth and adoption of DeFi platforms drive these tokens, which operate independently from traditional financial markets.

During favorable conditions, cryptocurrencies tend to move independently of traditional markets. The factors that drive crypto bull runs—such as positive adoption news or improvements in infrastructure—are often unrelated to macroeconomic factors affecting equities and fixed income (Saef et al. 2024). This independence reinforces the role of digital assets as diversification tools, providing portfolios with exposure to uncorrelated growth opportunities.

Yousaf and Yarovaya (2022) examined the return and volatility transmission between NFTs, DeFi assets, and other assets such as oil, gold, Bitcoin, and the S&P 500 using the TVP-VAR framework. Their results revealed weak static return and volatility spillovers between NFTs, DeFi assets, and selected markets, suggesting that these new digital assets remain relatively decoupled from traditional asset classes. They found that Bitcoin, oil, and about half of the NFTs and DeFi assets are net transmitters of return and volatility spillovers, while the remaining markets are net recipients.

As Bitcoin and other major cryptocurrencies experience gains not necessarily tied to economic fundamentals or corporate performance, they can serve as complementary assets in a broader investment strategy. For investors seeking both growth potential and portfolio diversification, the ability of digital assets to perform independently during bull markets enhances their appeal.

Correlation During Market Stress.   During periods of financial stress or economic downturns, the correlations between digital assets and traditional asset classes can increase, undermining their diversification benefits. For instance, during the COVID-19 pandemic crash in early 2020, Bitcoin and equities showed a temporary positive correlation as investors rushed to liquidate positions and sought cash, indiscriminately selling off risky assets across the board (Abakah et al. 2024). In such instances, digital assets—despite their long-term growth potential and appeal as alternative investments—were treated similarly to equities, reflecting a marketwide flight from risk.

This phenomenon, known as *"correlation breakdown,"* occurs when assets that typically exhibit low or negative correlations begin to move in tandem during times of market stress. It underscores a significant limitation of digital assets: their effectiveness as a hedge may diminish during extreme market conditions. In these situations, investor behavior tends to prioritize liquidity and capital preservation over portfolio construction strategies, leading to a temporary alignment between traditionally uncorrelated assets. The increased correlations during downturns indicate that while cryptocurrencies can enhance portfolio diversification in stable market environments, they may not always provide protection during crises.

Demiralay and Bayracı (2021) developed six portfolios that included cryptocurrencies along with both developed and emerging equity markets. Their findings indicated that the correlations between cryptocurrencies and stock markets are generally low. However, these correlations significantly increase during turbulent periods, such as the Brexit referendum and the Coincheck hack. Yousaf and Yarovaya (2022) provided evidence that dynamic return and volatility interconnectedness increased during the initial phase of the COVID-19 pandemic and the cryptocurrency bubble of 2021.

As digital assets gain wider acceptance and institutional investors begin to include them in diversified portfolios, the correlation between cryptocurrencies and traditional asset classes may stabilize or even rise over time. This trend presents a double-edged sword: while greater adoption can help reduce volatility and legitimize digital assets, it may also make them more vulnerable to macroeconomic events and cryptocurrency-specific developments, such as regulatory changes and technological advancements.

How Digital Assets Deviate From Modern Portfolio Theory Assumptions

Exponential Growth Phases

The traditional portfolio analysis approach of Markowitz is not appropriate for use with portfolios containing crypto-assets, as the model requires that the investor have a quadratic utility function or that the returns be normally distributed, which is not the case for crypto-assets (Castro et al. 2020). Digital assets, especially cryptocurrencies, have experienced periods of rapid growth that differ significantly from traditional asset classes. These sudden spikes in value are often driven by speculative behavior, where investor sentiment, network effects, and technological advancements create a feedback loop that pushes prices higher. For instance, as the adoption of a blockchain network increases, the utility—and thus the value—of its native token can rise, attracting more participants and investors, which further accelerates price appreciation. This cycle of positive reinforcement contributes to the high volatility and explosive growth that is rarely seen in traditional markets.

MPT, which focuses on the trade-offs between risk and return and assumes that returns follow a more predictable, normal distribution, may struggle to account for these extreme price dynamics. The nonlinear growth patterns of cryptocurrencies, propelled by technological breakthroughs, liquidity influxes, and speculation, can lead to short-term gains that far exceed what MPT's traditional models would predict for a given level of risk. This reveals the limitations of conventional portfolio theory when applied to digital assets, as it may not fully capture the significant upside potential these assets offer.

Liquidity Constraints

Many digital assets, especially smaller altcoins, encounter significant liquidity challenges. This means that large trades can cause substantial fluctuations in market prices. In highly liquid markets, the entry and exit of investors do not dramatically affect prices. However, in thinly traded markets, even moderate buy or sell orders can lead to noticeable price swings. This situation deviates from one of MPT's core assumptions: that markets are efficient and liquid, allowing asset prices to remain stable regardless of individual trade volumes.

The illiquidity of certain digital assets introduces additional risks, such as slippage, which is when the actual execution price of a trade differs from the intended price, especially for large orders. High transaction costs—such as network fees and spreads—can further diminish returns, complicating portfolio rebalancing and efficient allocation. Consequently, managing portfolios that include illiquid digital assets requires more strategic planning and careful timing of trades to minimize the impact of market movements. These liquidity challenges also heighten the likelihood of price volatility during market stress, when many investors attempt to exit positions at the same time, worsening price declines.

Behavioral Factors

Cryptocurrencies are significantly influenced by market sentiment, speculation, and media hype, leading to frequent price bubbles and sharp crashes. Behavioral finance challenges the traditional assumption of MPT that investors are rational actors who make decisions solely based on risk and return trade-offs. In reality, the behavior of digital asset markets often reflects emotion-driven trading, where fear, greed, and the FOMO play central roles. This can lead to significant deviations from the expected risk-return profiles predicted by traditional financial models.

Periods of hype and speculative mania can drive prices well beyond their intrinsic value, resulting in price bubbles that eventually burst, leading to significant corrections. For example, Bitcoin and other cryptocurrencies have experienced multiple cycles of boom and bust, with prices soaring during bullish phases before collapsing when sentiment changes. This volatility is further exacerbated by influential events—such as social media trends, celebrity endorsements, or regulatory announcements—that can trigger rapid buying or panic selling.

Using the conditional autoregressive value-at-risk (CAViaR) models, Li et al. (2022) found that Bitcoin's volatility is significantly linked to the volatility of its returns. The main factors influencing this volatility include speculation, investor attention, market interoperability, and the interaction between speculation and market interoperability. Additionally, Li et al. provided evidence that investor attention is the primary driver of volatility. The relationship between speculation and the interaction term is U-shaped, while investor attention and market interoperability exhibit a linear trend regarding Bitcoin's volatility.

Behavioral finance highlights how cognitive biases, such as herding behavior and confirmation bias, influence irrational decision making in financial markets. Specifically in the context of digital assets, investors often pursue short-term gains or follow the crowd, creating feedback loops that increase volatility. This emotional trading complicates the ability of MPT models to predict the performance of cryptocurrency portfolios accurately, as these models assume that returns are normally distributed and primarily driven by underlying fundamentals.

To address estimation risk, Huang et al. (2023) used the Bayes–Stein model without short-selling and applied variance-based constraints. They found that lower levels of investor risk aversion make crypto-currencies more effective as portfolio diversifiers. Interestingly, during uncertain economic periods, such as the post-COVID-19 environment, cryptocurrencies offer the same diversification benefits as they do in more stable times.

Market Inefficiencies

In theory, digital asset markets should be highly efficient due to their global nature, 24/7 trading hours, and the transparency provided by blockchain technology. The decentralized structure of these markets ensures that real-time information is accessible to all participants, offering open access to transaction histories, wallet activity, on-chain data, and price movements. This democratization of information, combined with continuous trading, theoretically allows prices to adjust quickly to new information, promoting efficient market behavior.

However, in practice, informational asymmetry still exists, leading to market inefficiencies. Many digital assets remain highly speculative, with prices often driven by events that are not easily observable or trans-parent. For example, insider activities, developer decisions, or sudden regulatory announcements can significantly impact prices, sometimes giving certain investors early access to crucial information. Additionally, technical developments—such as blockchain upgrades or security vulnerabilities—can be difficult for many market participants to fully understand or predict, complicating price discovery.

Furthermore, the lack of centralized oversight and fragmentation across multiple exchanges make it challenging for participants to track all relevant information consistently. While on-chain data offers transparency, it does not always present the complete picture, especially for newer or less established cryptocurrencies. Whale activity—large trades by individuals or institutions—can significantly influence price movements, often catching smaller investors off guard. Social media platforms, news outlets, and messaging groups can amplify rumors and speculation, leading to delayed or distorted interpretations of market events.

Diversification Benefits of Digital Assets

Portfolio diversification is crucial for most investors in the cryptocurrency market, as virtual currencies are significantly riskier than traditional assets (Mazanec 2021). In recent years, numerous studies have explored the benefits of incorporating alternative assets into traditional portfolios that include stocks and bonds (Castro et al. 2020; Colombo et al. 2021; Jeribi and Fakhfekh 2021; Ma et al. 2020; Mazanec 2021; Platanakis et al. 2020).

Investment strategies during the fourth industrial revolution should address the needs of all societal segments by incorporating exposure to technological and digital financial innovations (Ma et al. 2020). Holovatiuk (2020) confirmed that crypto assets have diversification properties, and portfolio optimization with the MPT showed an increase in the Sharpe ratio of tangency portfolios with the inclusion of CRIX.

Ma et al. (2020) examined the impact of adding five cryptocurrencies to four traditional asset portfolios from November 2015 to November 2019. Their findings revealed that diversification generally increased returns in most cases and reduced volatility across all portfolios. Additionally, they found that this diversification provided higher returns for the same level of risk compared to traditional portfolios. The study also suggested that the benefits of diversification could be enhanced when short sales are permitted.

Colombo et al. (2021) conducted a country-specific analysis using a sample of 21 developing and developed countries. They indicated that cryptocurrencies typically fit within the tangent portfolio (maximum Sharpe ratio) in conjunction with stocks, bonds, real estate, and commodities. Their research further illustrated that even global portfolios benefiting from international diversification can gain additional advantages by investing marginally in cryptocurrencies. Specifically, both mean-variance optimal and naive strategies that included cryptocurrencies outperformed identical portfolios without them in terms of risk-adjusted returns. Notably, their results showed that exchange rate movements did not influence this better performance, as it held true for both local returns (denominated in local currency) and global returns (denominated in USD). Furthermore, Colombo et al. (2021) provided evidence that the diversification benefits of cryptocurrencies existed both before and after the COVID-19 pandemic, with the 1/N portfolio including cryptocurrencies yielding the highest risk-adjusted returns.

Platanakis et al. (2020) found that incorporating Bitcoin into an investment portfolio could lead to significantly higher risk-adjusted returns. They noted, in line with Ma et al. (2020), that Ethereum might offer superior diversification opportunities compared to Bitcoin. Platanakis et al. utilized data up to June 2018 to explore the potential out-of-sample benefits of including Bitcoin in a stock-bond portfolio across various asset allocation strategies. Their analysis demonstrated significant advantages in incorporating Bitcoin, irrespective of the asset allocation strategy or level of risk aversion, resulting in substantially higher risk-adjusted returns. The robustness of their findings was strengthened by considering transaction costs, including a commodity portfolio, alternative indexes, short-selling strategies, and applying additional optimization techniques that accounted for higher moments, both with and without variance-based constraints.

Further, holding Bitcoin can also reduce the liquidity risk under the mean-variance-liquidity framework. By examining the dependence structure between Bitcoin and several financial assets, Ghabri et al. found evidence of a low time-varying correlation of liquidity innovations over the period 2014 to 2019, which suggests the existence of a potential gain in diversifying the liquidity risk using Bitcoin instead of traditional assets.

Diversifying With Stablecoins

Stablecoins are a type of digital asset designed to maintain a stable value by being pegged to traditional currencies, such as the U.S. dollar. They have gained significance in the cryptocurrency ecosystem due to their stability compared to more volatile assets such as Bitcoin, Ethereum, and other altcoins. This stability makes stablecoins an appealing option for risk management.

The primary purpose of stablecoins is to provide price stability within a typically volatile cryptocurrency market. They serve as a store of value or a medium of exchange during times of market uncertainty. For investors who want to maintain exposure to digital assets without facing significant price fluctuations, stablecoins such as USD Coin, Tether, and Dai offer a safer alternative.

Key Diversification Benefits of Stablecoins

Liquidity Management and Cash Alternative. Stablecoins serve as a cash-equivalent asset within the digital ecosystem, enabling quick reallocation of capital during volatile market conditions. They facilitate instant settlement, thus avoiding the delays typical of traditional banking.

Low Correlation With Traditional Markets. Unlike Bitcoin or equities, stablecoins are designed to maintain a fixed value, which helps to reduce exposure to market downturns. During periods of high stock market volatility, stablecoins provide a safe haven within the crypto ecosystem.

Yield Generation and Passive Income. Stablecoins can be staked, loaned, or deposited into DeFi protocols to earn yields, which are often higher than those of traditional fixed-income assets. For example, USD Coin on platforms like Aave and Compound can yield between 3 percent and 6 percent annually. Additionally, institutional yield products, such as Circle Yield, offer regulated exposure.

Hedge Against Inflation and Currency Risks.   Holding USD-pegged stablecoins can protect against local currency devaluation, particularly in emerging markets. Gold-backed stablecoins, like Paxos Gold and Tether Gold, offer a digital alternative to gold ETFs, combining inflation protection with liquidity.

Enhanced Portfolio Flexibility.   Investors can quickly rebalance their portfolios without needing to exit the crypto ecosystem. This allows for tactical asset allocation, enabling shifts between riskier assets (such as cryptocurrencies and equities) and stable-value holdings (stablecoins).

Arbitrage and Trading Opportunities.   Stablecoins provide arbitrage traders with the ability to hedge against market movements effectively. They also serve as a stable base currency for executing algorithmic and quantitative trading strategies.

While stablecoins offer these diversification benefits, investors should be aware of potential risks, including:

1. Counterparty Risk: Centralized stablecoins, such as USD Coin and Tether, rely on the solvency of their issuers.
2. Regulatory Uncertainty: Governments are tightening oversight of stablecoin issuers and their usage.
3. Depegging Risks: Algorithmic stablecoins, exemplified by the collapse of TerraUSD in May 2022, have demonstrated systemic vulnerabilities.

Tokenized Assets in Diversification

The tokenization of assets, driven by blockchain technology, is changing how investors approach diversification. By converting traditional assets such as real estate, art, and commodities into digital tokens, this process broadens access to these asset classes and creates new opportunities for portfolio diversification.

Tokenization Adds New Layers of Diversification

Tokenization is the process of converting ownership of tangible or intangible assets into digital tokens, which are recorded and transacted on a blockchain (Benedetti and Garnica 2023). This innovation makes traditionally illiquid and high-value assets—such as real estate, fine art, and commodities—more accessible, divisible, and tradable (Heines et al. 2021).

Tokenization can enhance the standard features and characteristics of assets and securities (Benedetti and Garnica 2023). It offers several benefits, including reduced issuance and trading costs, decreased reliance on intermediaries, increased market liquidity, and enhanced transparency regarding an asset's life cycle for all parties involved (Benedetti and Garnica 2023).

Furthermore, tokenization creates new opportunities for investors to diversify their portfolios by including assets that were previously difficult to access due to high costs or liquidity constraints.

Real Estate.   Real estate is one of the most significant sectors undergoing transformation through tokenization. Traditionally, investing in real estate requires substantial capital and poses liquidity challenges. Asset tokenization in real estate involves converting ownership of real estate assets into digital tokens, which can be traded on blockchain-based platforms (Alnabulsi 2024).

Tokenized real estate enables fractional ownership, allowing investors to purchase small portions of a property through these digital tokens. These tokens represent ownership rights, giving investors access to the real estate market without needing to buy an entire property. Alnabulsi (2024) analyzed the impact of asset tokenization on real estate markets, investment behavior, and financial stability. The findings suggest that asset tokenization has the potential to increase market liquidity, reduce transaction costs associated with real estate trading, and enhance investment diversification. Additionally, tokenized real estate can provide a stable, income-generating asset, helping to balance the volatility of other investments, such as equities or cryptocurrencies.

Art and Collectibles.   Art and collectibles, typically considered illiquid assets reserved for high-net-worth individuals, can now be tokenized and traded on digital platforms. By tokenizing ownership of paintings, sculptures, and other rare items, investors can purchase fractional shares of these valuable assets. This democratization of art investment simplifies the process of including rare, alternative assets in a portfolio, potentially providing returns that are uncorrelated with broader financial markets. Consequently, tokenized art and collectibles can serve as effective diversification tools, particularly during times of economic uncertainty when traditional markets may be volatile.

Commodities.   Commodities such as gold, oil, and agricultural products have long been integral to diversified portfolios, serving as hedges against inflation and economic downturns. Tokenization enables these commodities to be traded digitally, allowing investors direct access to commodity markets without the need for physical ownership or complicated financial instruments like futures contracts. For instance, a token representing a specific quantity of gold can be easily bought, sold, or transferred via blockchain technology, offering a more accessible and liquid means to gain exposure to commodities. Tokenized commodities can thus act as effective hedges in a diversified portfolio.

How Tokenization Adds New Layers of Diversification.   Tokenization expands the range of investable assets. Traditional portfolios have typically been limited to a few broad categories, such as stocks, bonds, and real estate. However, with tokenized assets, investors can explore a wider array of options, including real estate, fine art, commodities, digital currencies, synthetic assets, and even intellectual property. This broader access to various asset classes creates more opportunities for diversification, enabling investors to customize their portfolios for better risk-adjusted returns.

Tokenization allows for fractional ownership, introducing a new level of microdiversification. Even small investors can spread their capital across a diverse set of assets. For example, an investor might own fractions of a tokenized real estate property, a piece of fine art, and some commodities—all while maintaining liquidity and flexibility. This approach contrasts with traditional investments, which typically require substantial capital commitments and come with liquidity constraints.

Blockchain technology enhances interoperability between asset classes by enabling tokens representing different assets to be easily traded or exchanged on decentralized exchanges. This fosters new opportunities for cross-asset diversification, allowing investors to move seamlessly between types of tokenized assets without relying on centralized intermediaries. DeFi platforms facilitate this process, enabling users to hold various assets within a single ecosystem, often at lower costs than those found in traditional financial systems.

Tokenization benefits from the global and 24/7 accessibility of blockchain technology. Investors can access tokenized assets at any time and from any location, free from the time-zone constraints that traditional markets impose. This global accessibility enhances liquidity and reduces trading friction in various markets, allowing for more dynamic portfolio adjustments and improved risk management (Farabegoli and Fucile 2023).

Adhami et al. (2020) developed indexes to represent both the overall token asset class and its subclasses. They modeled dynamic conditional correlations among all asset classes in their sample to obtain time-varying correlations for each token-asset pair. Their study found that tokens serve as effective diversifiers but are neither a hedge nor a safe haven asset. This research demonstrated significant systematic differences between tokens and the two asset classes they are most often compared to: cryptocurrencies and equities.

Kantaphayao (2021) applied both static and dynamic conditional correlation to form portfolio optimization, calculating the dynamic conditional correlation using the Dynamic Conditional Correlation(DCC)-GARCH (1,1) model. Kantaphayao found that coins and tokens are moderately positively correlated with each other; however, they exhibit extremely low correlations with other traditional assets. Therefore, cryptocurrencies may serve as an alternative asset class beneficial for portfolio diversification.

BenMabrouk et al. (2024) examined dynamic spillover effects and hedging effectiveness among five main segments of NFTs—collectibles, art, gaming, metaverse, and utility—compared to other asset classes such as Bitcoin and American stocks (S&P 500). Their study covered the period from April 27, 2018 to September 15, 2022. Utilizing a time-varying connectedness approach through the TVP-VAR model, inspired by the Diebold and Yilmaz spillover index, they found weak dynamic return spillovers between NFTs and traditional assets, indicating that these new digital assets remain relatively decoupled from them and Bitcoin. The results showed that Bitcoin is a significant transmitter of spillover effects, while collectibles, utility assets, and the S&P 500 are net recipients of these spillovers.

The Rise of Synthetic Assets

Synthetic assets are digital tokens that represent real-world or financial assets, such as stocks, bonds, commodities, or currencies. These assets are created and traded within DeFi ecosystems. By using synthetic assets, investors can gain exposure to traditional financial assets without having to hold the underlying assets directly. This bridges the gap between traditional finance and DeFi, providing a powerful tool for diversification and risk management.

Within DeFi platforms, synthetic assets allow investors to access stocks or bonds without using traditional brokerage services. For instance, a synthetic token might track the price of Apple stock or the value of a government bond, enabling DeFi users to trade or invest in these assets in a decentralized environment. This creates a seamless connection between traditional finance and DeFi, broadening the range of assets available for a diversified portfolio without relying on centralized intermediaries.

Risk Management and Hedging.   Synthetic assets also offer opportunities for hedging and managing risk within investment portfolios. Investors can use synthetic assets to gain exposure to assets that move inversely to their other holdings, providing protection against downside risk. Additionally, these assets can mimic complex financial derivatives such as options or futures, enabling more sophisticated portfolio strategies to be executed on DeFi platforms (Benedetti and Labbé 2021). This adds significant diversification benefits, especially for those seeking a wider variety of financial instruments.

One major advantage of synthetic assets is the increased liquidity they bring to traditionally illiquid markets. By tokenizing financial instruments and enabling their trade on decentralized exchanges, synthetic assets help eliminate barriers associated with certain investments, such as high fees, regulatory constraints, and limited access (Benedetti and Labbé 2021). This increased liquidity facilitates more dynamic portfolio management and better opportunities for diversification.

Summary

The integration of digital assets into portfolio management presents both exciting opportunities and significant challenges for investors. While MPT offers a valuable framework for balancing risk and return, the unique characteristics of digital assets introduce complexities due to their extreme volatility, speculative nature, and departure from traditional assumptions, such as efficient markets and rational behavior.

When used strategically, digital assets can enhance portfolio diversification and improve risk-adjusted returns. Innovations such as stablecoins and tokenized assets provide lower volatility and additional diversification options. The key takeaway is that, despite their deviation from traditional MPT assumptions, digital assets offer unique benefits and potential returns, making them valuable components of modern portfolios.

PART 3

Integrating and Managing Digital Assets

Strategies, Risk, and Regulatory Considerations

CHAPTER 5

Asset Allocation Strategies

Asset allocation is a crucial element of investment strategy, determining how capital is distributed among various asset classes to balance risk and return. As financial markets evolve, so do the models and approaches that investors use for asset allocation. This chapter explores both traditional asset allocation models—such as the classic 60/40 portfolio—and the emerging role of digital assets, including cryptocurrencies and altcoins, in modern portfolios.

By comparing case studies of traditional portfolios with those that incorporate digital assets, we examine how asset allocation strategies can be adjusted to address new risks and opportunities. Additionally, we delve into advanced asset allocation techniques, such as risk parity, volatility-based allocation, and trend-following, which provide dynamic methods for navigating today's increasingly complex and volatile markets.

This chapter serves as a comprehensive guide to understanding the evolution of asset allocation and how modern portfolios can be structured to optimize performance in an ever-changing financial landscape.

Traditional Asset Allocation Models

Asset allocation is a crucial aspect of portfolio management, determining how an investor's funds are distributed across various asset classes. Traditional asset allocation models aim to balance risk and return by considering factors such as time horizon, risk tolerance, and market conditions.

Strategic Versus Tactical Asset Allocation

Strategic Asset Allocation

Strategic asset allocation focuses on long-term investment goals. It involves setting a target mix of asset classes that aligns with an investor's risk tolerance, financial objectives, and time horizon. The asset allocation remains relatively stable over time, with periodic rebalancing to maintain the target proportions. Strategic asset allocation is based on the belief that markets are generally efficient over the long term. The key to success lies in maintaining a diversified portfolio that reflects the investor's overall strategy (Zhong 2013). This method typically minimizes trading and transaction costs, making it suitable for long-term investors, such as those saving for retirement.

Tactical Asset Allocation

In contrast, *tactical asset allocation* is a short-term, dynamic strategy where investors actively adjust their portfolio weightings to take advantage of market opportunities or to defend against perceived risks. These tactical adjustments are based on market conditions, economic data, or asset price trends, aiming to exploit short-term inefficiencies. While the core principles of strategic allocation still apply, tactical shifts allow for temporary deviations from the long-term allocation to enhance returns or reduce risk during volatile periods. This approach requires more frequent monitoring and incurs higher trading costs, but it offers greater flexibility for investors looking to adapt to changing market environments.

The 60/40 Portfolio—Does It Still Work?

The 60/40 portfolio—typically composed of 60 percent equities and 40 percent bonds—has long served as a benchmark for investors seeking a balanced approach to growth and risk management (Correia 2023). In this model, the equities portion usually drives capital appreciation, while the bond allocation provides income stability and downside protection during stock market downturns. However, the evolving financial landscape has raised questions about the continuing viability of the 60/40 portfolio in today's market.

Declining Bond Yields

Historically, bonds have been essential for generating stable returns and serving as a hedge against stock market volatility. Recently, however, persistently low interest rates have significantly reduced the yields that bonds can offer. With central banks implementing low interest rate policies and quantitative easing to stimulate economic growth, bond yields have become compressed, limiting their potential for income generation. This situation calls into question whether bonds can still provide meaningful returns and protection within a 60/40 portfolio.

Furthermore, lower yields mean that bonds may no longer fulfill their traditional role as a safe haven. In past economic downturns, bonds have reliably buffered equity losses, but the diminished income and potential for price appreciation in a low-interest-rate environment weaken this protective function.

Inflation and the Erosion of Fixed-Income Returns

Another significant challenge for the traditional 60/40 portfolio is rising inflation. When inflation increases, the purchasing power of fixed-income assets like bonds diminishes. Bonds typically offer fixed interest payments, but in a high-inflation environment, these payments may not keep pace with rising costs, thereby eroding real returns. As a result, investors risk that their bond investments may not provide sufficient returns to compensate for inflation, further undermining the overall defensive role that bonds usually play in a balanced portfolio.

Shifting to Alternative Asset Classes

In response to these challenges, investors are increasingly diversifying their portfolios beyond the traditional 60/40 model by incorporating alternative asset classes such as real estate, commodities, and digital assets like cryptocurrencies. These alternatives offer potential inflation protection and improved diversification, as they tend to exhibit lower correlations with traditional assets like stocks and bonds.

Real estate and commodities are viewed as natural hedges against inflation, as their prices often rise in line with general price levels. Digital assets, including Bitcoin and Ethereum, are attracting attention due to their high potential returns and unique status as uncorrelated assets, although they come with increased volatility and regulatory uncertainty.

Given the changing market environment, many investors are exploring adjustments to the traditional 60/40 portfolio. However, incorporating these alternative assets introduces new risks, such as volatility, liquidity constraints, and, in the case of digital assets, regulatory uncertainty. Balancing these risks with the traditional goals of growth and stability necessitates a more nuanced approach to portfolio construction.

Portfolios Including Digital Assets

Traditional 60/40 Portfolio Versus 60/30/10

With the rise of digital assets, especially Bitcoin, investors are increasingly exploring the option of adding a small allocation of Bitcoin to their portfolios in order to capture its high growth potential. In a traditional 60/40 portfolio, digital assets could fit into the "alternatives" allocation, balancing their volatility with more stable assets such as bonds and cash.

Diversification

Historically, Bitcoin has shown low correlation with traditional assets such as equities and bonds. This means that when stock prices decline, Bitcoin does not always follow the same pattern, which could help cushion losses in a diversified portfolio. However, it is important to note that correlations can fluctuate—during market crises, Bitcoin has occasionally moved in sync with risk assets, such as technology stocks.

Yousaf and Yarovaya (2022) calculated the static and dynamic optimal weights, hedge ratios, and hedging effectiveness for portfolios that included NFTs and other assets (including oil, gold, Bitcoin, and the S&P 500). Their findings suggested that investors and portfolio managers should consider adding NFTs and DeFi assets to their portfolios of gold, oil, and stocks to achieve diversification benefits. Utilizing the DCC-GARCH model, BenMabrouk et al. (2024) found that adding NFTs to portfolios composed of either the S&P 500 or Bitcoin could enhance diversification advantages. Furthermore, using a TVP-VAR model, Goodell et al. (2023) concluded that NFTs are highly suitable for inclusion in portfolios due to their low correlation with the other examined asset classes.

Inflation Hedge

Bitcoin has a hard cap of 21 million coins, which makes it scarce, similar to gold. Furthermore, unlike fiat currencies, no central authority (such as the Federal Reserve or the ECB) can print more Bitcoin. Every four years, the rate at which new Bitcoin is issued is cut in half, further increasing its scarcity over time.

Liquidity and Accessibility

Bitcoin is one of the most liquid assets in the digital marketplace, with a market capitalization exceeding US$1 trillion as of December 31, 2024. It is traded 24/7, unlike stocks and bonds, which have specific market hours. Transactions involving Bitcoin can also be conducted within seconds via exchanges, funds, or ETFs.

Volatility

However, including Bitcoin in a portfolio also brings significantly higher volatility. Bitcoin is notorious for its extreme price fluctuations, often experiencing daily swings of 10 percent or more, with annualized volatility much greater than that of both equities and bonds (Conlon et al. 2024). Although long-term returns may be impressive, the short-term volatility can have a major impact on the overall portfolio, particularly during bearish cryptocurrency cycles.

During downturns in the cryptocurrency market, Bitcoin has been known to undergo severe declines, sometimes losing more than 50 percent of its value within weeks or months. When Bitcoin enters such periods of drastic correction, its presence can amplify losses, leading to larger drawdowns than a traditional 60/40 portfolio would typically encounter (Kawai et al. 2024). This risk is especially relevant for investors with shorter time horizons or those who are less tolerant of volatility (Olabanji et al. 2024).

The volatility of Bitcoin can also prompt emotional reactions from investors, resulting in decisions driven by fear or excitement rather than sound investment principles (Hafishina et al. 2023). This may lead to panic selling during downturns or overexposure during bullish trends, complicating portfolio management.

Asymmetric Return Profile

Bitcoin has demonstrated remarkable growth since its inception, boasting annualized returns that significantly surpass those of traditional asset classes over certain periods. Research indicates that during Bitcoin's bull runs, portfolios with even a modest allocation to Bitcoin have outperformed traditional 60/40 portfolios (Platanakis and Urquhart 2020). The substantial growth of Bitcoin during these periods can lead to impressive returns, enhancing portfolio performance in the short to medium term (Wang et al. 2023). Consequently, adjusting the portfolio to 60 percent equities, 30 percent bonds, and 10 percent Bitcoin— a 60/30/10 portfolio—can increase returns, especially during bullish phases in the cryptocurrency market.

Additionally, Bitcoin has an asymmetric return profile, meaning that its potential gains significantly outweigh potential losses. While Bitcoin has historically exhibited high volatility, its long-term trajectory has been overwhelmingly positive.

Risk-Adjusted Returns

Despite Bitcoin's extreme volatility, its long-term positive returns can significantly enhance a portfolio's risk-adjusted performance, as measured by metrics such as the *Sharpe ratio* and the *Sortino ratio*. These ratios evaluate a portfolio's returns relative to the risks it incurs. The Sharpe ratio assesses total volatility (Honerød-Bentsen and Knutli 2023). Evidence shows that during bull markets, Bitcoin's gains often lead to an increased Sharpe ratio, indicating better risk-adjusted returns compared to a traditional 60/40 portfolio (Honerød-Bentsen and Knutli 2023). Backtest also suggests that even a small allocation to Bitcoin, e.g., 1-5 percent, can enhance Sharpe ratio without significantly increasing portfolio volatility, assuming a long-term investment horizon.

In analyzing optimal portfolios using the DCC-GARCH (1,1) model, Kantaphayao (2021) found that actively adjusted weight portfolios yield much higher average annual returns, although they also exhibit a higher standard deviation compared to fixed-weight investment portfolios. Notably, the increase in average return outweighs the relatively small rise in standard deviation.

Similarly, Dhillon and Nikbakht (2023) reported that adding crypto assets to simulated portfolios of equities, bonds, and real estate improved the reward-to-risk ratio, as measured by the Sharpe ratio. It is important to note, however, that the contribution of crypto assets to a well-diversified traditional portfolio differs significantly from the performance of investing in a single, isolated crypto asset.

The Sortino ratio focuses specifically on downside risk (Honerød-Bentsen and Knutli 2023). In favorable market conditions, the Sortino ratio also improves as strong upside performance compensates for downside volatility, particularly when risks are managed with small position sizes.

Umar et al. (2023) examined the risks and returns associated with NFTs, considering tail dependence, higher order moments, and various portfolio characteristics. They analyzed a range of asset classes, including equities, fixed-income securities, and commodities. Their findings highlighted the beneficial hedging and portfolio attributes of NFTs, utilizing conditional value-at-risk (CoVaR) and ΔCoVaR with different copula functions. The results indicate that NFTs offer valuable investment and hedging characteristics across various market conditions, including during the COVID-19 pandemic.

However, while adding Bitcoin can improve risk-adjusted performance in favorable market conditions, it also increases vulnerability to rapid corrections. During bearish cycles or periods of extreme market stress, this heightened vulnerability to sudden price drops underscores the need for careful consideration regarding timing and market conditions, as the volatility of digital assets can work against investors during adverse situations.

El Alaoui et al. (2021) explored the effects of adding digital currencies to an Islamic portfolio by relying on a mean-variance efficient frontier. They compared the risk-return profiles of portfolios with and without digital currencies across different scenarios. The results indicated that incorporating digital currencies into Shariah-compliant portfolios can enhance performance; however, this improvement is primarily driven by an increase in returns, rather than a reduction in total risk. Specifically, digital currencies can introduce significant speculative risks into portfolio diversification.

Kantaphayao (2021) suggested that the optimal allocation of investments in cryptocurrencies should be lower compared to traditional assets known for their fundamental movements. For investors with a long-term perspective and a high tolerance for risk, including Bitcoin in a traditional 60/40 portfolio can be an effective strategy to enhance returns. Additionally, Castro et al. (2020) developed a portfolio optimization model based on the Omega measure, which offers a more comprehensive approach than the Markowitz model. Their findings indicated no clear preference for any specific cryptocurrency when creating portfolios composed exclusively of crypto assets.

Mixed Portfolio With Altcoins

Altcoins can significantly enhance a portfolio by increasing its growth potential, diversification, utility, and income generation. While Bitcoin primarily serves as a store of value, altcoins fulfill various functions, including powering smart contracts, DeFi, gaming, and AI applications. The main advantages of including altcoins in a portfolio are:

Higher Growth Potential

Although Bitcoin is the largest and most stable cryptocurrency, altcoins have delivered higher percentage gains during bull markets due to their smaller market capitalizations and innovation-driven growth. Many altcoins have historically outperformed Bitcoin during bullish market cycles. In strong uptrends, altcoins can offer returns multiples (5x, 10x, or more) greater than those of Bitcoin.

Diversification Within Crypto

Investing in altcoins allows for exposure to multiple blockchain ecosystems, reducing reliance on Bitcoin's price movements and creating a more balanced portfolio. Many altcoins facilitate real-world applications such as DeFi, smart contracts, gaming, and the tokenization of assets. Investing in altcoins provides an opportunity to engage with the future of blockchain technology and its real-world adoption.

Yield Generation

Unlike Bitcoin, which does not provide native yield, some altcoins enable investors to earn passive income through staking, lending, and liquidity provision within DeFi protocols. This approach enhances returns without necessitating the sale of assets.

For investors with a risk-tolerant mindset and a long-term perspective, a well-balanced digital asset portfolio that includes altcoins allows for diversified exposure within the crypto ecosystem while effectively managing risk. However, it is essential to note that allocating to altcoins alongside Bitcoin can increase volatility. Altcoins like Ethereum, Solana, and Cardano, which serve specific functions, often experience more significant price fluctuations compared to Bitcoin. Since many altcoins are associated with emerging technologies and particular use cases, they carry a higher degree of speculative risk and market uncertainty.

However, allocating to altcoins alongside Bitcoin in a portfolio also carries the risk of increased volatility. Altcoins such as Ethereum, Solana, and Cardano, which serve specific functions, often experience more significant price fluctuations than Bitcoin. As many altcoins are linked to emerging technologies and particular use cases, they come with a higher degree of speculative risk and market uncertainty.

Several factors contribute to the higher volatility of altcoins compared to Bitcoin:

1. Market Capitalization: Many altcoins have significantly smaller market caps than Bitcoin, making them more vulnerable to large price swings due to relatively modest trades. Low liquidity in altcoin markets can exacerbate this volatility, causing price movements to be more pronounced in reaction to market sentiment or large buy/sell orders.

2. Evolving Technologies: Altcoins are often associated with innovative technologies or platforms, such as smart contract platforms (e.g., Ethereum, Solana) or DeFi projects that are still in early adoption stages. This speculative aspect increases price volatility, as investors react to news, project developments, or regulatory updates.

3. Ecosystem Development: Unlike Bitcoin, which has solidified its status as a more stable asset in the cryptocurrency market, many altcoins are still developing their ecosystems. The success or failure of updates, security issues, or competition from other blockchain platforms can lead to significant price fluctuations.

During bearish market cycles, altcoins typically experience sharper declines due to their smaller size and higher speculative nature. Investors often perceive these assets as riskier and tend to liquidate positions quickly when market sentiment shifts, which can cause dramatic price drops. The rush to invest in altcoins can reverse just as rapidly, resulting in substantial losses during market stress.

When incorporating altcoins into a portfolio alongside Bitcoin, it is essential to recognize the potential for increased price fluctuations that can lead to heightened portfolio volatility. While diversifying among various altcoins may reduce exposure to the risk of any single project, the overall correlations within the crypto market tend to increase during market downturns. This means that if Bitcoin falls, altcoins often decline even more sharply, concentrating risk rather than alleviating it.

Those investors seeking short-term gains might face significant challenges due to unpredictable price swings and the potential for capital loss during market downturns.

Factors Affecting Allocation

Risk Tolerance

Risk tolerance is a critical factor in determining how much to allocate to digital assets. It refers to an investor's ability and willingness to endure the volatility and potential loss of value in their portfolio. Investors with a high risk tolerance are comfortable with significant fluctuations in asset prices and can withstand market downturns, leading them to allocate more heavily to equities and alternative investments. Conversely, those with a low risk tolerance prioritize capital preservation and income generation. Assessing risk tolerance is essential to ensure that an investor's portfolio aligns with their comfort level regarding risk and their financial capacity to absorb losses.

Cryptocurrencies are known for their high volatility, which can result in both substantial gains and steep losses. Investors with high risk tolerance may be more inclined to allocate a larger portion of their portfolios to digital assets, seeking the potential for outsized returns despite the associated volatility. In contrast, conservative investors with lower risk tolerance may prefer minimal or no exposure to digital assets, favoring more stable investment options. It is crucial to allocate digital assets in a way that corresponds to an investor's ability to endure potential losses without jeopardizing their overall financial security.

Time Horizon

Time horizon refers to the length of time an investor intends to hold investments before needing to withdraw funds. Long-term investors can benefit from the growth prospects of digital assets over time, even amidst short-term volatility. A longer time horizon allows investors to ride out market cycles and take advantage of the potential upside of emerging technologies. On the other hand, short-term investors, or those approaching a specific financial goal, such as retirement, may be less inclined to allocate heavily to volatile digital assets, as they might not have sufficient time to recover from potential market downturns. Therefore, time horizon significantly impacts the level of risk an investor can afford to undertake.

Liquidity

Liquidity refers to how easily an asset can be converted into cash without significantly affecting its price. Major cryptocurrencies such as Bitcoin and Ethereum are generally liquid and can be traded quickly. However, some altcoins or tokens linked to smaller projects may have liquidity constraints, making them harder to buy or sell without impacting the price, especially during market downturns. For those who might need quick access to capital, it's important to ensure that their portfolio includes liquid assets alongside any more illiquid digital investments to avoid being forced to sell at unfavorable prices.

Regulatory Environment

The regulatory landscape for digital assets is still evolving, with significant variations across jurisdictions. Regulatory uncertainty adds another layer of risk, as future regulations could affect the market, trading, and taxation of cryptocurrencies. While some countries have embraced digital assets, others have imposed strict regulations or outright bans. Investors should carefully assess the regulatory environment in their region and globally when determining the level of exposure they're comfortable with. Additionally, regulatory changes may influence the tax treatment of digital assets, making compliance and tax efficiency important to consider.

Advanced Asset Allocation Strategies

Risk Parity Strategy

Risk parity is an asset allocation strategy designed to distribute risk equally across various asset classes, rather than relying solely on capital or expected returns. The main goal is to create a balanced portfolio where each asset contributes equally to the overall risk, which can help reduce volatility and smooth returns over time.

When applying risk parity to digital assets, the focus is on balancing the risk that each asset contributes to the overall portfolio, ensuring that no single asset or asset class dominates the portfolio's volatility. Given the high volatility of cryptocurrencies such as Bitcoin and Ethereum, this approach can be especially beneficial for investors who want exposure to digital assets without being heavily affected by their inherent risks.

In a risk parity strategy, the weight allocated to Bitcoin or Ethereum is not based purely on their high expected returns; rather, their volatility is also considered. This often leads to a reduced allocation to these high-volatility assets to balance their impact on the overall portfolio risk. For example, if Bitcoin's annualized volatility is around 80 percent, while other assets in the portfolio, such as bonds or equities, exhibit much lower volatility, holding a significant amount of Bitcoin could disproportionately increase the portfolio's risk. Thus, a risk parity approach would involve decreasing the allocations to Bitcoin and Ethereum to align their risk contributions with the rest of the portfolio.

To counterbalance the volatility of high-risk digital assets, a risk parity strategy may increase allocations to less volatile assets, such as stablecoins or lower-risk altcoins. By raising the proportion of stablecoins, investors can stabilize the overall portfolio and mitigate the impact of fluctuations in the more volatile segments of the crypto market. Lower-risk altcoins, such as Chainlink or Litecoin, generally display less extreme price swings than Bitcoin or Ethereum while still providing exposure to the broader cryptocurrency market. Although these altcoins are still subject to market fluctuations, their reduced volatility can be advantageous in a risk parity strategy.

During cryptocurrency bear markets, where Bitcoin or Ethereum may experience significant drawdowns, a portfolio constructed using risk parity principles tends to be less impacted. The inclusion of stablecoins or lower volatility assets helps maintain overall portfolio stability, preventing large fluctuations in value.

Koutsouri et al. (2020) built on the risk parity theory by allowing for weighting based on the desired contribution to volatility. Their research indicated that a crypto-gold weighting based on weighted risk contribution historically achieved a better Sharpe ratio compared to various other asset allocation strategies. Within their crypto basket—composed of selected assets that are rebalanced monthly—they found that an equal weighting scheme outperformed market capitalization weighting in terms of the Sharpe ratio.

Kashyap (2024) developed blockchain-based risk-managed portfolios by creating three distinct funds with varying risk and return profiles: (1) Alpha—a high-risk portfolio; (2) Beta—which mirrors the broader market; and (3) Gamma—representing the risk-free rate adjusted for inflation. Kashyap set the weight of each asset in its respective portfolio inversely proportional to the risk involved in investing in that asset. This structure ensures equal risk contributions from each asset toward the overall portfolio risk within the subfunds (Alpha, Beta, and Gamma). The study illustrated that any investor could utilize decentralized ledger technology to select their preferred level of risk or return and allocate their wealth accordingly among the subfunds, which balance one another under varying market conditions. This evolution of the risk parity principle leads to a framework designed to perform well across all market cycles, which can be termed conceptual parity.

Hierarchical risk parity (HRP) incorporates a filtered correlation structure and is less sensitive to noise compared to quadratic optimization. Papenbrock et al. (2021) showcased the robustness of the HRP approach by comparing various extensions, finding that a specific type of adaptive HRP strategy outperformed others on a risk-adjusted basis. They also noted that structural breaks in crypto correlations are common, and the optimal hierarchical cluster representations change over time—insights best captured by distance matrix-based adaptive HRP approaches.

Volatility-Based Allocation

In traditional asset allocation, portfolios are periodically rebalanced to maintain predefined asset class weights. In contrast, volatility-based rebalancing adjusts allocations dynamically based on the observed volatility of each asset. This approach is particularly important for digital assets, which can experience extreme price fluctuations compared to traditional investments.

When market volatility increases—such as during corrections or periods of uncertainty—the allocation to digital assets is reduced to mitigate risk. For example, during the COVID-19 market crash in March 2020, Bitcoin lost over 50 percent of its value within a short time (Wu et al. 2022). A portfolio employing volatility-based rebalancing would have lowered exposure as volatility rose, thus limiting losses during this period. The rationale behind this strategy is to lower risk when market uncertainty is high, as prices are likely to be erratic, leading to greater downside risk compared to potential upside.

Conversely, during stable or bullish market conditions, when volatility decreases, dynamic rebalancing allows for higher allocations to digital assets. This strategy enables investors to benefit from price appreciation while the market is less volatile and more predictable. For instance, in a prolonged Bitcoin bull market, volatility often declines as prices steadily increase. During such times, increasing allocations to digital assets can enhance returns without taking on excessive risk, given that market conditions are favorable.

This approach helps investors capture upside potential while maintaining a disciplined approach to risk management. Dynamic adjustments keep the portfolio's risk exposure in check, ensuring that high-volatility periods do not lead to disproportionately large swings in portfolio value. Additionally, by smoothing out overall portfolio volatility, investors can better manage their risk-return profiles.

Another significant benefit of dynamic rebalancing based on volatility is that it minimizes emotional decision making during market extremes. Investors often make impulsive decisions, selling when markets crash and buying during euphoric bull runs. A volatility-based strategy removes emotion from the equation by providing a systematic way to increase or decrease exposure based on objective measures like market volatility.

During periods of extreme fear, when volatility is high, this strategy automatically reduces risk, preventing overexposure to digital assets at the wrong time. Conversely, during periods of overconfidence, when volatility is low, it ensures that exposure to digital assets can increase without the risk of being caught off guard by unpredictable market shifts.

- Example: Consider a portfolio with a target allocation of 20 percent to digital assets, such as Bitcoin and Ethereum. During a period of high volatility, when Bitcoin's price experiences large swings, the allocation to digital assets could be reduced to 10 percent or even 5 percent, depending on the severity of the volatility. Conversely, during calm market conditions when volatility is low, the allocation could be increased to 25 percent or even higher, depending on the investor's risk tolerance and market outlook.

Market Timing With Trend-Following

Trend-following strategies employ fixed trading mechanisms to capitalize on long-term market movements, regardless of past price performance (Fong and Tai 2009). These strategies, particularly those that utilize long-term indicators such as the 200-day *moving average* (200-DMA), provide a systematic approach to managing exposure to digital assets in response to market trends. By increasing exposure during upward trends and reducing it during downward trends, trend-following strategies help investors navigate the extreme price volatility characteristic of digital asset markets. The objective is to capture upward momentum during bull markets while minimizing the risk of significant drawdowns during bearish cycles.

The 200-DMA is one of the most commonly used long-term trend indicators in both traditional and digital asset markets. It calculates the average price of an asset over the past 200 days, smoothing out short-term fluctuations to offer a clearer view of the underlying trend. When a digital asset's current price (e.g., Bitcoin, Ethereum) is above its 200-DMA, it indicates an upward trend. This suggests that bullish momentum is present, prompting investors to increase their exposure to the asset, anticipating further price appreciation. Conversely, if the current price falls below the 200-DMA, it indicates a downward trend. This signals potential weakness, urging investors to reduce their exposure or exit their positions to avoid being caught in a prolonged bear market. The 200-DMA is effective at filtering out short-term noise, allowing investors to make decisions based on sustained movements rather than reacting to daily volatility.

In the context of digital assets, trend-following strategies enable investors to participate in bull markets without attempting to perfectly time the market. By following the 200-DMA, investors can gradually increase their exposure when the price breaks above this average, indicating that bullish momentum is building. Digital assets, especially cryptocurrencies, often experience explosive price growth during bull markets, frequently posting exponential gains in a short time. A trend-following strategy based on the 200-DMA allows investors to ride this upward momentum, ensuring that they capitalize on the majority of the price appreciation while minimizing the risk of missing out on gains.

Le and Ruthbah (2023) developed and evaluated trend-following investment strategies in the context of cryptocurrencies and examined the commonly held belief regarding the correlation between the movements of the Nasdaq 100 index and cryptocurrencies, which has significant implications for investment strategy development. Their findings suggest that trend-following strategies perform well over the researched period. Moreover, they discovered that the impact of transaction costs on portfolio performance is substantial. Additionally, Le and Ruthbah found no correlation between the Nasdaq 100 index and the cryptocurrencies examined, which contradicts widespread market perceptions.

A key benefit of a 200-DMA strategy is its ability to signal when to reduce exposure during bear markets. Given the crypto market's high volatility and steep drawdowns, a downward break below the 200-DMA can serve as a warning sign that prices are likely to decline further. This capital preservation strategy is crucial in the volatile crypto space, where unchecked losses can adversely affect long-term portfolio performance.

The volatility of the crypto market can make it challenging for investors to maintain consistent exposure without facing significant drawdowns. Trend-following strategies, such as the 200-DMA, help mitigate this risk by providing a systematic approach to adjusting exposure based on price trends. Instead of relying on emotional decision making, investors can use clear, rules-based signals to navigate extreme price fluctuations effectively.

These strategies also help eliminate emotional bias by offering a structured method for making buy and sell decisions based on actual price trends rather than personal emotions. Furthermore, using longer term indicators such as the 200-DMA filters out short-term price movements or "noise," which can often lead to false buy or sell signals in short-term trading strategies. This longer term perspective is particularly beneficial in the crypto market, where price spikes or drops can occur frequently but do not necessarily reflect a change in the underlying trend.

- Case Study: Historically, applying a 200-DMA strategy to Bitcoin has provided valuable signals for navigating bull and bear markets. During Bitcoin's bull run from late 2020 to early 2021, Bitcoin's price consistently stayed above the 200-DMA, indicating strong upward momentum (Kanani et al. 2021). Investors following this strategy would have increased their exposure early in the rally, capturing substantial gains. However, during the mid-2021 correction, when Bitcoin's price fell sharply and crossed below the 200-DMA, it would have signaled a need to reduce exposure, helping investors preserve capital.

Summary

In the rapidly changing financial landscape, asset allocation strategies must evolve to keep up with market dynamics, investor requirements, and new asset classes. Traditional models, like the 60/40 portfolio, have historically provided a stable framework for balancing risk and return. However, the emergence of digital assets such as Bitcoin and altcoins challenges the assumptions behind these strategies.

Empirical evidence shows that incorporating digital assets into investment portfolios can enhance returns, but it also introduces new levels of volatility and risk, complicating the allocation process. At the same time, advanced asset allocation strategies—such as risk parity, volatility-based allocation, and trend-following—provide investors with tools to dynamically adjust their portfolios in response to changing market conditions, aiming for improved risk-adjusted returns.

Ultimately, the most effective asset allocation strategy takes into account individual risk tolerance, investment time horizon, and the specific features of both traditional and digital assets. This approach helps investors navigate the complexities of modern markets while optimizing performance.

CHAPTER 6

Assessing Digital Asset Investments

As digital assets continue to gain prominence in global financial markets, effectively assessing their value and growth potential has become crucial for investors. Unlike traditional assets, digital assets such as cryptocurrencies and tokenized assets require a unique blend of analytical approaches.

In this chapter, we explore the key methodologies used to evaluate digital assets:

1. *Fundamental analysis* (FA) examines use cases and adoption metrics.
2. *Technical analysis* (TA) focuses on price trends, chart patterns, and market indicators.
3. *Sentiment analysis* gauges market psychology and investor sentiment by analyzing social media, news, and other public sources.

Together, these approaches provide a comprehensive framework for understanding the factors driving digital asset markets, helping investors make informed decisions in this rapidly evolving and highly volatile space.

Fundamental Analysis of Digital Assets

FA is a method used by investors to evaluate the intrinsic value of an asset by examining various economic, financial, and qualitative factors. In traditional finance, FA focuses on metrics such as earnings, revenue, and balance sheets. However, when analyzing digital assets, FA takes a different approach because many digital assets do not represent ownership in a company or produce cash flows. Instead, investors must rely on unique metrics tailored to blockchain technology, network activity, and the underlying utility of the digital asset.

Utility and Use Cases

One of the most critical aspects of evaluating a digital asset is understanding its utility and use case within the broader ecosystem. This involves analyzing the asset's purpose, the problem it aims to solve, and the potential demand for the solution it provides.

For example, Bitcoin is often viewed as "digital gold," serving as a store of value, whereas Ethereum powers dApps through smart contracts. Some tokens are used for governance, staking, or as a medium of exchange within specific DeFi protocols.

Assessing real-world adoption and demand for the digital asset is essential. A project with a strong use case and a growing user base— such as Ethereum for DeFi applications or Chainlink for decentralized data oracles—is more likely to succeed in the long term. By analyzing the asset's adoption rate and the strength of its use case, investors can gauge future demand for the token and its potential for value appreciation.

Tokenomics

Tokenomics refers to the economic structure and incentives that govern the digital asset, including the token's supply dynamics, distribution model, and inflation rate. Understanding tokenomics is crucial for assessing the long-term sustainability and price appreciation potential of a digital asset.

Factors such as the maximum supply of tokens, the current circulating supply, and how new tokens are issued (e.g., mining, staking rewards, or inflation) can significantly affect price dynamics. For instance, Bitcoin has a fixed maximum supply of 21 million coins, which creates scarcity and helps drive its value over time.

Some digital assets have inflationary supply models, meaning new tokens are continuously added, which can dilute the value of existing tokens. In contrast, deflationary models, like Bitcoin's, have a capped supply, which generally favors long-term price appreciation. It is also important to evaluate how the token is used within its network. Some tokens may serve as utility tokens, while others may be utilized for governance or staking. Projects with multiple use cases for their tokens tend to have stronger demand drivers.

Network Activity and On-Chain Metrics

FA of digital assets also entails evaluating on-chain metrics—data directly observable on the blockchain. These metrics provide insights into the health and usage of the network and can serve as powerful indicators of demand and value.

1. High and increasing transaction volumes often signal healthy network activity, indicating that the digital asset is being actively used for payments, smart contracts, or dApps. The number of unique active addresses on the network is another valuable metric; a rising number suggests growing user adoption, while a decline may signal waning interest.
2. For PoW assets like Bitcoin, the network's hash rate (the computing power dedicated to securing the network) is a crucial indicator of security and robustness. A higher hash rate often indicates a more secure and resilient network.
3. In PoS assets, the amount of tokens being staked is an important indicator of network participation and investor confidence. Staking reduces the liquid supply of tokens, which can create upward price pressure.

Development Activity and Team

The success of a digital asset heavily relies on the quality and activity of its development team and the broader community supporting the project. Development activity serves as a proxy for ongoing progress and innovation, both essential for long-term viability.

Tools like GitHub can track the number of commits, code updates, and releases in the project's repository. Active development suggests that the team is continually improving the platform, fixing bugs, and introducing new features. This is particularly important in blockchain networks, where technological innovation drives value.

A project's founding team, advisers, and partners can also indicate its likelihood of success. Experienced teams with backgrounds in blockchain, software development, or finance are better positioned to overcome challenges. Investors should look for backing from reputable venture capital (VC) firms, partnerships with established companies, or alliances with other blockchain projects.

External Factors

Regulatory Environment

The regulatory landscape for digital assets is constantly evolving, and changes in regulations can significantly impact a project's viability. Investors must stay informed about both local and international regulations that affect the asset. Compliance with emerging rules regarding AML, securities laws, and taxation can influence adoption rates, exchange listings, and institutional interest.

Competitive Landscape

Competition in the digital asset space is intense. It is essential to evaluate how a project compares to its competitors. Is it a first mover, or does it possess unique advantages over others? For example, while Ethereum is a leader in smart contract platforms, newer competitors like Solana and Avalanche offer faster transaction processing. Understanding the competitive landscape helps investors assess a project's potential for long-term success or vulnerability to being overtaken by rivals.

Case Study: Fundamental Analysis of Ethereum

This framework evaluates Ethereum based on five key aspects: utility, tokenomics, network activity and on-chain metrics, development activity and team, and external factors.

Utility and Use Cases

Ethereum's wide range of applications makes it one of the most versatile and widely adopted blockchain networks.

Key Use Cases:

1. Smart Contracts:Self-executing agreements that operate without intermediaries.
2. DeFi: Decentralized finance applications for lending, borrowing, and trading protocols (e.g., Aave, Uniswap).
3. NFTs: Enabling digital ownership of assets in areas like art, gaming, and collectibles.
4. Layer 2 Scaling Solutions: Solutions like Polygon, Arbitrum, and Optimism enhance Ethereum's efficiency.
5. Enterprise Adoption: Institutions utilize Ethereum for tokenized assets and blockchain integration.

Tokenomics

The tokenomics of Ethereum directly impact its value proposition and long-term sustainability.

Key Tokenomics Metrics:

- Total Supply: No fixed cap (issuance reduced post-Merge).
- Circulating Supply: Approximately 120 million ETH.
- Consensus Mechanism: Transitioned to PoS following the Ethereum Merge.

- Staking Rewards: Validators earn an annual yield of roughly 3–5 percent.
- Burn Mechanism: Ethereum Improvement Proposals (EIP)-1559 burn transaction fees, contributing to its deflationary nature.
- Inflation Rate: Ranges from approximately 0 to -2 percent annually (deflationary after the Merge).

Ethereum's deflationary model and staking incentives enhance its value retention, making it an appealing long-term asset:

- The transition from PoW to PoS in 2022 reduced energy consumption by around 99.9 percent.
- The fee burn mechanism has made Ethereum potentially deflationary during periods of high network usage.
- Staking locks up supply, which reduces market sell pressure and strengthens long-term value.

Network Activity and On-Chain Metrics

A blockchain's adoption and health can be assessed through on-chain metrics. Ethereum maintains high levels of activity, strong dominance in DeFi, and increasing participation in staking, reinforcing its fundamental strength.

Key On-Chain Metrics (as of 2024):

- Daily Active Addresses: Approximately 500,000, indicating strong adoption.
- Total Transactions: Around 1.2 million per day, demonstrating active ecosystem demand.
- Total Value Locked in DeFi: Approximately US$50 billion, reflecting Ethereum's dominance in DeFi.
- NFT Marketplace Volume: Over $500 million per month, highlighting Ethereum's significant role in the NFT economy.
- Average Gas Fees: Ranging from US$5 to US$10 per transaction, suggesting network congestion and demand.

- ETH Staked in PoS: Approximately 27 million ETH (about 22% of total supply), indicating reduced sell pressure.

Development Activity and Team

The pace of Ethereum's development and innovation is crucial to its long-term success. Continuous development, strong leadership, and the largest developer ecosystem ensure ongoing innovation and relevance.

Developer Contributions and Updates:

- Largest Developer Ecosystem: Over 5,000 active developers monthly, the highest in the crypto space.
- Frequent Protocol Upgrades: The Shanghai Upgrade (2023) enabled Ethereum staking withdrawals.
- Upcoming Scaling Improvements: Proto-Danksharding aims to reduce Layer 2 fees.
- Strong Leadership: The Ethereum Foundation is led by Vitalik Buterin and a dedicated team.

External Factors

Ethereum's growth is also influenced by external factors such as regulation and market competition.

Regulatory Environment.

- SEC and CFTC Stance: Ethereum is not currently classified as a security, reducing risks compared to some altcoins.
- Ethereum Staking and Securities Concerns: Regulatory scrutiny on PoS staking rewards may impact centralized staking providers.
- Institutional Adoption: Growth in Ethereum ETFs and regulated DeFi initiatives is increasing institutional investment.

Competitive Landscape

Ethereum faces competition from newer blockchains that offer faster speeds and lower fees. While competitors like Solana, Avalanche, and Polkadot are emerging, Ethereum maintains an advantage in security, decentralization, and adoption. Layer 2 solutions such as Arbitrum and Polygon are helping Ethereum compete with these faster networks.

Conclusion

Ethereum remains the leading smart contract platform, supported by a robust ecosystem and deflationary supply dynamics. Growing institutional adoption and staking participation bolster its long-term value. Although faced with challenges like high gas fees and competition from faster chains, Layer 2 scaling solutions are improving efficiency. Overall, Ethereum represents a strong long-term investment opportunity, with increasing adoption and constant innovation.

Technical Analysis of Digital Assets

TA is a method used to predict future price movements based on historical market data, such as price charts, volume, and other market indicators. Unlike FA, which focuses on intrinsic value, TA aims to identify patterns, trends, and market psychology to make informed trading decisions. In the highly volatile and speculative world of digital assets, TA is widely employed to time trades and capitalize on short-term market movements.

Price Charts

Price charts are fundamental to TA. Various types of charts visualize the price action of digital assets, helping traders identify trends and patterns that can predict future movements.

Candlestick Charts

The most common chart used in the TA of digital assets is the candlestick chart. Each "candle" represents a specific time frame (e.g., one hour, one day) and displays the asset's opening, closing, high, and low prices during that period. Candlestick patterns, such as dojis, engulfing patterns, and hammers, can indicate potential reversals or continuations of trends.

Support and Resistance Levels

Support is a price level where demand is sufficient to prevent the price from falling further, while resistance is a price level where selling pressure is strong enough to halt price increases. Identifying these levels helps investors make decisions about entry and exit points. Owing to their speculative nature, digital asset markets often respect these technical levels; breakouts from support or resistance can signal significant future price movements.

Chart Patterns

Common chart patterns used in the TA of digital assets include:

- Head and Shoulders: A reversal pattern indicating a trend shift.
- Triangles (Ascending, Descending, Symmetrical): Continuation patterns signaling potential price movement after a period of consolidation.
- Double Tops and Bottoms: Patterns that suggest a reversal from an existing trend.

Chart patterns are useful for identifying potential buying or selling opportunities based on historical price movements and trader psychology.

Technical Indicators

Technical indicators are mathematical calculations based on price, volume, or other market data. Momentum strategies are commonly used in TA to take advantage of trends and price movements in financial markets. These strategies assume that assets that have been trending in a particular direction—either upward or downward—are likely to continue moving in that same direction in the short to medium term. This is especially true in digital asset markets, which are often influenced by sentiment, market cycles, and speculation. As a result, momentum and trend-following approaches can be particularly effective.

Moving Averages

Moving averages (MAs) are among the most fundamental tools in technical analysis. They help smooth out short-term price fluctuations and reveal the underlying trend by averaging past prices over a specific period. There are two main types of MAs:

1. Simple Moving Average (SMA): This calculates the average of an asset's closing prices over a set period (e.g., 50 or 200 days). Each data point in the SMA carries equal weight.
2. Exponential Moving Average (EMA): This is similar to the SMA but gives more weight to recent prices, making it more responsive to new data and short-term price movements.

A popular momentum strategy involving MAs is the MA crossover. This strategy signals potential buy or sell opportunities based on the interaction between two MAs—typically a short-term MA and a long-term MA. The short-term average reacts more quickly to price changes, while the long-term average is slower and smoother.

A buy opportunity is indicated when the short-term MA crosses above the long-term MA, known as a bullish crossover. This pattern suggests the beginning of an upward trend. For example, a 50-DMA crossing above a 200-DMA indicates increasing momentum and signals a good time to buy.

Conversely, a sell opportunity arises when the short-term MA crosses below the long-term MA, referred to as a bearish crossover. This suggests the start of a downward trend, signaling traders to sell the asset. For instance, if the 50-DMA falls below the 200-DMA, it may indicate declining momentum. These crossovers can help traders identify shifts in market sentiment and potential trend reversals, making them valuable tools for momentum-based trading.

Relative Strength Index

The *relative strength index (RSI)* is a key momentum indicator that helps assess the speed and magnitude of recent price changes. It allows traders to determine whether an asset is overbought or oversold and evaluates the likelihood of a price reversal. The RSI is usually calculated over a 14-day period and ranges from 0 to 100. It compares the magnitude of recent gains to recent losses, producing a value that reflects the strength of the price movement.

An RSI above 70 indicates that an asset is overbought, suggesting it has risen too quickly, and a price correction may be imminent. In this scenario, traders might look for a selling opportunity or prepare for a potential trend reversal. Conversely, an RSI below 30 indicates that an asset is oversold, meaning it has declined too rapidly and may be due for a rebound, which traders may interpret as a buying opportunity.

The RSI is often used alongside other indicators, such as MAs, to confirm signals. For example, if a MA crossover suggests a buying signal and the RSI indicates that the asset is oversold, it reinforces the potential for an upward price movement.

Moving Average Convergence Divergence

Moving average convergence divergence (MACD) is another momentum indicator that helps traders identify trend direction, strength, and potential reversals. It is based on the relationship between two MAs and is represented by the MACD line and a signal line, along with a histogram that shows the difference between the two. The MACD line is calculated by subtracting the 26-day EMA from the 12-day EMA. The signal line is a 9-day EMA of the MACD line.

A buy signal occurs when the MACD line crosses above the signal line, indicating that short-term momentum is stronger than long-term momentum, which suggests a potential upward trend. Conversely, when the MACD line crosses below the signal line, it signals a weakening trend, indicating a possible downward movement and a selling opportunity.

The MACD histogram visually represents the difference between the MACD line and the signal line. When the two lines converge (move closer together), it signals a weakening trend. When they diverge (move further apart), it indicates a strengthening trend. MACD is particularly effective for identifying momentum shifts and confirming trend strength, making it a vital tool for traders who employ momentum strategies.

Momentum traders often use a combination of technical indicators to make more informed decisions. While any single indicator can suggest a potential opportunity, combining multiple indicators—such as MAs, RSI, and MACD—provides stronger confirmation of a trend.

For instance, if an MA crossover occurs while the RSI indicates that the asset is in overbought territory, it may signal caution before entering a trade. On the other hand, if both the MACD and MAs show a bullish trend while the RSI suggests that the asset is not yet overbought, this may indicate a stronger buying opportunity.

Bollinger Bands

Bollinger Bands are a widely used TA tool that helps investors and traders assess the volatility and potential price movements of assets, including digital assets. These bands consist of three lines: a middle band, which is typically a MA (commonly a 20-day SMA), and two outer bands that are situated two standard deviations above and below the middle band. The outer bands expand and contract based on market volatility, creating a dynamic range for price movement.

Bollinger Bands are often used to identify overbought and oversold conditions in the market:

- When the price approaches or touches the upper band, it may signal that the asset is overbought—meaning it has risen too quickly—and a price correction or pullback might be imminent. In such cases, traders may consider selling or reducing their positions, expecting a potential reversal.

- Conversely, when the price nears or touches the lower band, it can indicate that the asset is oversold. This suggests that the price has fallen sharply and may be due for a rebound. Traders often view this as a buying opportunity, anticipating an upward price movement.

One of the key functions of Bollinger Bands is to visually reflect the volatility of an asset. The distance between the upper and lower bands widens and contracts based on the asset's price volatility:

- When the bands widen, it indicates a period of increased market volatility, where large price swings or disruptions are more likely to occur. This can signal that a significant price movement—either upward or downward—may be on the horizon.
- When the bands narrow, it suggests a period of reduced volatility or market consolidation, where prices remain relatively stable. Narrow bands often precede a potential breakout, where prices could move sharply in either direction once volatility increases.

Bollinger Bands are also effective for identifying potential breakouts—sharp price movements that follow periods of low volatility. After a period of band tightening (indicating low volatility), an expansion often follows, signaling the possibility of a breakout:

- If the price moves outside the upper band during the breakout, it could indicate the beginning of a strong bullish trend, suggesting a potential buying opportunity.
- Conversely, if the price moves below the lower band, it might signal that a bearish trend is forming, providing a potential sell signal or shorting opportunity.

In digital asset markets, where price swings and volatility are common, Bollinger Bands are particularly valuable for traders looking to time their entry and exit points. Cryptocurrencies such as Bitcoin and Ethereum often experience periods of consolidation followed by sharp moves, making Bollinger Bands a useful tool for predicting these breakouts and identifying potential trading opportunities.

Fibonacci Retracement Levels

Fibonacci retracement is a popular tool in TA, based on the Fibonacci sequence. It helps traders identify potential levels of support and resistance where price retracements or reversals may occur. In the context of digital assets, Fibonacci retracements can provide crucial guidance for entering or exiting trades, especially during corrections or temporary pullbacks within an ongoing trend.

The Fibonacci retracement tool is grounded in the mathematical Fibonacci sequence, where each number is the sum of the two preceding numbers. The potential levels are derived from key Fibonacci ratios: 23.6, 38.2, 50, 61.8, and 78.6 percent. These percentages represent areas where the price of an asset could reverse or stall during a pullback in a broader trend. The 61.8 percent level, known as the golden ratio, is particularly significant in technical analysis, as it often marks strong reversal points.

Traders utilize Fibonacci retracement levels to predict how far a market might retrace before resuming its previous trend. After a significant price movement (either upward or downward), these levels help identify key areas where the price may pause, reverse, or consolidate. This tool is especially effective in trending markets where pullbacks or corrections are common.

To use the Fibonacci retracement tool, traders first identify a swing high and swing low on the price chart of a digital asset. These are the highest and lowest points over a specific period. The Fibonacci levels are then drawn between these two points, creating horizontal lines at the Fibonacci ratios (23.6%, 38.2%, 50%, 61.8%, and 78.6%). These levels function as potential areas of support during an uptrend or resistance during a downtrend.

In an uptrend, Fibonacci retracement levels can act as support, where the price might pause or bounce back after a pullback. Conversely, in a downtrend, these levels serve as potential resistance areas where the price might stall or reverse before continuing lower.

In the volatile world of digital assets, Fibonacci retracements are useful for identifying key price levels where traders might consider entering or exiting trades. For example, during a correction within an overall uptrend, such as with Bitcoin or Ethereum, traders may look at Fibonacci levels to find support and anticipate a resumption of upward movement. If Bitcoin retraces 50 percent of its recent gains, traders may regard the 50 percent Fibonacci level as a possible entry point, assuming that the broader uptrend remains intact.

Fibonacci retracement levels can also help traders identify profit-taking zones or points where they may wish to exit a position. For instance, if a digital asset is in a downtrend and begins to retrace upward, the 38.2 or 61.8 percent levels may act as strong resistance areas where traders might lock in profits before the price potentially resumes its downward trend.

These retracements are particularly effective for identifying reversal points or continuation patterns. If an asset approaches a key Fibonacci level (like 61.8%), traders often look for other technical indicators—such as candlestick patterns, RSI divergence, or volume spikes—to confirm whether the price is likely to reverse. For example, should Bitcoin reach the 61.8 percent retracement level after a pullback and form a bullish reversal candlestick pattern, this could signal the potential resumption of the upward trend.

Sometimes, instead of reversing, the price consolidates near Fibonacci levels before continuing in the direction of the broader trend. In such cases, traders might consider increasing their position size if the price holds above a key Fibonacci support level, anticipating a continuation of the trend.

Key Fibonacci Levels to Watch:

- A 23.6 Percent Retracement: A relatively shallow retracement that often indicates minor corrections. If the price reverses here, it suggests strong underlying momentum in the trend.
- A 38.2 Percent Retracement: Often viewed as a key support or resistance point in a strong trend.
- A 50 Percent Retracement: While not an official Fibonacci ratio, the 50 percent level is psychologically important and frequently acts as support or resistance during corrections.

- A 61.8 Percent Retracement: Known as the golden ratio, this level is especially significant in technical analysis and often acts as a major turning point in both uptrends and downtrends.
- A 78.6 Percent Retracement: A deeper retracement that may indicate a stronger reversal is likely if the price holds at this level.

Fibonacci retracements can also aid in managing risk in digital asset trading. Traders often set stop-loss orders just below a key Fibonacci support level to minimize losses if the price breaks below it. Similarly, they can establish profit targets at Fibonacci resistance levels to ensure they lock in gains before the price potentially reverses.

Whale Activity

In digital asset markets, *"whales"*—large holders of cryptocurrencies—can significantly influence price movements due to their ability to execute large trades. Monitoring whale activity can provide valuable insights into potential market trends.

Tracking the number and size of large transactions (whale trades) helps identify periods of increased buying or selling activity. For instance, substantial transfers of Bitcoin to an exchange may indicate that a whale is preparing to sell, which could increase selling pressure and lead to a price drop.

Whale wallets, which contain large amounts of a specific cryptocurrency, can be monitored using on-chain data to observe changes in their holdings. A sudden reduction in whale holdings may signal an impending major sell-off, while an increase in holdings could suggest that whales are accumulating assets in anticipation of future price appreciation.

Case Study: Technical Analysis of Bitcoin

This case study presents a TA of Bitcoin using price charts, trend analysis, and technical indicators to identify potential market direction.

Step 1: Analyzing the Price Chart

- Chart Type: Candlestick Chart (Daily Timeframe)
- Trend Analysis: Determine whether Bitcoin is in an uptrend, downtrend, or experiencing range-bound movement.

Key Levels to Watch:

- Support Levels: Areas where the Bitcoin price tends to bounce upward.
- Resistance Levels: Areas where the Bitcoin price struggles to move higher

Bitcoin Price Chart Analysis (Example as of 2024)

Key Observations:

1. Bitcoin has been forming higher highs and higher lows, indicating an uptrend.
2. There is strong support at US$40,000 and resistance at US$50,000 (a psychological level).
3. Bitcoin broke out above the US$48,000 resistance, suggesting bullish momentum.

If Bitcoin holds above US$48,000, it could continue its uptrend toward US$55,000 and above. Conversely, a failure to hold this level may lead to a retest of the US$45,000–US$40,000 support levels.

Step 2: Using Technical Indicators for Confirmation

Moving Averages:

- 50-Day MA (MA50): A short-term trend indicator.
- 200-Day MA: A long-term trend indicator.

Observation:

1. Bitcoin is trading above both the MA50 and the 200-Day MA, which is a bullish sign.
2. A Golden Cross (the MA50 crossing above the 200-Day MA) has occurred, historically signaling strong continuation of an uptrend.

The MAs support a bullish bias, confirming upward momentum.

Relative Strength Index:

- The RSI (14-day) indicates whether Bitcoin is overbought or oversold.
- Above 70 = Overbought (possible correction).
- Below 30 = Oversold (potential buying opportunity).

For Bitcoin, the RSI is approximately 65.
This means:

- The RSI is not yet overbought but is approaching high levels.
- If Bitcoin crosses above 70, it may face a short-term pullback before continuing its uptrend.

Momentum is strong but nearing the overbought zone, suggesting a potential pullback before further gains.

Moving Average Convergence Divergence:

- This indicator identifies trend strength and potential reversals.
- MACD Line crossing above the Signal Line = Bullish.
- MACD Line crossing below the Signal Line = Bearish.

For Bitcoin, the MACD has crossed above the Signal Line, confirming bullish momentum. Additionally, the MACD histogram shows increasing positive momentum, suggesting further upside. The MACD confirms a strong uptrend, aligning with the MAs.

Fibonacci Retracement:

Fibonacci retracement levels identify potential pullback areas before trend continuation.

- Key Fibonacci Levels: 38.2 percent, 50 percent, and 61.8 percent retracements.

Based on the recent rally from US$40,000 to US$50,000, the Fibonacci levels are as follows:

- 38.2 percent Retracement: US$46,200 (Potential Support)
- 50 percent Retracement: US$45,000 (Stronger Support Level)
- 61.8 percent Retracement: US$43,800 (Deep Support Zone)

If Bitcoin retraces, these levels may serve as buying opportunities.

Conclusion

Bitcoin remains in a bullish trend, with technical indicators aligning for further upside. A breakout above US$50,000 could target US$55,000–US$60,000. However, a short-term pullback to the US$46,000–US$45,000 range is possible before continuation. Overall sentiment is bullish, with the potential for a healthy pullback before additional gains.

Sentiment Analysis in Digital Asset Markets

Sentiment analysis is a vital tool for understanding and predicting price movements in digital asset markets. In these highly speculative and emotionally driven environments, sentiment—the collective attitude and behavior of market participants—can serve as a strong indicator of future trends. This analysis involves gauging the mood of investors and traders through various data sources, such as social media, news outlets, and market metrics, to assess whether the market is characterized by fear, greed, optimism, or pessimism.

Social Media Monitoring

Social media plays a crucial role in shaping sentiment in digital asset markets. Platforms such as Twitter, Reddit, Telegram, and Discord have become central hubs where both retail and institutional investors discuss market developments, new projects, and price changes. Monitoring social media activity provides real-time insights into market sentiment. Moreover, by analyzing big data from these networks, researchers can identify correlations between community sentiment and the value of traded assets (Casillo et al. 2022).

Zhu et al. (2022) examined user perceptions of NFT markets as reflected in their social media posts. They found that, despite market turmoil, users generally had a positive view of the digital asset markets. Their findings indicate that positive sentiment has increased over the past five months, while negative sentiment has remained relatively low and stable.

Tracking the volume of mentions or discussions about specific cryptocurrencies can also reveal clues about market sentiment. Sudden spikes in social media activity, especially positive mentions, may indicate growing interest or excitement about a digital asset, often leading to price increases. Conversely, a surge in negative sentiment or discussions about potential risks can signal an impending price drop. Qian et al. (2022) analyzed emotions expressed in tweets on platforms such as Twitter related to NFTs, conducting secondary market analysis to explore reasons for the growing acceptance of NFTs through sentiment and emotion analysis. They classified tweets using the Pearson Product Moment Correlation Coefficient (PPMCC) and examined eight emotions (Anger, Anticipation, Disgust, Fear, Joy, Sadness, Surprise, and Trust), along with positive and negative sentiments. The results revealed that approximately 72 percent of the tweets contained a positive sentiment, with anticipation and trust being the dominant emotions globally.

Identifying trending hashtags and keywords related to specific projects or tokens can also provide insight into the market's collective mood. For example, hashtags such as #BitcoinBullRun or #ETHAllTimeHigh may signify bullish sentiment, while #FUD (Fear, Uncertainty, and Doubt) often indicates a more negative or cautious outlook.

Sentiment Indexes

Sentiment indexes provide a structured and aggregated view of investor sentiment. These indexes compile various metrics, including social media activity, volatility, and price momentum, to offer a clear picture of the market's emotional state.

One well-known tool for assessing overall market sentiment is the Crypto Fear and Greed Index. This index ranges from 0 (indicating extreme fear) to 100 (indicating extreme greed). It is derived from several factors, including volatility, market volume, social media sentiment, and surveys. High levels of greed suggest overbought conditions, which may lead to market corrections, while extreme fear indicates oversold conditions and potential buying opportunities (Gunay and Muhammed 2022).

Sentiment indexes often incorporate metrics such as volatility and price momentum as proxies for investor sentiment. For example, periods of low volatility paired with steady upward price trends generally correlate with positive sentiment. In contrast, high volatility and sharp price declines are typically associated with fear and uncertainty. Xing et al. (2018) explored the role of market sentiment in asset allocation and proposed generating sentiment time series from social media using sentiment analysis and text mining techniques. Their neural network model, which combined evolving clustering and long short-term memory, successfully formalized sentiment information into market views. The experimental results demonstrated that this model outperformed many established forecasting techniques.

In addition to social and sentiment data, on-chain metrics—such as active wallet addresses, transaction volumes, and the number of new addresses created—can also reflect shifts in sentiment. Increased network activity often correlates with growing confidence in a project, while stagnation or declines in activity may indicate waning interest.

The Role of News and Influencer Impact

The news cycle significantly influences sentiment in the digital asset space, often leading to rapid changes in market conditions. News related to regulatory developments, technological upgrades, partnerships, or security breaches can have an immediate and dramatic impact on asset prices.

For instance, news about government regulations—such as a country imposing a ban on cryptocurrencies, tax rulings, or the launch of a central bank digital currency—can either boost confidence or incite fear. Positive regulatory news, like the approval of a Bitcoin ETF or clear legal frameworks for digital assets, can encourage bullish sentiment. Conversely, negative news, such as regulatory crackdowns, often triggers fear-driven sell-offs.

Announcements about major upgrades to blockchain platforms (like the Ethereum 2.0 upgrade) or innovations in DeFi protocols typically foster optimism, which is reflected in bullish sentiment and increased demand for the associated tokens.

High-profile figures, including tech entrepreneurs and social media influencers, can also significantly impact digital asset markets. For example, tweets or statements from individuals like Elon Musk have caused substantial short-term price movements in assets such as Bitcoin and Dogecoin. Monitoring influential accounts and their public statements can provide insights into market sentiment and potential short-term price actions.

While sentiment analysis can be a powerful tool, it has limitations, particularly in the fast-paced and sometimes irrational world of digital assets. Sentiment analysis is often more suitable for short-term trading decisions rather than long-term investment strategies. Additionally, digital asset markets may be subject to manipulation through social media or coordinated efforts to sway sentiment. Pump-and-dump schemes—where traders artificially inflate the price of an asset through misleading positive sentiment and then sell at the peak—can mislead investors. Therefore, it is crucial to cross-reference sentiment data with other analytical methods to avoid being misled by manipulated market trends.

Gurrib and Kamalov (2022) proposed a method for predicting the direction of Bitcoin (BTC) prices using linear discriminant analysis (LDA) alongside sentiment analysis. They demonstrated that including news sentiment resulted in the highest forecast accuracy of 0.585 on the test data. The LDA (support vector machine [SVM]) model, using asset-specific inputs (both news sentiment and asset-specific features), ranked first among their respective model classifiers. These findings suggest that both BTC news sentiment and asset-specific factors are vital for predicting the next day's price direction.

Moreover, social media can generate substantial "noise," and not all sentiment data is equally reliable. The challenge for investors is to sift through irrelevant or misleading information and concentrate on genuine sentiment shifts that are likely to influence market behavior.

Funding Rates in Derivatives Markets

The emergence of cryptocurrency derivatives, such as futures and perpetual contracts, has made funding rates a crucial market indicator. These rates indicate the cost of holding long or short positions and offer insights into market sentiment.

When the funding rate is positive, traders with long positions (those betting on price increases) must pay fees to traders with short positions. This generally signals a bullish market. However, excessively high funding rates can indicate overleveraging, which increases the risk of a market correction.

Conversely, a negative funding rate occurs when short traders pay fees to long traders, suggesting bearish sentiment. Yet, an extremely negative funding rate might signal that the market is oversold, potentially presenting a buying opportunity.

Case Study: Sentiment Analysis of Bitcoin

Below is an example of Bitcoin sentiment analysis by examining social media trends, sentiment indices, news influence, and derivatives market funding rates.

Social Media Monitoring

Social media platforms such as Twitter, Reddit, Telegram, and Discord significantly influence Bitcoin sentiment.

- Mentions and Hashtags: An increase in posts related to Bitcoin (e.g., "#Bitcoin," "#BTC") can indicate growing interest.
- Engagement (Likes, Shares, Comments): High interaction levels suggest either excitement (bullish) or panic (bearish).
- Tone of Conversations: Are users optimistic about price movements, or is fear prevailing in the discussions?

Example: Bitcoin's Social Media Sentiment (example as of 2024)

Data from Twitter and Reddit over the past 30 days shows:

1. Mentions of #Bitcoin increased by 80 percent, especially after Bitcoin surpassed US$50,000.
2. Sentiment analysis indicates that 70 percent of posts are bullish, while 30 percent are bearish.
3. Major discussion topics include institutional adoption, ETF approvals, and hype surrounding the Bitcoin halving.

Overall, the social media buzz is overwhelmingly bullish, reflecting strong market interest and potential FOMO.

Sentiment Indices: Fear and Greed Index

The Crypto Fear and Greed Index combines data from various sources (volatility, volume, social media, and market momentum) to gauge investor sentiment on a scale from 0 (Extreme Fear) to 100 (Extreme Greed).

Bitcoin Sentiment Score (December 2024):

- Fear (0-30): Indicates a bearish market, which may present a buying opportunity.
- Neutral (31-50): Suggests market indecision.

- Greed (51-75): Reflects a bullish market with increasing demand.
- Extreme Greed (76-100): Signals an overheated market, indicating a potential crrection.

Bitcoin Fear and Greed Index: 82 (Extreme Greed).

1. Investors exhibit high optimism, possibly leading to over-leverage.
2. Extreme greed often precedes short-term pullbacks or corrections, suggesting the market is overheated and profit-taking might occur soon.

The Role of News and Influencer Impact

Bitcoin sentiment is highly responsive to news events and commentary from influencers.

Positive News (Bullish Sentiment):

1. Bitcoin ETF Approval (2024): Major institutions like Black-Rock, Fidelity, and VanEck launched Bitcoin ETFs, increasing institutional demand.
2. Bitcoin Halving (April 2024): Historically, Bitcoin halvings reduce supply and trigger bull markets.
3. MicroStrategy and Tesla Increasing BTC Holdings: Institutional purchases bolster market confidence.

Negative News (Bearish Sentiment):

1. Regulatory Crackdowns: SEC lawsuits against cryptocurrency exchanges instill fear.
2. Hawkish Federal Reserve Rate Decisions: Rising interest rates could slow Bitcoin adoption.

Influencer and Whale Impact:

1. Elon Musk's tweets about Bitcoin can cause instant price fluctuations.
2. Michael Saylor (CEO of MicroStrategy) promoting Bitcoin can enhance institutional confidence.
3. Large holders (whales) moving Bitcoin to exchanges may signal potential sell-offs.

Bitcoin's price sentiment is heavily influenced by institutional adoption and macroeconomic news. Traders should be vigilant about regulatory updates and whale activity.

Funding Rates in Derivatives Markets

Funding rates in Bitcoin futures markets help determine whether traders are over-leveraged in long or short positions:

- Positive Funding Rate: Long positions pay shorts, indicating excessive bullish leverage.
- Negative Funding Rate: Short positions pay longs, suggesting excessive bearish sentiment.

Bitcoin Funding Rate Analysis: +0.08 percent (Elevated Levels)

- Traders are paying a premium to hold long positions, indicating over-leveraged bullish sentiment.
- Historically, high funding rates precede corrections, as long traders may need to close positions.

Conclusion

Bitcoin sentiment appears strongly bullish, driven by ETF approvals, the upcoming halving, and institutional demand. However, the Extreme Greed levels and high funding rates signify that a short-term correction might be on the horizon. Investors should exercise caution near local highs and consider profit-taking or hedging against potential pullbacks.

Summary

In the complex and rapidly evolving world of digital asset investments, understanding various analytical approaches is crucial for making informed decisions. FA offers insights into the underlying value of digital assets by evaluating factors such as technology, utility, adoption, and the strength of development teams. TA provides a data-driven perspective, focusing on price patterns, trends, and market indicators to predict future price movements. Sentiment analysis gauges the emotional and psychological drivers of the market, reflecting how news, social media, and public opinion can influence asset prices. By combining these three approaches—fundamental, technical, and sentiment analysis—investors can develop a comprehensive strategy for assessing digital assets. This holistic approach helps navigate the inherent volatility of the market, ultimately enhancing their ability to seize opportunities and manage risks effectively.

CHAPTER 7

Risk and Portfolio Management

In the rapidly changing world of digital assets, effective risk and portfolio management is essential for achieving long-term success while navigating the market's inherent volatility and unpredictability. This chapter discusses key strategies that investors can use to manage the risks associated with their portfolios, particularly in the context of highly volatile digital assets.

By focusing on managing volatility through tools such as diversification, position sizing, and hedging, investors can better protect their portfolios from significant losses. The chapter also highlights the importance of managing liquidity risk, ensuring that a portion of the portfolio remains accessible for swift action during periods of market stress.

Finally, we examine the crucial role of rebalancing in maintaining target allocations, locking in gains, and ensuring a balanced approach to risk management in an ever-shifting market landscape.

Managing Volatility

Volatility is a defining characteristic of digital asset markets, where cryptocurrencies often experience frequent and dramatic price swings. While this volatility can create opportunities for high returns, it also exposes investors to significant risks. Effective risk management is essential for navigating these turbulent markets and protecting portfolios from substantial losses.

Diversification

Diversifying Across Asset Classes

One of the most effective strategies to reduce portfolio volatility and mitigate risk is diversification. By including noncorrelated asset classes, investors can create a balanced portfolio that performs more consistently over time, regardless of market conditions. During periods of high volatility in the cryptocurrency market, these noncorrelated assets can help smooth returns and prevent large drawdowns that could significantly impact a portfolio's overall performance.

Equities. Equities, particularly growth stocks, can complement the speculative aspects of cryptocurrencies by offering exposure to both traditional markets and disruptive technologies. By incorporating equities into a portfolio, investors benefit from the more predictable performance of stocks compared to the rapid price fluctuations of cryptocurrencies.

Bonds. Bonds are generally less volatile than equities or digital assets and are considered safer investments, especially government bonds like U.S. Treasuries. They serve as a stabilizing force in portfolios heavily weighted toward volatile assets. Historically, bonds tend to have a negative correlation with riskier asset classes, including cryptocurrencies. When digital assets experience sharp declines, bond prices may rise as investors seek safe-haven investments. Additionally, bonds provide a steady stream of income through interest payments, which can help offset potential losses in the cryptocurrency portion of the portfolio during bear markets.

Real Estate. Real estate is typically regarded as a long-term hedge against inflation, offering income through rental yields or real estate investment trusts. As a noncorrelated asset, real estate often moves independently of equity markets and cryptocurrencies. It provides a layer of stability, as property values and rental income are less influenced by market speculation and more by supply and demand in the physical economy. During periods of high volatility in digital asset markets, real estate investments can serve as a buffer, delivering more consistent returns and reducing overall portfolio risk.

Commodities.   Commodities, such as gold, silver, oil, and agricultural products, have historically been seen as safe-haven assets during periods of market uncertainty. Including commodities in a portfolio that is heavily concentrated in cryptocurrencies can help hedge against both market volatility and inflation. Gold, in particular, is known as a store of value and often performs well during times of economic stress or financial instability. When cryptocurrencies endure steep corrections, gold can help protect the portfolio's value. Additionally, commodities like oil and agricultural products can serve as a hedge against inflation, safeguarding purchasing power when rising prices potentially impact digital asset markets.

Aggarwal et al. (2018) utilized eight indexes to construct a portfolio spread across six asset classes in India: equity, fixed income, commodities, real estate, gold, and alternative investments. They employed "long only," "constrained," and "equally weighted" strategies to create optimal portfolios using a mean-CVaR approach for asset weight allocation. The findings suggest that portfolios including Bitcoin yield superior risk-adjusted returns compared to those without Bitcoin for both the "long only" and "equally weighted" strategies. The results also indicate relatively stable weights for Bitcoin over the investment horizon in the "long only" strategy compared to the "constrained framework."

In another study, Ali et al. (2023) examined the connectedness between precious metals, industrial metals, and DeFi assets during prepandemic and COVID-19 subperiods. Their findings indicate that all DeFi assets, along with palladium, aluminum, zinc, and nickel, are net importers of return spillover, whereas gold, silver, platinum, and copper are net exporters. The return transmission between these markets is dynamic, with rapid fluctuations during the COVID-19 period. The optimal portfolio analysis suggests that incorporating DeFi assets into a metals-based portfolio enhances diversification.

The degree of diversification depends on an investor's risk tolerance, investment horizon, and financial goals. For those with lower risk tolerance, a higher allocation to stable, income-generating assets such as bonds and real estate may be more suitable. In contrast, investors with a higher risk tolerance may choose to allocate a larger portion to cryptocurrencies and growth stocks, seeking higher potential returns.

Diversification Within Digital Assets

Diversification within the cryptocurrency space is as crucial as it is in traditional markets. While Bitcoin often dominates discussions as the most prominent digital asset, the broader cryptocurrency ecosystem includes a wide array of other assets, each with unique use cases, risk profiles, and volatility levels.

By diversifying across different digital assets, investors can mitigate the risk that a sharp downturn in one cryptocurrency will significantly impact the entire portfolio. Cryptocurrencies often move independently or exhibit varying levels of volatility, meaning a decline in one asset does not necessarily imply a decline across the entire portfolio.

- For example, during periods of market correction, Bitcoin might experience sharp declines, while Ethereum or other altcoins could outperform due to their specific use cases, such as DeFi or technological advancements.

Holding a mix of altcoins reduces reliance on the success or failure of any single project.

- For instance, if Cardano experiences delays in its blockchain upgrades and suffers a price drop, having exposure to other altcoins like Polkadot or Binance Coin can help offset those losses.

This risk-spreading strategy is especially important in the cryptocurrency market. A diversified crypto portfolio helps manage risks by ensuring that no single asset can dominate the overall performance of the portfolio.

Mensi et al. (2019) utilized wavelet coherence and cross-wavelet transform approaches to examine the comovement between Bitcoin and five major cryptocurrencies—Dash, Ethereum, Litecoin, Monero, and Ripple—and their portfolio risk implications. The results demonstrated evidence of comovements in time-frequency space, showing leading relationships of Bitcoin with Dash, Monero, and Ripple, a lagging relationship with Ethereum, and out-of-phase movements with Litecoin. By considering different portfolios—risk-minimizing, equally weighted, and hedging portfolios—Mensi et al. found that a mixed portfolio (featuring Bitcoin alongside other cryptocurrencies) offers better diversification benefits.

Additionally, Mensi et al. showed that an Ethereum-Bitcoin (or Monero-Bitcoin) hedging portfolio provides the highest risk reduction and hedging effectiveness over medium and long-term horizons. The results regarding downside risk reductions are dependent on the time horizon.

Using MPT, Mazanec (2021) analyzed a total of 16 virtual currencies from October 1, 2017, to January 13, 2020. He found that the optimal portfolio, based on the Markowitz approach, included Cardano, Binance Coin, and Bitcoin.

Global and Sector Diversification

Investors can enhance the diversification of their digital asset portfolios by expanding beyond individual cryptocurrencies and focusing on geographical and sectoral diversification. This approach allows for exposure to a broader range of projects, technological innovations, and regional markets. By diversifying across various geographical locations and different sectors of the blockchain economy—such as DeFi, NFTs, layer-1 protocols, and privacy coins—investors can spread risk and capitalize on various growth drivers within the blockchain ecosystem.

Geographical Diversification.   Geographical diversification is a crucial risk management strategy, particularly in the rapidly evolving and heavily regulated world of digital assets. The global nature of the cryptocurrency and blockchain ecosystem means that regulatory environments, market dynamics, and adoption rates can vary significantly across regions. By diversifying investments across different geographical markets, investors can mitigate risks associated with regional regulations, economic conditions, or political developments.

Different regions have vastly different regulatory approaches to digital assets. For instance, countries such as the United States and China have implemented stricter regulations, while Singapore and Switzerland have adopted more crypto-friendly policies. By holding assets or participating in projects based in regions with diverse regulatory landscapes, investors reduce the risk of being overly exposed to a market that may suddenly impose restrictions or bans on digital assets.

The level of cryptocurrency adoption also varies widely among countries. For example, South Korea and Japan feature rapidly growing retail crypto markets, while Africa is increasingly using cryptocurrencies to address economic instability. Geographic diversification enables investors to benefit from regional differences in market maturity and adoption rates. By investing in digital assets or projects from multiple regions, investors can tap into growth from emerging crypto hubs while lessening their dependence on any single market.

Emerging markets such as Latin America and Southeast Asia are witnessing rising crypto adoption as a means of financial inclusion and protection against inflation. Investing in projects or assets that cater to these regions can provide exposure to high-growth markets that may be insulated from downturns in more mature crypto economies.

Sectoral Diversification. The blockchain economy consists of various sectors, each representing a unique use case and technological advancement. By diversifying investments across these different sectors, investors can mitigate their reliance on any single use case or market segment.

For instance, if the DeFi sector experiences a downturn, strong performance in NFTs or layer-1 protocols could offset potential losses. Similarly, while privacy coins may encounter regulatory challenges, DeFi tokens or NFT platforms could thrive due to innovation and increased adoption in other areas of the crypto economy.

This kind of cross-sector diversification allows investors to engage with multiple blockchain innovations, which not only reduces the overall risk of their portfolio but also provides exposure to various growth opportunities.

Position Sizing

Position sizing is a crucial risk management technique that involves determining the right amount of capital to allocate to a specific asset within a portfolio. This is especially important in the context of digital assets, where volatility is much higher than in traditional financial markets. Effective position sizing is essential for balancing potential rewards with risk management. It helps investors manage downside risk, avoid overexposure to a single asset, and optimize the risk-return profile of their portfolio.

Risk Per Trade

A fundamental principle of position sizing is defining how much of the portfolio an investor is willing to risk on a single trade. For volatile assets like cryptocurrencies, the recommended risk per trade typically ranges from 1 to 3 percent of the total portfolio. This range depends on the investor's risk tolerance and investment horizon.

- For example, if an investor has a portfolio worth US$100,000 and decides to risk 2 percent of their capital per trade, they are willing to lose US$2,000 on a specific digital asset. This approach ensures that even if a trade does not go as planned, the overall portfolio remains largely intact.

Volatility and Position Sizing

Given the extreme volatility of digital assets like Bitcoin, Ethereum, and various altcoins, it is important to adjust position sizing based on an asset's historical volatility or expected price fluctuations. Generally, assets with higher volatility should have smaller position sizes to minimize the risk of large losses from sudden price changes.

One effective method for position sizing is to scale the allocation according to an asset's volatility. For example, if Bitcoin has lower volatility compared to a more speculative altcoin like Dogecoin or Solana, the position in Bitcoin could be larger, while the position in Dogecoin would be smaller to account for its higher volatility.

- For instance, if Bitcoin's average daily price movement is 5 percent, while an altcoin's average daily movement is 15 percent, an investor might allocate three times more capital to Bitcoin than to the altcoin. This approach reflects the differences in volatility and helps mitigate risk.

Stop-Loss Orders

Stop-loss orders play a crucial role in position sizing by limiting potential losses on a given trade. A stop-loss is established at a predetermined price level, at which the asset will be automatically sold if its price falls to or below that level. The position size is then determined based on the distance between the entry price and the stop-loss level, ensuring that the investor's risk per trade aligns with their risk tolerance.

- For example, if an investor buys Bitcoin at US$40,000 and sets a stop-loss at US$36,000, they are willing to risk a loss of US$4,000 per Bitcoin. If they are only willing to risk US$2000 on this trade, they should purchase 0.5 BTC to adhere to their risk parameters.

Position Sizing Based on Market Conditions

The digital asset markets are highly influenced by market sentiment and trends. Position sizing should be dynamic, adapting to changing market conditions. During periods of extreme market volatility or uncertainty, investors may opt to reduce their position sizes to protect their portfolios. Conversely, in a bull market with strong momentum, they might choose to increase their position sizes, while still prioritizing prudent risk management.

- For instance, if an investor recognizes that Bitcoin is experiencing high volatility due to regulatory news or macroeconomic uncertainty, they may reduce their exposure to Bitcoin by decreasing its position size and reallocating funds to more stable assets, such as stablecoins or less volatile investments in their portfolio.

Scholz (2012) systematically analyzed the impact of position sizing on timing strategies and found that the introduction of relative position sizing significantly affects trading results compared to erratic positions. Based on these findings, Scholz argued that smaller trading fractions tend to deliver the highest risk-adjusted returns in most scenarios.

Hedging

Hedging is a risk management strategy designed to reduce potential losses by taking offsetting positions in related assets or utilizing specific financial instruments. In the realm of digital assets, hedging helps investors protect their portfolios from significant drawdowns or price corrections. By mitigating risk, this strategy allows investors to manage their exposure to adverse price movements while still holding higher-risk digital assets such as Bitcoin, Ethereum, and various altcoins.

Hedging With Stablecoins

Stablecoins, such as USD Coin, Tether, and Dai, are pegged to fiat currencies (like the USD) and are intended to maintain a stable value. Since stablecoins exhibit minimal volatility compared to traditional cryptocurrencies, they can be an effective hedge during market instability or when investors expect a downturn.

When the crypto market becomes volatile, investors can convert a portion of their holdings into stablecoins, thereby reducing exposure to sharp price drops while retaining liquidity. For instance, if Bitcoin or Ethereum experiences a severe correction, holding stablecoins helps preserve capital and maintain purchasing power.

Stablecoins also provide instant liquidity, allowing investors to quickly re-enter the market when conditions improve, making them a flexible hedging tool in a volatile environment.

- For example, If an investor holds a portfolio heavily weighted in Bitcoin but anticipates a short-term market correction, they might convert a portion of their holdings into USD Coin. This reduces their exposure to volatility while keeping liquidity available for when the market stabilizes.

Hedging With Derivatives

Derivatives such as options and futures are popular hedging instruments that allow investors to lock in prices or benefit from adverse price movements. In the digital asset space, these tools are widely available on exchanges such as Chicago Mercantile Exchange (CME), Binance, and Futures Exchange (FTX), enabling investors to hedge against both upward and downward market fluctuations.

Put options give investors the right (but not the obligation) to sell an asset at a predetermined price before a specified expiration date. This serves as insurance against a decline in the price of the underlying asset.

- For example, if an investor holds a significant position in Ethereum and is concerned about a potential price drop, they can purchase Ethereum put options. This allows them to secure the right to sell Ethereum at a specific price, thereby reducing the risk of losses if the asset's price falls below that level.

Investors can also enter into futures contracts to hedge against price declines. Taking a short futures position allows an investor to benefit from falling prices. If the price of the digital asset drops, the gain from the short position offsets the loss in the spot position.

- For instance, if an investor is long on Bitcoin but fears a market correction, they can open a short position in Bitcoin futures.

If Bitcoin's price decreases, the gains from the short position will counterbalance the losses from the spot holdings, effectively providing a hedge.

Hedging With Inverse Exchange-Traded Products

Inverse exchange-traded products or inverse ETFs are designed to profit from declines in the price of specific assets or indexes. While not as common in traditional markets, there are emerging inverse crypto ETFs and inverse tokens that allow investors to bet on falling cryptocurrency prices.

Inverse ETFs aim to deliver the opposite performance of a particular cryptocurrency or index. For example, an inverse Bitcoin ETF would increase in value when Bitcoin's price falls. This feature enables investors to hedge their Bitcoin exposure without needing to sell their underlying Bitcoin holdings.

Some DeFi protocols offer inverse tokens, which are synthetic assets that gain value when the price of the underlying digital asset decreases. These tokens are typically available on platforms like Synthetix or Inverse Finance.

- For instance, if an investor has a long position in Bitcoin but wants to hedge against potential downside risk, they could invest in an inverse Bitcoin ETF or an inverse Bitcoin token. If Bitcoin's price declines, the value of the inverse ETF or token would rise, helping to offset the losses in their Bitcoin holdings.

Pair Trading

Pair trading involves taking opposite positions in correlated assets to hedge against risk. In the context of digital assets, this strategy allows investors to mitigate risk by simultaneously holding long and short positions in cryptocurrencies that tend to move together or have high correlations. Guesmi et al. (2019) demonstrated that maintaining a short position in the Bitcoin market can hedge investment risk for various financial assets.

- For example, an investor may take a long position in Bitcoin while shorting Ethereum, anticipating that the two assets will move in tandem. If Ethereum declines more sharply than Bitcoin during a market downturn, the investor could profit from the short position, effectively hedging the losses incurred from the long Bitcoin position.

Pritchard (2018) analyzed the Litecoin (LTC)/Bitcoin (BTC) pair by conducting statistical tests and implementing automated trading strategies to identify potential profit levels. The results indicate that pairs trading strategies can profit from price movement disparities in the digital asset market, without incurring the same risks associated with exchange-to-exchange arbitrage; however, varying profit levels can be attained.

Guesmi et al. (2019) highlighted that hedging strategies involving gold, oil, equities, and Bitcoin considerably reduce portfolio risk compared to a portfolio composed solely of gold, oil, and equities.

Aggarwal (2022) advised investors to create an optimized two-asset portfolio focused on minimizing exposure to Stellar while including Litecoin and Ripple. Market participants holding a long position in Ripple can achieve a cost-effective hedge by shorting Stellar.

Ben Mabrouk et al. (2024) forecasted the performance of hedged versus unhedged portfolios using long short-term memory (LSTM) networks. Their findings largely confirm the effectiveness of hedging, particularly highlighting NFTs and the metaverse assets as strong hedging candidates.

Additionally, some investors hedge their altcoin exposure by holding Bitcoin or stablecoins. For instance, during periods of high volatility or potential corrections in altcoins, a position in Bitcoin can act as a hedge since it typically tends to decline less than altcoins during bear markets.

Hedging With Cross-Asset Correlations

Cross-asset correlation hedging entails using traditional financial assets such as gold, stocks, or bonds to mitigate risks in digital asset portfolios. This approach is particularly beneficial during macroeconomic shifts when various asset classes respond to changes in the economic landscape.

Historically regarded as a safe-haven asset, gold can effectively hedge against the volatility of digital assets. During periods of financial uncertainty or inflation, gold prices often rise while cryptocurrencies may decline, providing a natural hedge.

Based on prevailing market conditions, certain equities or bonds may move inversely to digital assets, enabling investors to balance their risks.

- Example: If an investor holds a substantial portfolio of crypto-currencies and anticipates a potential market downturn due to macroeconomic factors, such as rising interest rates, they could take a long position in gold or defensive stocks to offset potential losses in their crypto portfolio.

Research by Wang et al. (2019) analyzed daily data from Bitcoin and six major financial assets (stocks, commodity futures, gold, foreign exchange, monetary assets, and bonds) in China from 2013 to 2017 using a VAR-GARCH-BEKK model. Their study explored the mean and volatility spillover effects between Bitcoin and other major assets, investigating whether Bitcoin could serve as a hedging asset or a safe haven. The findings revealed that:

1. Only the monetary market, specifically the Shanghai Interbank Offered Rate (SHIIBOR), had a mean spillover effect on Bitcoin.
2. Gold, monetary assets, and bond markets exhibited volatility spillover effects on Bitcoin, while Bitcoin itself had a volatility spillover effect solely on the gold market.

Additionally, Wang et al. found that Bitcoin can be hedged against stocks, bonds, and SHIBOR and acts as a safe haven during extreme price fluctuations in the monetary market.

Yang et al. (2022) studied the connectedness, hedging, and safe-haven properties of Bitcoin, gold, crude oil, and commodities against six currencies across various investment horizons, with a focus on asset performance during the COVID-19 outbreak. They concluded that the overall dependence between assets and the currency market is strongest in the short term, while Bitcoin exhibited the least dependence across all horizons. The relationships among these four assets and the currency market varied over time frames, showing Bitcoin's superior long-term hedging capabilities. Commodities emerged as the most favorable option for maintaining an optimal currency portfolio across all time horizons. The study also highlighted that these assets effectively reduced investment risk in the early stages of the pandemic.

Research by Maouchi et al. (2024) examined the financial properties, including diversification, safe-haven status, and hedging capabilities, of two gold-backed cryptocurrencies against traditional cryptocurrencies, NFTs, and DeFi tokens amid significant external and internal crises. They assessed hedge ratios and the effectiveness of hedging for the pairs studied. The results indicated that the gold-backed cryptocurrencies serve as effective diversifiers, with varying hedging and safe-haven properties depending on the crisis nature, including the COVID-19 pandemic and the Russia–Ukraine War.

Using a time-varying Student's copula to explore linkages among different assets from February 11, 2021, to January 5, 2023, Belguith et al. (2024) found that the dependence between gold-backed cryptocurrencies and both NFT and DeFi tokens fluctuated over time. Their results showed that gold-backed cryptocurrencies function as suitable hedging or diversifying assets in normal market conditions, while during the 2022 bear market, they proved to be robust safe havens for most NFT and DeFi assets. Specifically, Pax Gold (PAXG) and Perth MInt Gold Token (PMGT) were identified as the best safe-haven instruments for NFT and DeFi tokens. Although Digix Gold (DGX) also acted as a safe haven for some NFTs and DeFi assets, its risk-mitigation capacity was lower compared to PAXG and PMGT. In general, DGX functioned primarily as a strong diversifier, with its hedging capabilities noted only for the NFT protocol (xNFT) and the DeFi token Chainlink.

Using GARCH and VaR models, Li (2024) analyzed weekly return data from July 2017 to December 2021 for Bitcoin and traditional nondigital asset market indexes, such as stocks, bonds, gold, and commodities. The study found strong hedging effects of digital assets against the bond market but weaker effects against gold, stocks, and commodity markets.

Jeribi and Fakhfekh (2021) proposed a strategy based on the hedging ratio and mean-variance approach to minimize risk while maintaining the same expected returns in a digital-conventional financial asset portfolio. Their recommendation is for investors to hold more conventional financial assets than digital assets. However, exceptions apply to the pairs of crude oil with Bitcoin, Dash, and Ethereum, where the hedge ratios are significant according to ordinary least squares (OLS) regression.

Ali et al. (2023) assessed optimal portfolio weights, hedge ratios, and hedging effectiveness for portfolios consisting of metals and DeFi assets. Their findings indicate that the relationships between DeFi-precious metal and DeFi-industrial metal pairs are weaker compared to those between traditional precious and industrial metals. Additionally, the interconnectedness of these markets increased during the COVID-19 period.

Hedging Through Yield-Generating Strategies

Yield-generating strategies, such as staking, lending, and yield farming, can help offset losses by providing passive income, even when the prices of underlying assets decline. These strategies serve as a hedge, allowing investors to earn returns during periods of market volatility.

By staking assets such as Ethereum, Polkadot, or Cardano, investors can earn rewards that help mitigate the impact of price fluctuations. Platforms such as Aave and Compound enable investors to lend their assets and earn interest. Additionally, yield farming within DeFi protocols offers extra rewards in the form of tokens, which can further help offset losses if the price of the underlying asset decreases.

Managing Liquidity Risk

Liquidity risk is a crucial consideration for investors in both traditional and digital asset markets. In the realm of digital assets, liquidity risk can be particularly pronounced due to the market's nascent nature, the fragmentation of trading venues, and the extreme volatility associated with some assets. Effective management of liquidity risk is essential to safeguard portfolios from sudden market downturns, slippage, or forced liquidations during illiquid periods.

Liquidity in Digital Asset Markets

Liquidity in digital asset markets refers to how easily an asset can be bought or sold without causing significant price changes. Highly liquid assets can be traded quickly, even in large volumes, with minimal impact on market price. In contrast, illiquid assets are more challenging to trade, and even small transactions can lead to substantial price fluctuations.

Major cryptocurrencies such as Bitcoin and Ethereum are considered highly liquid because they are traded on multiple exchanges with deep order books and high trading volumes. This allows investors to enter or exit positions relatively quickly with minimal price impact.

On the other hand, smaller altcoins or tokens with lower market capitalizations are more susceptible to liquidity risks. These assets are often traded on fewer exchanges, resulting in thinner order books and fewer buy and sell orders at different price levels. Consequently, large trades can significantly affect the price, and during market stress, these assets may become difficult to sell at favorable prices.

In the DeFi space, liquidity risk can be exacerbated. While DeFi protocols, such as DEXs and lending platforms, provide innovative opportunities, they rely on liquidity providers (LPs) who supply tokens to liquidity pools. If LPs withdraw liquidity or if network congestion occurs during periods of high demand, the available liquidity can diminish quickly, leading to slippage and execution delays.

Several factors contribute to liquidity risk in digital asset markets, many of which are specific to this evolving asset class. Unlike traditional financial markets, which are typically centralized, digital asset markets are highly fragmented, with thousands of cryptocurrencies traded across hundreds of exchanges worldwide. This lack of a unified trading platform creates inconsistencies in liquidity across different exchanges, meaning the same asset could exhibit vastly different liquidity profiles on various platforms.

Liquidity can vary significantly between exchanges. While major centralized exchanges (CEXs) such as Binance, Coinbase, and Kraken generally offer higher liquidity, smaller or newer exchanges may have thinner order books, thereby increasing liquidity risk. Additionally, DEXs, although innovative, often possess less liquidity compared to their centralized counterparts.

The extreme price volatility that characterizes digital asset markets often correlates with liquidity risks. During market downturns or panic selling, liquidity can evaporate quickly as buyers retreat, leaving sellers unable to execute trades at reasonable prices. Similarly, during bull markets, prices may surge beyond available buy orders, resulting in increased slippage.

Regulatory changes or fears of crackdowns can also lead to a rapid decline in liquidity. For instance, when governments announce new cryptocurrency regulations or impose restrictions on certain exchanges, trading activity typically slows down, and liquidity may diminish as participants withdraw funds or exit positions.

Strategies for Managing Liquidity Risk

Effectively managing liquidity risk in digital asset markets requires a proactive approach that includes assessing the liquidity of assets, diversifying across multiple exchanges, employing suitable trading strategies, and maintaining access to cash or stablecoins. Petukhina and Sprünken (2021) found that liquidity-bounded strategies often perform very well, highlighting the non-normal distribution of returns and the need to control for liquidity constraints in alternative asset markets.

Investors should evaluate the liquidity profile of any digital asset before making an investment. After discussing the strengths and weaknesses of fiat-backed stablecoins (fsCOINs) and CBDCs, Marthinsen and Gordon (2024) concluded that synthetic central bank digital currencies (sCBDCs) offer the most significant net liquidity benefits when considering risks and returns.

Metrics such as trading volume, order book depth, and bid–ask spreads can provide insights into an asset's liquidity. High daily trading volumes and deep order books indicate that an asset is liquid, while wide bid–ask spreads suggest higher liquidity risk. Investors should prioritize assets with consistent liquidity over time, especially if they plan to hold substantial positions.

Trading on High-Liquidity Platforms

Choosing the right exchange is crucial for investors to manage liquidity risk effectively and ensure smooth trading of digital assets. The choice of exchange significantly impacts an investor's ability to enter and exit positions, especially in volatile markets. Different types of exchanges —such as CEXs and DEXs—offer varying levels of liquidity, trading volume, and security.

Centralized Exchanges.   CEXs, such as Binance, Coinbase, Kraken, and FTX, are traditional cryptocurrency trading platforms where a central authority manages order matching, trade execution, and asset custody. These exchanges typically provide high liquidity, making them ideal for investors who need to execute trades quickly and efficiently without significant price slippage.

CEXs generally have higher liquidity than DEXs, particularly for major digital assets such as Bitcoin, Ethereum, and large-cap altcoins. This higher liquidity is due to CEXs aggregating large pools of buyers and sellers, allowing for smooth and efficient trade execution, even for substantial orders. Investors can execute large transactions without significantly impacting the market price, thereby reducing the risk of slippage.

CEXs often handle billions of dollars in daily trading volume, ensuring tight bid–ask spreads and faster trade execution. High trading volumes make CEXs better suited for investors who frequently trade or hold large positions in liquid assets. For example, Binance typically handles over $20 billion in daily trading volume across various assets, providing ample liquidity for most trades.

Moreover, CEXs usually have more reliable infrastructure and stable uptime, which are essential during volatile trading periods. Major CEXs invest heavily to ensure low latency and system stability, reducing the risk of failed trades or service outages during high-demand situations. For instance, exchanges like Coinbase Pro are recognized for their efficiency in managing surges in trading activity during periods of heightened market volatility.

CEXs also offer a variety of trading features such as limit orders, stop-loss orders, and margin trading, which help investors manage liquidity risk more effectively by automating trade execution at specific price points.

- Example: If an investor wishes to trade a large volume of Ethereum (e.g., US$500,000), a CEX like Binance or Kraken would likely provide sufficient liquidity to complete the trade without considerable price slippage. The exchange's high trading volume and deep order book ensure that the trade is executed quickly and at a competitive price.

Decentralized Exchanges.   DEXs, such as Uniswap, SushiSwap, and PancakeSwap, enable users to trade cryptocurrencies directly from their wallets using smart contracts, without depending on a central authority to manage funds. While DEXs offer greater control over assets and access to niche tokens, they may face liquidity challenges compared to CEXs, especially for large trades or less popular assets.

In general, DEXs have lower liquidity than major CEXs, particularly for large-cap assets like Bitcoin or Ethereum. This is because DEX liquidity is provided through liquidity pools, which vary significantly in size based on the asset and the incentives offered to liquidity providers. Smaller pools can result in greater price slippage for large trades, as the available liquidity may be inadequate to handle significant orders without affecting the price.

One notable advantage of DEXs is their ability to provide a wider variety of niche tokens and assets that may not be listed on larger CEXs. DEXs often support newly launched tokens, DeFi assets, and governance tokens that cater to specific ecosystems. For investors interested in accessing early-stage projects or less mainstream assets, DEXs can be an appealing option.

DEXs operate on a noncustodial basis, which means that investors maintain control over their private keys and funds throughout the trading process. This setup reduces the risk of exchange hacks or insolvency associated with centralized platforms. For security-conscious investors who prioritize control over their assets, DEXs provide a safer alternative to CEXs.

The liquidity on DEXs is often dependent on automated market makers, which utilize liquidity pools funded by users. Insufficient liquidity can lead to significant slippage for large trades, especially during periods of market stress when liquidity providers may withdraw funds from pools. Additionally, DEXs typically have wider bid–ask spreads, which can increase transaction costs.

- For example, an investor looking to trade a newly launched DeFi token that is not available on CEXs might turn to Uniswap for liquidity. However, due to the token's relatively low liquidity, a large trade could result in substantial slippage; therefore, the investor should carefully assess the pool's depth before executing the transaction.

Stable Uptime and Reliable Infrastructure. Exchanges with stable uptime and reliable trading infrastructure are critical for investors, especially during periods of high volatility when trading volumes surge. System outages or delayed order execution can lead to missed trades or price slippage, which is particularly concerning in volatile digital asset markets.

Large CEXs like Coinbase and Binance invest heavily in server capacity, load balancing, and trading engines to effectively manage extreme volatility and increased demand. These platforms are more likely to maintain stable uptime during market surges, ensuring that traders can access the market and execute trades without disruption.

While DEXs are less vulnerable to centralized failures, they can still experience network congestion during times of high demand, especially on popular blockchain networks like Ethereum. Increased gas fees and slower transaction speeds during such congestion can raise the cost and risk of trading on DEXs.

- For example, during Bitcoin's significant price rally in 2021, some CEXs like Coinbase experienced brief outages due to surging demand. Investors who chose platforms with stable uptime and robust infrastructure were able to continue trading smoothly, emphasizing the importance of selecting an exchange capable of handling market spikes.

Using Limit Orders

Using limit orders is a crucial strategy for managing slippage and avoiding unfavorable trades in volatile or thinly traded markets, such as those often found in the digital asset space. A limit order allows an investor to specify a particular price for buying or selling an asset, meaning the order will only be executed if the market price meets or exceeds their desired price.

A buy limit order is placed below the current market price and indicates the maximum price the investor is willing to pay for the asset. This order will only be executed if the market price falls to or below the limit price. In contrast, a sell limit order is placed above the current market price, indicating the minimum price at which the investor is willing to sell the asset. This order will only be executed if the market price rises to or above the limit price.

- For example, if an investor wants to buy Ethereum (ETH) and the current market price is US$1,800, they could place a buy limit order at US$1,750. This means they are willing to purchase Ethereum only if the price drops to US$1,750 or lower. Conversely, if they own Ethereum and wish to sell it when the price reaches US$2,000, they could place a sell limit order at that price. The order would then be executed only if the market price reaches US$2,000 or higher.

Limit orders offer several advantages, particularly in volatile or illiquid markets where prices can change rapidly, potentially leading to poor trade execution if market orders are used.

One of the main benefits of using a limit order is that it helps prevent slippage—the difference between the expected price of a trade and the actual price at which it is executed. In fast-moving or thinly traded markets, a market order could result in buying or selling at a significantly less favorable price than anticipated. A limit order ensures that the trade is executed only at the predetermined price, protecting the investor from unwanted price swings.

Limit orders provide investors with precise control over the price at which their trades are executed. This is especially useful in thinly traded markets or when dealing with less liquid altcoins, where prices can fluctuate significantly due to low trading volumes or shallow order books. Investors can set a specific price that reflects their target entry or exit point, allowing them to avoid executing trades at less advantageous prices.

Digital assets, especially smaller altcoins or newly launched tokens, can experience extreme volatility, leading to significant price fluctuations in a short time. A limit order allows investors to take advantage of these price movements by setting specific buy or sell levels, minimizing the risk of overpaying or underselling in a rapidly changing market.

Limit orders can also be part of a broader strategy for accumulating positions or taking profits. For example, if investors anticipate that the price of an asset will drop before rising again, they can place buy limit orders at various levels below the current price to secure lower entry points. Conversely, they can set sell limit orders at different levels above the current price to take profits incrementally as the price increases.

- For instance, imagine an investor believes that Bitcoin (BTC), currently trading at US$25,000, will decrease in price before rebounding. They could set multiple buy limit orders at US$24,000, US$23,000, and US$22,000 to accumulate BTC at progressively lower prices, ensuring they only buy when their conditions are met.

Limit orders offer investors greater control over their trades, but they come with potential downsides, especially in fast-moving or highly liquid markets. The main risk associated with limit orders is that they may not be executed if the market price does not reach the designated limit price. For instance, if an investor sets a buy limit order too far below the current market price, it is possible that the price may never drop low enough to fill the order. Similarly, if a sell limit order is set too high, the market may never reach that price, leaving the investor holding their position longer than intended.

In rapidly rising markets, a buy limit order can lead to missed opportunities if the price does not decline to the set limit before continuing to rise. Conversely, in a falling market, a sell limit order set too high may go unexecuted, resulting in the investor missing the chance to sell before prices drop further.

- Example: An investor might set a buy limit order for Solana at US$80 when the market price is US$85, anticipating a short-term dip. If the price never falls to US$80 and instead increases to US$100, the investor would miss the opportunity to buy Solana at US$85 and may need to reconsider their entry point.

In thinly traded markets, where there are fewer participants buying and selling, the bid–ask spreads can be wider, and price volatility may be more pronounced due to lower liquidity. Here, limit orders are particularly important to avoid the potential drawbacks of market orders, such as buying at inflated prices or selling at significant discounts, as there may be insufficient counterparties available at the expected price.

When a large market order is placed in a market with a shallow order book, it may cause a significant price movement if there aren't enough buy or sell orders at the current price. For example, if an investor places a large market buy order in a thin market, they may unintentionally raise the price significantly, leading to costs that exceed their expectations. A limit order helps ensure that transactions occur only at a prespecified price or better.

- Example: In a less liquid token like SushiSwap, placing a large buy order could result in slippage, particularly if there are few sell orders available. Using a limit order at a specific price—say US$10—ensures that the investor does not inadvertently trigger a large price increase by buying progressively higher to fill their order.

Investors need to strike a balance between the speed of trade execution and the price certainty provided by limit orders. While market orders are ideal for immediate execution, they expose investors to slippage, especially in volatile markets. On the other hand, limit orders grant price certainty but may not get filled, presenting a risk for investors needing to enter or exit positions quickly.

Limit orders are especially useful when controlling price is a priority and immediate execution is not necessary. They are suitable for situations where an investor anticipates market volatility or is dealing with low liquidity, making them reluctant to risk executing a market order at an unfavorable price.

If speed is essential, such as during market breakouts or when trading in highly liquid environments, market orders may be more suitable to ensure quick execution, even if some slippage occurs.

Time-in-Force Instructions for Limit Orders:

1. Good-Til-Canceled (GTC): The GTC limit order remains active until it is either executed or manually canceled by the investor. It is useful for longer-term strategies where the investor is willing to wait for the market to reach the target price.
2. Immediate-Or-Cancel (IOC): An IOC order attempts to execute as much of the order as possible immediately, while the unfilled portion is canceled. This option helps investors minimize exposure to slippage while still aiming to get part of their order filled quickly.

Maintaining Liquidity Buffers

To effectively manage liquidity risk, it is essential for investors—especially those with exposure to highly volatile digital assets—to maintain a portion of their portfolio in highly liquid assets such as stablecoins (e.g., USDC, USDT) or cash. These liquid assets serve as a buffer, providing quick access to capital during times of market stress. This access allows for timely rebalancing or the opportunity to capitalize on emerging situations without needing to sell less liquid or more volatile assets at unfavorable prices.

By holding these highly liquid assets, investors ensure that they have immediate capital available when needed. Whether for rebalancing, making new investments, or protecting against market downturns, liquid assets offer flexibility without the necessity of selling more volatile or illiquid positions.

- For example, if an investor holds a significant portion of their portfolio in volatile altcoins, they can allocate a portion of their capital to USDC. During a sharp market downturn, they can quickly use these stablecoins to buy assets at discounted prices or to reallocate to other positions, avoiding the need to sell their altcoins at a loss.

Stablecoins, which are typically pegged to traditional fiat currencies like the U.S. dollar, provide a unique advantage for liquidity management within the crypto ecosystem. Unlike cash, which requires moving funds in and out of crypto exchanges (often incurring fees and processing delays), stablecoins allow investors to maintain on-chain liquidity while shielding their capital from the volatility of traditional cryptocurrencies.

Stablecoins such as USD Coin, Tether, and Dai are designed to maintain a stable value, protecting investors' portfolios from the price swings associated with other digital assets like Bitcoin or Ethereum. In this sense, stablecoins act as safe-haven assets during times of market volatility. They provide the benefits of cash while remaining within the crypto ecosystem, making them ideal for fast, efficient trades when market conditions improve.

With stablecoins, investors can easily move funds between different DeFi protocols, exchanges, and wallets without the friction associated with fiat currencies. This facilitates quick capital deployment into new opportunities or effective portfolio management without waiting for traditional banking systems to process transactions.

- For instance, an investor with a significant allocation to Bitcoin and Ethereum might hold 10 to 20 percent of their portfolio in USDC. This allocation allows them immediate access to funds for rebalancing, taking advantage of yield opportunities in DeFi protocols, or reducing risk without exiting the crypto space entirely.

During times of market stress or significant volatility, having access to highly liquid assets is essential for timely portfolio rebalancing. Without a liquidity buffer, investors may be forced to sell volatile assets at depressed prices, locking in losses. Maintaining stablecoins or cash as part of a portfolio allows investors to rebalance without selling other holdings at inopportune times.

When markets experience a downturn, highly volatile assets like altcoins or even Bitcoin can see sharp price declines. In such scenarios, having stablecoins on hand enables investors to rebalance their portfolios without selling volatile assets at a loss. Instead, they can use stablecoins to buy undervalued assets or increase their allocation to more stable investments.

Liquidity from stablecoins or cash gives investors the ability to strategically rebalance during volatile conditions. They can gradually reenter the market when conditions stabilize or allocate more capital to high-conviction investments without being at the mercy of market timing.

- For example, if an investor's portfolio is primarily composed of altcoins and Bitcoin, and Bitcoin's price suddenly drops by 20 percent, the investor can use their stablecoin reserves to buy more Bitcoin at a discount and rebalance their portfolio.

This allows them to avoid panic-selling other volatile assets and instead capitalize on the price dip.

Stablecoins also provide a key advantage in the growing world of DeFi, where liquidity is often rewarded through various protocols. Investors can deploy stablecoins in lending protocols, liquidity pools, or yield farming strategies, generating passive income while maintaining liquidity.

Since stablecoins are already part of the crypto ecosystem, investors can quickly redeploy them into other assets or yield opportunities. This flexibility is crucial for those who want to remain agile and respond to market opportunities as they arise.

- For instance, an investor holding USD Coin in a compound lending pool could earn interest on their stablecoin while waiting for the right moment to reenter the market. When they identify an opportunity, they can quickly withdraw their funds to buy crypto assets or participate in new projects, all while maintaining liquidity during market downturns.

While cash (fiat currency) remains the ultimate liquid asset in traditional finance, its utility in the digital asset space is more limited due to the friction involved in moving funds in and out of exchanges. However, some investors may find it beneficial to maintain a portion of their portfolio in cash, especially if they frequently convert crypto holdings back to fiat, providing an added layer of security.

- For example, an investor using a CEX like Coinbase or Binance might hold part of their portfolio in cash for immediate access to fiat for personal expenses or security reasons. Although not as fast or flexible as stablecoins in the crypto ecosystem, cash offers a sense of liquidity in the traditional financial world.

Cryptocurrencies are notorious for extreme volatility, which can lead to market shocks where liquidity dries up, especially in smaller markets or during significant corrections. Holding stablecoins or cash ensures that investors are better prepared to weather these market shocks, giving them the option to wait out downturns or take advantage of market dislocations.

By keeping liquid assets in stablecoins or cash, investors reduce the pressure to sell volatile positions during a market crash. Instead of panic-selling to free up cash, they can maintain their positions and use their liquid assets to strategically buy when prices are low.

Market corrections often present opportunities to purchase valuable assets at discounted prices. Having stablecoins on hand allows investors to capitalize on these opportunities without the need to sell other holdings at a loss or wait for funds to transfer from fiat accounts.

- For example, during the March 2020 market crash, many investors who had a liquidity buffer in stablecoins were able to buy Bitcoin at significantly lower prices. They benefited from the subsequent price recovery without having to sell other digital assets during the panic.

Additionally, diversifying across different digital assets with varying liquidity profiles can help mitigate the risk of being overexposed to illiquid assets. By balancing positions between high-liquidity assets like Bitcoin or Ethereum and smaller, more speculative tokens, investors can reduce the risk of being unable to liquidate their positions when needed.

For investors who wish to include illiquid tokens in their portfolios, position sizing is crucial. Allocating a smaller percentage of the portfolio to illiquid or speculative assets can help limit the impact of liquidity risk. Furthermore, it's important to conduct thorough due diligence on the trading activity of these tokens and to avoid placing large bets in assets that might become difficult to sell during market downturns.

Rebalancing

Rebalancing is a key risk management strategy designed to maintain a specific asset allocation in an investment portfolio, ensuring that it aligns with investors' goals, risk tolerance, and market conditions. This strategy is particularly important in the context of digital assets. Digital assets—such as Bitcoin, Ethereum, altcoins, DeFi tokens, and stablecoins—exhibit extreme price volatility compared to traditional investments like stocks or bonds. Consequently, portfolios containing cryptocurrencies can experience significant changes in asset weightings over short periods. Without regular rebalancing, an investor's portfolio may drift from its original allocation strategy, which could expose them to unintended risks or cause them to miss opportunities to lock in profits.

Cryptocurrencies can experience substantial price fluctuations in a brief time frame. For instance, if Bitcoin's value surges, it could come to dominate a portfolio that was initially balanced between Bitcoin, Ethereum, and stablecoins. Rebalancing helps maintain the desired risk profile by allowing investors to trim gains from overperforming assets and reallocate funds to other holdings.

Rebalancing enables investors to lock in profits from winning assets by selling high and reinvesting in underperforming or more stable assets. This process ensures that investors capture profits while minimizing exposure to additional price swings in a single asset.

Over time, a portfolio's asset mix may drift, leading to greater exposure to riskier assets like altcoins or speculative tokens. By rebalancing, investors can keep their portfolio aligned with their risk tolerance and investment goals, avoiding excessive exposure to high-risk digital assets.

Rebalancing a portfolio generally involves two main steps: assessing the current asset allocation and then adjusting it back to the target allocation. The approach can vary based on the investor's strategy, market conditions, and personal preferences.

First, investors should determine their ideal asset allocation to reflect their risk tolerance and investment objectives. A common strategy for a moderate-risk investor might allocate:

- 50 percent to Bitcoin and Ethereum (the two largest and most established digital assets);
- 30 percent to altcoins and DeFi tokens (for growth potential); and
- 20 percent to stablecoins (for liquidity and stability).

Over time, as prices fluctuate, these percentages can drift. For example, if Bitcoin experiences a significant price increase, it might now account for 60 percent of the portfolio, while altcoins could drop to 20 percent.

Threshold-Based Rebalancing

One common approach to rebalancing is threshold-based rebalancing. In this method, investors rebalance their portfolio whenever an asset's weighting deviates from its target allocation by a specific percentage (e.g., 5% or 10%). Threshold-based rebalancing is particularly beneficial for portfolios that include highly volatile assets, such as Bitcoin and altcoins. This strategy helps prevent overexposure while capitalizing on market fluctuations.

How Threshold-Based Rebalancing Works:

Step 1: Predefine a Target Allocation for Each Asset Class

Before implementing threshold-based rebalancing, investors should decide on the target allocation for each asset in the portfolio. This allocation should be determined based on factors such as risk tolerance, investment horizon, and diversification goals—namely, the balance between traditional assets (like stocks and bonds) and digital assets (such as Bitcoin and Ethereum). The target allocation establishes the baseline from which deviations will be measured.

Step 2: Set Allowable Deviation Limits

Given that asset prices fluctuate, allowable thresholds define the maximum deviation permitted before rebalancing is triggered.
How to Set the Threshold:

- Low-Volatility Assets (Stocks, Bonds): Tighter thresholds (e.g., ±5%)

- High-Volatility Assets (Bitcoin, Altcoins): Wider thresholds (e.g., ±10-20%)

For instance, a 10 percent threshold for Bitcoin means that rebalancing will take place only if Bitcoin's allocation moves beyond 5.5 percent or drops below 4.5 percent.

Step 3: Regularly Monitor Portfolio Weights

To effectively apply threshold-based rebalancing, investors must continuously track asset weights over time.
Factors to Monitor:

1. Bitcoin's Price Fluctuations: Rapid gains or losses in Bitcoin can trigger rebalancing.
2. Market Cycles: Bull and bear markets can impact allocation dynamics.
3. Correlations Between Assets: If stocks and Bitcoin move in tandem, threshold breaches may occur more frequently.

Frequent monitoring ensures timely rebalancing and prevents the risk of overexposure.

Step 4: Trigger Rebalancing When an Asset Exceeds Its Threshold to Restore the Portfolio's Target Allocation

When an asset surpasses its threshold, the portfolio must be adjusted back to the target weight.

Scenario 1: Bitcoin Surges Beyond Its Upper Threshold. If Bitcoin's price increases sharply and its portfolio allocation rises to 7 percent (exceeding the 5.5 percent threshold):
Action:

1. Sell the excess Bitcoin (1.5% of the portfolio).

2. Reinvest the proceeds into underweight assets (such as stocks or bonds).

This action locks in Bitcoin gains while maintaining the target allocation.

Scenario 2: Bitcoin Drops Below Its Lower Threshold.   If Bitcoin's price declines and its allocation falls to 3.5 percent (below the 4.5% threshold):

Action:

• Purchase Bitcoin using funds from overweight assets (like stocks or bonds).

This approach allows for accumulating Bitcoin at a lower price, effectively "buying the dip."

Time-Based Rebalancing

Another method is time-based rebalancing, where investors review and adjust their portfolio at regular intervals—monthly, quarterly, or annually—regardless of how much the allocations have drifted. Unlike threshold-based rebalancing, which reacts to price deviations, time-based rebalancing follows a fixed schedule, ensuring consistent risk management and profit-taking. This method is simpler to execute and can often be automated on various platforms, although it may not be as responsive to sudden market changes.

• Example: An investor may choose to rebalance their portfolio every quarter. Even if market conditions change significantly within that quarter, they will adhere to the plan of rebalancing at the set intervals. Time-based rebalancing helps eliminate emotional decision making during trading, especially in volatile markets like cryptocurrencies, ensuring that investors remain disciplined.

Dynamic Rebalancing

Dynamic rebalancing involves adjusting asset allocations more frequently, often based on market conditions or levels of volatility. This approach entails increasing exposure to assets during periods of low volatility and decreasing exposure during times of high volatility.

- Example: If market conditions are stable and Bitcoin's price volatility is low, an investor may choose to increase their allocation to Bitcoin. Conversely, during periods of high market uncertainty, they might reduce their allocation to Bitcoin and increase their position in stablecoins to mitigate risk. Dynamic rebalancing is typically favored by more experienced or active traders who closely monitor market trends and are comfortable making frequent adjustments to their portfolio.

Rebalancing in the Context of Volatility

Volatility in digital asset markets presents both opportunities and risks. By rebalancing during high volatility, investors can capture gains from overperforming assets while reducing the risks associated with underperforming or highly volatile assets. However, frequent rebalancing in such markets also carries risks, as investors may lock in losses if the market rebounds after a temporary dip.

Large price fluctuations can cause an asset's weighting in a portfolio to change dramatically. Rebalancing allows investors to take profits from rapidly appreciating assets and reallocate funds to those with lower performance, potentially buying them at a discount.

During market rallies, specific asset classes—such as altcoins or DeFi tokens—may become overly dominant in a portfolio. Rebalancing during these times helps ensure diversification, preventing overexposure to a single asset class or sector, and reduces the risk of significant drawdowns in the future.

- Example: During the DeFi boom, many DeFi tokens (e.g., Aave, SushiSwap) saw substantial price increases. An investor who had allocated 20 percent of their portfolio to DeFi tokens might find that this allocation has grown to 40 percent or more. To maintain their original risk profile, they can rebalance by selling some of their DeFi holdings and reallocating to Bitcoin or stablecoins.

Summary

Effective risk and portfolio management is crucial for navigating the dynamic and often volatile world of digital assets. By strategically managing volatility through diversification, position sizing, and hedging, investors can reduce potential losses while balancing opportunities for growth.

Managing liquidity risk is also essential; keeping a portion of the portfolio in highly liquid assets ensures quick access to capital during times of market stress or when rebalancing is needed. Additionally, regular rebalancing helps maintain the desired asset allocation, allowing investors to lock in gains and avoid overexposure to any single asset or market trend.

Together, these strategies provide a framework that enables investors to build resilient portfolios, withstand market fluctuations, and achieve their long-term investment goals.

CHAPTER 8

Taxation and Regulatory Compliance

As digital assets such as cryptocurrencies, DeFi tokens, and NFTs continue to reshape the global financial landscape, it is essential for both investors and institutions to understand the complex tax implications and evolving regulatory frameworks.

In this chapter, we explore the key tax considerations involved in investing in digital assets. This includes capital gains tax on trades, income tax on staking rewards, the strategic use of tax-loss harvesting, and the challenges of navigating international tax obligations. We also discuss how DeFi activities and NFTs introduce additional layers of tax complexity.

In addition to tax considerations, the chapter examines the global regulatory landscape, highlighting the approaches taken by major jurisdictions, such as the United States, the EU, Asia-Pacific, and the Middle East and Africa. As digital asset markets evolve, so too do regulatory responses, which create both opportunities and challenges for investors. This chapter provides a comprehensive overview of the intersection of taxation and regulation in the digital asset space, equipping readers with the knowledge needed to navigate these critical areas effectively.

Tax Implications of Investing in Digital Assets

Investing in digital assets, such as cryptocurrencies, can lead to substantial returns, but it also involves significant tax implications that investors need to understand. Tax authorities worldwide, including the Internal Revenue Service (IRS) in the United States and various global agencies, have established regulations for reporting and taxing digital asset transactions.

In many jurisdictions, cryptocurrencies are classified as property rather than currency. This means that transactions involving digital assets are subject to capital gains taxes when they are sold or exchanged for a profit. Additionally, other taxable events can occur, such as receiving digital assets as income through methods like staking, mining, or airdrops.

Investors should also be aware of important considerations such as tax-loss harvesting, crypto-to-crypto transactions, and international tax regulations to ensure compliance and optimize their tax liabilities. Effectively managing the tax implications of digital assets is crucial for investors who want to maximize their net returns and avoid potential legal penalties.

Capital Gains Tax

In the United States and many other countries, cryptocurrencies are classified as property for tax purposes, similar to stocks or real estate. This means that when you sell a cryptocurrency or exchange it for another asset, you need to calculate the capital gain or loss from the transaction.

Capital Gains Taxation on Digital Assets

A capital gain is the difference between the cost basis (the price at which you originally purchased the cryptocurrency) and the sale price (the amount you received when selling or exchanging the cryptocurrency). You must report the resulting gain or loss to the tax authorities, and the tax rate applied depends on how long you held the asset before selling it.

If you hold the cryptocurrency for less than one year before selling or exchanging it, any gains are taxed at short-term capital gains rates, which are the same as ordinary income tax rates. In the United States, these rates can be as high as 37 percent for high-income earners (Kesselman 2024).

If you hold the cryptocurrency for more than one year, gains are taxed at long-term capital gains rates, which are generally lower than short-term rates. In the United States, these rates can be 0, 15, or 20 percent, depending on the taxpayer's income level (Ali et al. 2001). Long-term capital gains tax rates incentivize holding assets for a longer period to take advantage of the lower tax rates.

- For instance, if an investor buys Bitcoin for US$30,000 and then sells it for US$50,000, the capital gain is US$20,000. If the Bitcoin is held for less than a year, the investor will pay short-term capital gains tax on the US$20,000, taxed at their ordinary income tax rate. However, if the Bitcoin is held for more than a year, the US$20,000 gain would be subject to the more favorable long-term capital gains tax rates.

Crypto-to-Crypto Transactions as Taxable Events

One unique aspect of cryptocurrency taxation is that crypto-to-crypto trades—where one cryptocurrency is exchanged for another—are also considered taxable events. Even though no fiat currency is involved, tax authorities such as the IRS treat the exchange of one cryptocurrency for another as a sale of the first cryptocurrency. This means that when an investor trades Bitcoin for Ethereum, for example, they must report any gain or loss on the Bitcoin based on the value of the Ethereum they receive.

When exchanging one cryptocurrency for another, the fair market value of the cryptocurrency being acquired (Ethereum, in this case) at the time of the transaction is considered the sale price of the cryptocurrency being exchanged (Bitcoin). The capital gain or loss is calculated as the difference between the cost basis of the cryptocurrency being exchanged (Bitcoin) and its value at the time of the transaction.

- For example, let's say an investor initially bought 1 BTC for US$30,000. They later trade that Bitcoin for 10 ETH, and the total market value of the 10 ETH at the time of the exchange is US$40,000. The investor realizes a capital gain of US$10,000 (US$40,000 – US$30,000), even though no fiat currency was involved. This US$10,000 gain must be reported and is subject to capital gains tax, either at short-term or long-term rates, depending on the holding period of the Bitcoin.

This situation can be particularly challenging for active traders who frequently exchange cryptocurrencies, as each trade is a taxable event that must be reported. Investors need to maintain accurate records of all their trades, including the cost basis and the fair market value of the cryptocurrencies at the time of the exchange.

Tracking and Reporting Cryptocurrency Transactions

Investing in digital assets presents the challenge of accurately tracking and reporting all transactions to calculate capital gains or losses. Cryptocurrency transactions often occur across multiple exchanges and platforms, making record-keeping complicated. Investors need to monitor key details for each transaction, including:

1. Date of acquisition of the cryptocurrency
2. Cost basis (the original purchase price)
3. Fair market value of the cryptocurrency at the time of sale or exchange
4. Date of sale or exchange
5. Gain or loss on each transaction

While most cryptocurrency exchanges offer transaction reports, the responsibility for accurate record-keeping and ensuring all relevant transactions are reported on tax returns ultimately falls on the investor. For those who trade frequently, using cryptocurrency tax software—such as CoinTracking, Koinly, or TokenTax—can simplify the process by automatically tracking transactions, calculating gains and losses, and generating reports for tax filings.

Tax Implications for Losses and Offsetting Gains

Gains from the sale of cryptocurrencies are taxable, but losses can also be used to offset those gains. If an investor experiences a capital loss— meaning the sale price of a cryptocurrency is lower than its cost basis— they can use that loss to reduce their taxable income by offsetting it against gains from other cryptocurrency or investment sales.

In the United States, investors can deduct up to US$3,000 of net capital losses from their ordinary income each year. Any additional losses can be carried forward to future tax years to offset gains in those years (Gotham et al. 2020).

- For example, if an investor sells Bitcoin for a US$20,000 profit but also sells Litecoin at a US$5,000 loss, the loss can reduce the taxable gain from the Bitcoin sale to US$15,000. If the total losses exceed the gains, the investor can deduct up to US$3,000 from their regular income and carry over any remaining losses to future years.

Income Tax

When digital assets are received as income through activities such as mining, staking, airdrops, or DeFi lending, they are typically taxed as ordinary income at their fair market value (FMV) at the time of receipt. This tax treatment applies because receiving digital assets is considered a form of compensation, even if the compensation comes in cryptocurrency rather than cash. Once the digital assets are received and taxed as income, any subsequent appreciation or depreciation in their value is treated separately and taxed as a capital gain or loss when the assets are sold or exchanged.

Income Taxation on Digital Assets

When an individual receives digital assets as part of an income-generating activity, the IRS and other tax authorities treat the value of the assets at the time they are received as ordinary income. This income must be reported on the individual's tax return and taxed at their ordinary income tax rate.

The taxable income is based on the FMV of the digital asset when it is received. For example, if an investor receives staking rewards in ETH, they need to calculate the USD value of the Ethereum at the time it enters their wallet. This value will be regarded as income and taxed at ordinary income rates.

Ordinary income tax rates in the United States vary based on the taxpayer's total income, ranging from 10 to 37 percent. The same principle generally applies in most jurisdictions, where digital asset income is taxed at the recipient's standard income tax rate.

- Example: If an investor is staking Ethereum and receives 0.5 ETH in rewards when the price of Ethereum is US$2,000, the income from staking would be US$1,000 (0.5 ETH * US$2,000). This US$1,000 must be reported as income on their tax return for the year in which it was received, with the tax owed depending on the taxpayer's ordinary income tax rate.

Mining and Staking Income

Investors commonly earn digital assets as income through two main methods: mining and staking:

Mining Income. Cryptocurrency mining involves verifying transactions on a blockchain network, and miners receive rewards in the form of new cryptocurrency (e.g., Bitcoin) for contributing computational power. When a miner successfully mines a block, the fair market value of the newly mined cryptocurrency is recognized as ordinary income at the time it is received.

- Example: If a Bitcoin miner receives 0.1 BTC as a reward when Bitcoin is valued at US$30,000, the miner must report US$3,000 (0.1 BTC * US$30,000) as income on their tax return. This amount is subject to ordinary income tax rates.

Miners may also deduct operating expenses related to mining, such as electricity costs, hardware, and maintenance. These deductions can reduce the taxable income from mining operations, though specific rules vary by jurisdiction and whether the mining is classified as a business or a hobby.

Staking Income.   Staking involves locking up a certain amount of cryptocurrency to participate in the network's consensus mechanism (PoS) and earn rewards for validating transactions. The value of the rewards gained through staking is also considered ordinary income at the time they are distributed.

- Example: If an investor stakes a certain amount and receives 0.2 ETH in rewards when Ethereum is valued at US$2,500, they must report US$500 (0.2 ETH * $2,500) as income. This income is also subject to ordinary income tax rates.

Other Income-Generating Activities

Other common ways to earn digital assets as income include airdrops and interest from DeFi lending. These income sources are taxed similarly to mining and staking rewards.

Airdrop Income.   Airdrops involve the distribution of free tokens to users, often as part of a marketing campaign or to reward holders of another cryptocurrency. The FMV of the tokens received during an airdrop is considered ordinary income at the time they are received.

- For example, if an investor receives 100 tokens in an airdrop, and each token is valued at US$5 when received, they must report US$500 as income. If the tokens appreciate in value and are sold later, any additional gains will be subject to capital gains tax.

Tax-Loss Harvesting

Tax-loss harvesting is a valuable strategy that enables investors to minimize their tax liability by selling underperforming assets at a loss. These losses can then be used to offset gains from other investments. This practice is especially relevant in the volatile cryptocurrency market, where sharp price fluctuations can lead to both significant gains and losses within a single tax year. By strategically harvesting losses, investors can lower the amount of capital gains tax they owe, potentially enhancing their overall portfolio performance.

How Tax-Loss Harvesting Works

Tax-loss harvesting involves selling digital assets that have declined in value, thereby realizing the loss. These losses can offset both short-term and long-term capital gains. This strategy is particularly beneficial in the cryptocurrency market due to the frequent and often substantial price swings that digital assets experience.

- Example: If an investor sells Bitcoin, realizing a US$10,000 profit, but also sells Ethereum at a US$5,000 loss, they can use the Ethereum loss to offset the Bitcoin gain. This reduces their taxable capital gain from US$10,000 to US$5,000, lowering their capital gains tax for that year.

In situations where an investor's capital losses exceed their capital gains, they can deduct up to US$3,000 (in the United States) of those losses from their ordinary income. Any losses beyond this limit can be carried forward to future tax years, allowing the investor to offset future gains or income with unused losses.

Benefits of Tax-Loss Harvesting in a Volatile Market

Cryptocurrencies are known for their volatility, presenting both opportunities for significant gains and risks of substantial losses. Tax-loss harvesting provides key advantages in this environment.

Capitalizing on Losses.   In a volatile market, some digital assets may decline sharply in value after purchase. Instead of holding these assets indefinitely, investors can sell them, realize the loss, and use that loss to offset gains elsewhere in their portfolio. Even if the investor still believes in the long-term potential of the asset, they can take advantage of the tax benefits in the short term.

Tax Efficiency.   By strategically harvesting losses, investors can improve the tax efficiency of their portfolios, ultimately enhancing after-tax returns. This is especially useful for active crypto traders who may realize significant gains from certain positions while also holding losing positions.

Ongoing Opportunity.   In a market as volatile as cryptocurrency, where prices can fluctuate dramatically within a single tax year, the opportunity for tax-loss harvesting often arises repeatedly. By periodically reviewing their portfolios, investors can identify new chances to harvest losses.

- Example: Suppose an investor buys Cardano for US$3,000, but its value drops to US$1,500. The investor may choose to sell Cardano, realizing a US$1,500 loss, and apply that loss to offset gains elsewhere. If the investor also sold Bitcoin that year and realized a US$10,000 gain, the Cardano loss would reduce the taxable gain to US$8,500, thereby lowering the tax liability.

Wash Sale Rules

Wash sale rules are designed to prevent investors from claiming a tax loss by selling an asset and then immediately repurchasing the same or a substantially identical asset within a short period. In traditional markets, such as stocks and bonds, if an investor repurchases the same asset within 30 days of selling it at a loss, the IRS disallows the loss for tax purposes. Instead, the loss is added to the cost basis of the newly acquired asset, delaying any tax benefits until a future sale.

As of this writing, wash sale rules generally do not apply to digital assets in many jurisdictions, including the United States. This creates a unique opportunity for crypto investors to engage in tax-loss harvesting while maintaining exposure to their assets. Investors can sell a cryptocurrency at a loss, immediately repurchase it (or a similar asset), and still claim the loss for tax purposes, maximizing their tax benefits.

- Example: If an investor owns Ethereum, which they purchased for US$4,000, and the price drops to US$2,000, they could sell the Ethereum at a loss, realizing a US$2,000 loss for tax purposes. They can then immediately repurchase the same Ethereum or another similar cryptocurrency. This allows them to retain their exposure to the asset while taking advantage of the tax benefit.

While wash sale rules currently do not apply to digital assets in the United States, tax regulations regarding cryptocurrencies are evolving. Discussions in Congress have considered expanding wash sale rules to include cryptocurrencies. Investors should remain aware of potential changes in the future and consult with a tax professional before engaging in strategies that rely on the absence of these rules.

Tax-Loss Harvesting in Practice

Successful tax-loss harvesting requires careful tracking of gains and losses throughout the year. Investors should do the following:

1. Track the Cost Basis: For every cryptocurrency transaction, it is crucial to record the cost basis (the original purchase price). Many crypto exchanges and tax software platforms can assist with this tracking, ensuring that investors know the precise gain or loss when they sell.
2. Monitor Market Movements: Given the volatility of the cryptocurrency market, prices can fluctuate rapidly. Investors should regularly review their portfolios to identify underperforming assets that might be sold for a loss to offset gains.

3. Execute the Harvest Strategically: Harvesting losses near the end of the year can effectively manage taxes, especially if the investor is aware of realized gains that could be offset. However, this can also be done throughout the year as opportunities arise.

4. Avoid Overtrading: While frequent tax-loss harvesting can reduce tax liability, it should be done considering trading costs (e.g., transaction fees) and the investor's broader portfolio strategy. Overtrading to capture small losses may undermine the benefits of long-term investing.

International Tax Considerations

International investors in digital assets must carefully navigate tax obligations across multiple jurisdictions, as their investments are often conducted through global cryptocurrency exchanges. The tax treatment of digital assets varies significantly from one country to another. Some nations have lenient tax regimes that do not heavily regulate tax digital assets. In contrast, others, such as the United States, impose strict reporting requirements and require citizens to declare their worldwide income, including gains from cryptocurrency trading, regardless of where the assets are held.

Global Nature of Cryptocurrency Trading

Cryptocurrencies are traded on a global scale, with exchanges serving users from multiple countries. As a result, international investors often interact with exchanges that are located in jurisdictions different from their home country. This discrepancy creates tax reporting challenges, as investors may be subject to tax laws in multiple countries, depending on their residency and the location of the exchange.

Certain countries, such as Portugal and Germany, have more lenient tax policies for cryptocurrencies. For example, capital gains from personal cryptocurrency investments are generally tax-free in Portugal. In Germany, gains on crypto assets held for more than one year are not subject to taxation. Conversely, countries like the United States impose strict reporting requirements and tax digital assets at capital gains rates, with additional rules for reporting foreign holdings.

- Example: A U.S. citizen who trades on a European-based exchange, like Bitstamp, must report those holdings and gains to the IRS, even if the trading occurs outside the United States. Tax obligations depend not only on the location of the exchange but also on where the investor is—a tax resident or citizen.

Foreign Asset Reporting for U.S. Investors

U.S. taxpayers are required to report their foreign financial holdings, which include cryptocurrency accounts held on foreign exchanges, through forms such as the Foreign Bank Account Report (FBAR) and the Foreign Account Tax Compliance Act (FATCA) disclosures.

Foreign Bank Account Report.   U.S. citizens and residents must file an FBAR if they hold foreign financial accounts with an aggregate value exceeding US$10,000 at any point during the tax year. This requirement includes holdings in foreign cryptocurrency exchanges, provided the exchange qualifies as a "foreign financial account."

- Example: If an investor holds more than US$10,000 worth of Bitcoin on a foreign-based exchange such as Binance or Bitfinex, they must file an FBAR with the Financial Crimes Enforcement Network (FinCEN), even if they do not realize any gains or losses from trading. Failure to file an FBAR can result in substantial penalties ranging from US$10,000 to US$100,000 per violation.

Foreign Account Tax Compliance Act.   Under FATCA, U.S. taxpayers with foreign financial assets exceeding certain thresholds must report these assets to the IRS using Form 8938. The reporting thresholds vary based on the taxpayer's filing status (e.g., single or married) and whether they reside in or outside the United States. FATCA applies to digital assets held on foreign exchanges if they meet the criteria for foreign financial accounts.

- Example: If a single U.S. taxpayer holds more than US$50,000 in foreign cryptocurrency accounts at the end of the year or US$75,000 at any point during the year, they are required to file Form 8938 under FATCA. For married couples filing jointly, the thresholds are higher: US$100,000 at the end of the year or US$150,000 at any time during the year.

It is important to note that taxpayers who meet the FBAR and FATCA thresholds may need to file both reports (FBAR and Form 8938), as these are separate requirements with different filing rules.

Double Taxation

International investors must be aware of the potential for double taxation, which occurs when they are taxed on the same income in both their home country and the country where the cryptocurrency exchange is located. Many countries have established tax treaties to prevent this, offering relief to investors by allowing tax credits or exemptions that can reduce or eliminate the double tax burden.

Tax treaties between countries are designed to avoid double taxation by outlining which country has the primary right to tax specific types of income, such as capital gains from digital asset trading. Under most treaties, investors can claim a foreign tax credit in their home country for taxes paid on the same income in the foreign country, or vice versa.

- For example, a U.S. investor trading on a cryptocurrency exchange in Germany may be subject to German capital gains tax, depending on their holding period. If the United States and Germany have a tax treaty in place, the investor can claim a foreign tax credit on their U.S. tax return for taxes paid to Germany, thus avoiding double taxation on the same gains.

Claiming Foreign Tax Credits. If an investor is taxed on digital asset gains in a foreign country, they can often claim a foreign tax credit to offset taxes owed in their home country. This credit reduces the amount of tax owed domestically by the amount already paid in the foreign country.

- For example, if a U.S. investor pays US$5,000 in capital gains taxes on digital assets in a foreign country and owes US$8,000 in U.S. taxes on the same gains, they can claim a US$5,000 credit on their U.S. taxes. This reduces their total tax liability to US$3,000. If the foreign tax credit exceeds the amount of U.S. tax owed, the investor may be able to carry back the excess credit to the previous year or carry it forward to offset future tax liabilities.

Double Taxation Relief.   Tax treaties often include provisions to avoid double taxation through either tax exemption or tax credit mechanisms. Some treaties may specify that capital gains from investments made in one country are only taxable in that country, which would exempt investors from paying taxes on the same gains in their home country.

- For example, under certain treaties, if a U.S. investor realizes gains from cryptocurrency held in a European exchange, the treaty may stipulate that the United States has the primary taxing right, while the foreign country offers relief.

Cross-Border Cryptocurrency Compliance

International investors should also be aware that compliance with multiple tax authorities requires detailed record-keeping and cross-border reporting obligations, especially when assets are moved between different exchanges or converted into fiat currencies in various jurisdictions.

Investors trading across multiple exchanges—some based domestically and others internationally—must maintain detailed records of every transaction, including the date of purchase, cost basis, and fair market value of the digital asset at the time of sale or exchange. This information is crucial for calculating capital gains and losses and ensuring accurate reporting in both countries.

- For instance, if an investor trades Bitcoin on a U.S. exchange like Coinbase and later transfers the Bitcoin to a foreign exchange like Binance before selling it for fiat currency, they must track the complete transaction history to accurately report to both U.S. tax authorities and any foreign tax authority that may require reporting of the sale.

Tax Implications of DeFi and NFTs

As DeFi protocols provide innovative ways to earn interest, swap tokens, and engage in liquidity pools, and as NFTs reshape digital ownership of art, collectibles, and other assets, it's crucial for investors and creators to understand how these activities are taxed. The tax treatment of DeFi transactions and NFTs can vary based on local regulations, but it generally aligns with the principles of ordinary income, capital gains, and business income.

Taxation of Decentralized Finance Transactions

DeFi transactions can take various forms, including yield farming, liquidity mining, and crypto lending. These activities can generate different types of income, such as interest, staking rewards, or capital gains, and often involve complex interactions between various tokens and platforms.

Interest Earned From Lending Crypto. Lending cryptocurrency on DeFi platforms such as Aave, Compound, or Yearn Finance allows investors to earn interest or rewards for providing liquidity. This interest is typically classified as ordinary income and is taxable upon receipt (Trotz 2021).

- Example: If an investor lends USD Coin on a DeFi platform and earns US$500 in interest during the year, this US$500 must be reported as ordinary income. The FMV of the interest or rewards received at the time of distribution is used to calculate the taxable amount. Investors should track the FMV of the rewards in fiat currency (e.g., USD) when received, reporting this value as ordinary income on their tax returns, similar to interest earned from a bank.

Yield Farming and Liquidity Mining.   Both yield farming and liquidity mining can trigger tax liabilities in various ways. The rewards earned, often in the form of governance tokens (e.g., Uniswap, SushiSwap), are treated as ordinary income. A taxable event occurs when the investor receives the rewards, with the income determined by the FMV of the tokens at that time.

- Example: If an investor participates in Uniswap liquidity mining and earns US$2,000 worth of UNI tokens, this amount is treated as ordinary income and must be reported on the investor's tax return.

Providing liquidity to a DeFi protocol may involve swapping or pooling tokens, creating additional taxable events. For example, swapping ETH for a liquidity pool token is considered a sale of Etherreum, triggering a capital gains event based on the difference between the cost basis (the price originally paid for Etherreum) and its value at the time of the swap.

- Example: If an investor swaps ETH worth US$10,000 into a liquidity pool and originally purchased the Etherreum for US$8,000, they would realize a capital gain of US$2,000, which must be reported to tax authorities. If they later exchange the liquidity pool tokens back into ETH or another cryptocurrency, additional capital gains (or losses) must be calculated and reported based on the value at the time of the second swap.

When liquidity providers withdraw their tokens from a pool, they may experience impermanent loss (a loss incurred from price fluctuations between the pooled assets). This can affect the value of their withdrawal and may result in a capital gain or loss when converting liquidity pool tokens back into the underlying assets.

DeFi Token Swaps and Capital Gains.   Swapping tokens on DeFi platforms (e.g., exchanging Dai for USD Coin on Uniswap) is treated similarly to cryptocurrency trades on centralized exchanges. Each swap is a taxable event, and any gains or losses from the difference between the cost basis and the FMV at the time of the swap are subject to capital gains tax.

- Example: If an investor swaps DAI for USDC and the FMV of the USDC received is higher than the cost basis of the DAI, the investor must report the difference as a capital gain.

Investors in DeFi must diligently track every transaction and ensure that they account for capital gains or losses on each swap.

Taxation of Nonfungible Tokens

Both creators of NFTs and investors involved in buying, selling, or trading NFTs need to be aware of the tax implications, which can vary depending on their role in the transaction.

NFT Sales by Creators.   When an artist or creator mints and sells an NFT, the proceeds from the sale are usually considered ordinary income if the sale is part of their business activities. This applies to creators selling digital artwork, music, or other types of NFTs. The sale of an NFT by its creator is classified as business income or self-employment income. Consequently, the creator is responsible for paying income tax on the total amount received for the NFT, regardless of whether the payment is made in fiat currency or cryptocurrency.

- Example: If an artist sells an NFT for 10 ETH when Ethereum is valued at US$3,000 per token, the artist must report US$30,000 as income from that sale, even if the proceeds were received in cryptocurrency.

If the NFT creator holds onto the proceeds in cryptocurrency (e.g., ETH) and its value increases, any later sale or exchange of ETH will incur capital gains tax on the difference between the value at the time of receipt and its value at the time of sale.

- Example: If the creator receives 10 ETH as payment for an NFT and later sells that ETH for US$40,000, they would need to report a capital gain of US$10,000 (US$40,000 – US$30,000) on their tax return.

NFT Sales by Investors. For NFT investors buying and selling NFTs, the tax treatment is similar to that of other capital assets. If an investor purchases an NFT and later sells it at a profit, the gain is subject to capital gains tax. The amount of tax owed depends on whether the sale is classified as a short-term or long-term capital gain:

- If the NFT is sold within a year of purchase, any gains are taxed as short-term capital gains, which are taxed at ordinary income rates.
- If the NFT is held for more than a year, the gains are taxed at long-term capital gains rates, which are generally lower.
- Example: An investor buys an NFT for US$5,000 and sells it a few months later for US$10,000. The investor realizes a US$5,000 short-term capital gain, which is taxed at ordinary income tax rates. However, if they had held the NFT for over a year, the gain would be taxed at long-term capital gains rates.

Purchasing NFTs With Cryptocurrency. Purchasing an NFT with cryptocurrency is considered a taxable event because it involves the disposition of cryptocurrency. The IRS regards the use of cryptocurrency to purchase goods (such as NFTs) as a sale of the cryptocurrency. The difference between the cost basis of the cryptocurrency used for the NFT purchase and its value at the time of the transaction is a capital gain or loss.

- Example: If an investor uses 1 ETH to purchase an NFT, and the Ethereum was originally bought for US$2,000 but is worth

US$3,000 at the time of NFT purchase, the investor realizes a capital gain of US$1,000 on the sale of the Ethereum. This gain must be reported, in addition to tracking the tax basis for the newly acquired NFT.

Evolving Regulatory Landscape

The global regulatory landscape for digital assets—including cryptocurrencies, stablecoins, DeFi platforms, and NFTs—has rapidly evolved as governments and regulatory bodies aim to address the risks and opportunities these technologies present. Regulators face the challenge of balancing innovation and economic growth with concerns about consumer protection, financial stability, tax compliance, money laundering, and the potential misuse of cryptocurrencies for illicit activities.

As digital assets gain popularity, different jurisdictions have adopted varied approaches, ranging from proactive regulation and integration into financial systems to outright bans and restrictions.

United States

In the United States, the main regulatory bodies include the Securities and Exchange Commission (SEC), the IRS, and the Commodity Futures Trading Commission (CFTC).

Securities and Exchange Commission

The SEC views many cryptocurrencies as securities, applying traditional securities laws to regulate initial coin offerings (ICOs) and token sales (Wang 2023). The SEC has consistently utilized the Howey Test to determine whether certain cryptocurrencies or token sales qualify as securities, bringing enforcement actions against companies that fail to comply with these laws. One of the most notable enforcement actions is the SEC's lawsuit against Ripple Labs, the issuer of XRP, which argued that Ripple conducted an unregistered securities offering. This case has significant implications for how other digital assets may be classified in the United States.

The SEC's stance has created legal uncertainty for many crypto projects, as businesses must determine whether their tokens are classified as securities or commodities, subject to U.S. securities laws. This often leads to regulatory scrutiny and fines for noncompliance.

Internal Revenue Service

The IRS treats cryptocurrencies as property for tax purposes, meaning that capital gains taxes apply when digital assets are bought, sold, or exchanged. Each transaction triggers a taxable event, requiring individuals to report their capital gains or losses. The IRS has become increasingly aggressive in enforcing crypto tax compliance.

Commodity Futures Trading Commission

The CFTC has classified Bitcoin and Ethereum as commodities, placing them under its regulatory authority when used in derivatives or futures trading.

Overall, U.S. regulators have been relatively cautious, focusing on enforcing existing laws rather than creating a comprehensive new regulatory framework for digital assets. This approach has led to a patchwork regulatory environment, with different agencies asserting jurisdiction over various aspects of the crypto industry.

European Union

In Europe, regulation has been proactive and coordinated, particularly at the regional level through the EU. The EU has taken significant steps to establish a clear regulatory framework for digital assets, notably with the introduction of the Markets in Crypto-Assets (MiCA) regulation. This is one of the most comprehensive efforts to regulate digital assets at the regional level (Wronka 2024).

MiCA provides a thorough regulatory framework for issuers of cryptocurrencies, crypto exchanges, and wallet providers, offering clarity on how digital assets are treated across EU member states. Its aim is to harmonize regulations throughout the EU while fostering innovation and ensuring investor protection and market integrity.

Key elements of MiCA include:

- Licensing Requirements: Crypto exchanges and wallet providers must obtain a license to operate within the EU.
- Consumer Protections: MiCA enforces transparency and disclosure requirements for crypto issuers to protect investors from fraud and market manipulation.
- Stablecoin Regulation: MiCA introduces stringent rules for the issuance of stablecoins, ensuring they are adequately backed by reserves to prevent systemic risks.

MiCA is seen as a model for other regions as it balances regulation with innovation, providing legal certainty for businesses while protecting consumers and the financial system.

Additionally, the ECB has explored the regulation of CBDCs, particularly in connection with its development of a digital euro. The ECB aims to ensure that CBDCs operate within a clear regulatory framework while complementing the broader EU financial system.

Asia-Pacific

Asia has adopted a diverse approach to cryptocurrency regulation, with countries such as China, Japan, and Singapore leading the way in developing regulations that align with their economic and political priorities.

China has taken a strict regulatory stance by banning cryptocurrency trading and mining within its borders. However, it has also embraced blockchain technology and is at the forefront of developing a CBDC, known as the digital yuan.

In contrast, Japan has adopted a more permissive and forward-thinking attitude toward digital assets. The Financial Services Agency of Japan recognized Bitcoin as legal tender in 2017 and has established clear guidelines for crypto exchanges and ICOs (Kavaloski 2024). This progressive regulatory framework has made Japan one of the most crypto-friendly countries in Asia.

Singapore is another regional leader in crypto regulation. The Monetary Authority of Singapore has implemented a regulatory framework for digital payment tokens under the Payment Services Act, positioning the country as a global hub for blockchain innovation and crypto businesses.

One of the major challenges in regulating digital assets is the fragmentation of regulatory frameworks across different countries and regions. While some jurisdictions have established clear rules, others remain hesitant or have conflicting regulations, leading to uncertainty for businesses and investors.

Many industry leaders and policy makers argue that global harmonization of digital asset regulations is essential for the growth of the crypto industry. Uniform global standards would reduce regulatory arbitrage, where companies relocate to areas with more lenient rules, and create a level playing field for businesses operating across borders.

Efforts by international organizations, such as the Financial Action Task Force (FATF), aim to establish global standards on AML and counter-terrorism financing for digital assets. The FATF has issued guidelines that serve as a global benchmark for regulating these assets. In 2019, the FATF introduced the "Travel Rule," which requires virtual asset service providers, like crypto exchanges, to collect and share customer information for transactions exceeding a certain threshold (Takei and Kazuyuki 2024). These standards help ensure that crypto markets operate safely while providing some level of consistency across jurisdictions, although regional differences in regulation still exist.

Middle East and Africa

The Middle East and Africa are increasingly engaging with digital asset regulation, although the approaches differ significantly across the region.

Dubai and Abu Dhabi have established themselves as crypto-friendly jurisdictions, implementing dedicated frameworks for regulating digital assets. The ADGM and the Dubai Multi Commodities Centre both provide licenses to cryptocurrency firms and encourage blockchain innovation.

In South Africa, the government has indicated its intention to regulate cryptocurrencies as financial products. This will require exchanges and wallet providers to register with regulators and comply with AML laws. Additionally, South Africa is considering incorporating crypto asset regulation within its existing financial services legislation.

Global Trends in Regulations

As digital assets gain traction globally, regulators are increasingly responding to their growing influence on the financial system by introducing frameworks that balance innovation with consumer protection and financial stability.

1. Central Bank Digital Currencies: Many central banks are exploring or piloting CBDCs as a way to introduce digital assets into the financial system in a regulated manner. CBDCs offer a state-backed, digital alternative to cryptocurrencies, enabling governments to compete with or supplement existing digital assets while maintaining control over monetary policy.

2. Stablecoin Regulations: Stablecoins, which are pegged to traditional assets like fiat currency, are under increasing regulatory scrutiny. Many governments, including the United States and the EU, are developing regulations to ensure asset backing and reserve transparency, as well as to mitigate risks to payment systems and financial stability.

3. Anti Money Laundering and Know Your Customer (KYC) Requirements: To combat illegal activities, global regulators are tightening AML and KYC requirements for digital asset exchanges and service providers. The FATF has issued guidelines for virtual asset service providers, requiring them to adopt AML/KYC measures to prevent money laundering and fraud.

4. Taxation of Digital Assets: Tax authorities worldwide are establishing rules for digital asset taxation, including capital gains

and income tax on digital asset transactions. Many countries now require exchanges to report user transactions, and they have implemented guidelines to capture tax revenue from cryptocurrency trades, staking, and mining.

5. Consumer Protection and Market Integrity: Regulatory bodies are increasingly focused on ensuring transparency and fairness in digital asset markets. This includes measures to protect consumers from fraud, enforce trading standards, and address issues such as market manipulation and volatility, which have historically been challenges in cryptocurrency markets.

6. Cross-Border Collaboration: Digital assets are inherently global, prompting regulators to collaborate across borders. Initiatives such as the Financial Stability Board and FATF are fostering global cooperation to create standardized approaches to digital asset regulation, facilitating a consistent regulatory environment across jurisdictions.

These trends highlight a global push to integrate digital assets responsibly into financial systems, with an emphasis on stability, security, and transparency. As digital assets continue to evolve, regulatory frameworks are likely to adapt to protect consumers while supporting innovation in this dynamic financial landscape.

Summary

The landscape of taxation and regulatory compliance for digital assets is complex and rapidly evolving. Investors and institutions must stay informed and adaptable as they navigate this environment. Taxation of digital assets involves several aspects, including managing capital gains from trades, income tax on activities such as staking and mining, and utilizing strategies like tax-loss harvesting to optimize tax liabilities.

Additionally, international tax obligations introduce another layer of complexity, especially for those engaged in DeFi and the NFT markets. The global regulatory environment is diverse, with significant jurisdictions such as the United States and the EU, and regions such as Asia-Pacific and the Middle East adopting varying approaches to oversight.

As countries address the rise of stablecoins, CBDCs, and decentralized platforms, the regulatory landscape will continue to evolve to meet new challenges. Investors need to be diligent in understanding their tax obligations and the regulatory frameworks in their jurisdictions, as these factors will increasingly influence the future of digital assets and their role in global finance.

PART 4

The Path Forward

Institutional Integration and Key Considerations for Digital Assets

CHAPTER 9

Institutional Adoption of Digital Assets

The institutional adoption of digital assets marks a significant shift in the maturity and legitimacy of the cryptocurrency market. Initially, digital assets were primarily driven by retail investors and enthusiasts, but the entry of institutional players—ranging from hedge funds to asset managers and publicly traded companies—has dramatically altered the landscape.

In this chapter, we will examine early movers in this space, and analyze the investment vehicles they used to gain exposure to digital assets. We will also discuss the important implications of institutional involvement, including increased market stability and enhanced liquidity.

As crypto asset managers and hedge funds develop sophisticated strategies around digital assets, their roles in the market's growth and maturation become increasingly crucial. Additionally, we will explore how digital assets are being integrated into traditional financial products, such as ETFs and derivative instruments, making cryptocurrencies more accessible to a wider range of investors and shaping the future of finance.

Early Institutional Entrants

The digital asset market, once primarily dominated by retail investors and crypto enthusiasts, has increasingly attracted the attention of institutional players. Recently, large financial institutions, hedge funds, asset managers, and corporations have begun to recognize the potential of digital assets such as Bitcoin, Ethereum, and DeFi. These early institutional entrants have played a crucial role in legitimizing cryptocurrencies and accelerating their mainstream adoption. The entry of institutions into the digital asset market has been driven by a desire for portfolio diversification, the search for higher returns, the maturation of cryptocurrency infrastructure, and a growing acknowledgment of digital assets as a hedge against macroeconomic risks.

Portfolio Diversification

Institutional investors continually seek ways to diversify their portfolios and reduce risk. Digital assets, particularly Bitcoin, have demonstrated a low correlation with traditional asset classes like stocks and bonds, making them an attractive option for diversification. By allocating a small percentage of their portfolios to cryptocurrencies, institutions can potentially enhance their risk-adjusted returns.

Inflation Hedge

Amid concerns over inflation and unprecedented levels of monetary stimulus following the COVID-19 pandemic, many institutional investors began viewing Bitcoin as a hedge against inflation. Similar to gold, Bitcoin's fixed supply and decentralized nature make it an appealing alternative to fiat currencies, particularly in environments of low interest rates and currency devaluation.

Yield Generation in DeFi

DeFi platforms offer institutional investors opportunities to generate yield by lending, borrowing, and staking digital assets. This new frontier of DeFi services has piqued the interest of hedge funds and asset managers looking to explore innovative yield-generating strategies outside traditional finance.

Maturation of Market Infrastructure

The development of institutional-grade custody solutions, regulated crypto exchanges, and financial products such as Bitcoin futures and

ETFs has made it easier for institutions to enter the digital asset market. This maturation of market infrastructure has alleviated security and regulatory concerns, making digital assets more accessible to institutional investors.

Several high-profile institutions and corporations have paved the way for broader institutional adoption of digital assets. These early movers have validated cryptocurrencies as an asset class and driven significant inflows of institutional capital into the market.

- MicroStrategy: One of the earliest and most notable institutional entrants into Bitcoin was MicroStrategy, a publicly traded business intelligence company. In August 2020, led by CEO Michael Saylor, MicroStrategy made the bold decision to convert a substantial portion of its corporate treasury into Bitcoin, citing concerns over inflation and the devaluation of the U.S. dollar.
- Tesla: In February 2021, Tesla, the electric vehicle manufacturer led by Elon Musk, announced that it had purchased $1.5 billion worth of Bitcoin as part of its treasury management strategy. This investment marked a significant milestone, signaling that mainstream corporations were willing to hold digital assets on their balance sheets.
- Grayscale Investments: Grayscale Investments was among the first institutional vehicles to offer exposure to Bitcoin and other cryptocurrencies through its flagship product, the Grayscale Bitcoin Trust (GBTC). Launched in 2013, GBTC allows institutional and accredited investors to gain exposure to Bitcoin without needing to directly purchase or hold the cryptocurrency. Grayscale's suite of digital asset trusts for Ethereum, Litecoin, and others has made it easier for institutional investors to enter the market in a regulated environment.
- Fidelity Investments: In 2018, Fidelity Investments launched Fidelity Digital Assets, a platform offering institutional clients custody services, trade execution, and other digital asset solutions. Fidelity has since expanded its services to include Bitcoin and Ethereum custody for institutional clients such as hedge funds, family offices, and endowments.

- Square (Block): In October 2020, Square, the payments company led by Jack Dorsey (now known as Block), announced that it had invested US$50 million in Bitcoin, representing approximately 1 percent of its total assets. Square's investment was driven by the belief that Bitcoin could become the "native currency" of the internet.
- BlackRock: In 2021, BlackRock, the world's largest asset manager, began offering exposure to Bitcoin futures in two of its funds. This move marked a significant moment for institutional adoption, as BlackRock had previously been cautious about digital assets. Their entry into Bitcoin signaled that the largest institutional investors were starting to recognize the potential of cryptocurrencies.

Vehicles Employed by Early Institutional Entrants

The early institutional players in the digital asset space have adopted various strategies to gain exposure to cryptocurrencies, balancing risk management with the desire to harness the high-growth potential of these assets.

Direct Investment

Some institutions, such as MicroStrategy and Tesla, have opted for direct investments in Bitcoin, integrating it into their corporate treasury strategies. These direct investments aim to hedge against inflation, diversify reserves, and capitalize on Bitcoin's long-term appreciation potential. Ethereum, the second-largest cryptocurrency, has also garnered institutional interest due to its role in decentralized applications and DeFi platforms.

Digital Asset Funds

Other institutions, including pension funds, endowments, and family offices, prefer to invest in digital asset funds instead of purchasing cryptocurrencies directly. Products such as the GBTC, Grayscale Ethereum Trust, and Bitwise 10 Crypto Index Fund offer regulated and secure avenues for institutions to gain exposure to digital assets. These funds provide liquidity, custodial solutions, and regulatory compliance without the complexities of managing crypto wallets directly.

Futures, ETFs, and Derivatives

Many institutions are entering the market through derivatives and ETFs that offer exposure to digital assets without requiring ownership of the underlying cryptocurrency. The introduction of Bitcoin futures on the CME in 2017 and the subsequent approval of Bitcoin ETFs in the United States and Canada have simplified access for institutions, providing a regulated and familiar framework. These financial products allow institutions to hedge risks while gaining exposure to the price movements of cryptocurrencies.

Venture Capital

In addition to direct cryptocurrency exposure, institutional investors are increasingly participating in VC funding for blockchain start-ups. Prominent firms such as Andreessen Horowitz (a16z) and Sequoia Capital have been early investors in blockchain companies that are developing the infrastructure for DeFi, NFTs, and layer-1 protocols. This VC approach enables institutions to access the broader blockchain ecosystem and benefit from the technological advancements propelling the industry forward.

Implications of Institutional Involvement

The entry of institutions into the digital asset space has significant implications for both the cryptocurrency market and traditional finance.

Increased Legitimacy

The involvement of well-known institutions such as Tesla, Fidelity, and BlackRock has helped legitimize cryptocurrencies in the eyes of regulators, retail investors, and the broader financial industry. Institutional participation has sparked interest among more conservative investors, who now view digital assets as a viable component of a diversified portfolio.

Reduced Volatility Over Time

While the cryptocurrency market remains highly volatile, the presence of institutional investors could help stabilize it over time. Institutions often bring longer-term investment horizons and sophisticated risk management practices, which may reduce the speculative nature of crypto markets as the asset class matures.

Regulatory Focus

As institutions continue to invest in digital assets, regulators have increased their efforts to develop clearer frameworks and guidelines for the cryptocurrency industry. This growing institutional interest may accelerate the creation of regulations concerning crypto custody, market transparency, and investor protection, leading to a more robust and regulated market.

Increased Institutional Infrastructure

The rising demand for digital assets from institutional investors has driven the development of institutional-grade infrastructure, such as custodial services, compliance tools, and secure trading platforms. This infrastructure has made it easier for institutions to enter the market and for retail investors to access safer, more reliable crypto services.

Crypto Asset Managers and Hedge Funds

The cryptocurrency market has experienced explosive growth since Bitcoin was introduced in 2009, attracting traditional asset managers, hedge funds, and the establishment of new firms dedicated to digital assets. As the demand for institutional-grade investment products in the crypto space has surged, these firms have played a crucial role in providing professional management, security, and regulatory compliance.

Hedge funds were among the earliest institutional investors to explore cryptocurrencies. As early as 2013, a few pioneering hedge funds began investing in Bitcoin, motivated by its high volatility and potential for significant returns (Mokhtarian and Lindgren 2018). These early adopters helped validate cryptocurrencies as a legitimate asset class, paving the way for more traditional firms to follow suit.

As the market for digital assets expanded, a new type of specialized crypto asset management firm emerged. These firms focus exclusively on investing in cryptocurrencies, blockchain projects, and DeFi platforms. Notable examples include Pantera Capital, Grayscale Investments, Galaxy Digital, and Bitwise Asset Management, all of which offer institutional-grade products and services tailored to meet the needs of large investors.

Research by PwC and Elwood Asset Management indicates that the number of crypto hedge funds has increased significantly in recent years, with total assets under management rising swiftly as institutional interest continues to grow. Many of these funds focus on a diverse range of digital assets, including Bitcoin, Ethereum, altcoins, DeFi tokens, and even NFTs, reflecting the expanding opportunities in this space.

Investment Strategies of Crypto Asset Managers and Hedge Funds

Crypto asset managers and hedge funds utilize a range of sophisticated investment strategies based on their risk tolerance, target clients, and market outlook. These strategies vary from traditional buy-and-hold approaches to advanced trading techniques designed to take advantage of the cryptocurrency market's high volatility.

Long-Only Strategies

Some crypto asset managers and funds focus on long-only strategies, where they invest in digital assets for the long term, anticipating appreciation over time. This approach is commonly adopted by funds that are optimistic about the long-term potential of blockchain technology and the increasing adoption of cryptocurrencies as an asset class. Such funds typically allocate a significant portion of their portfolios to major cryptocurrencies such as Bitcoin and Ethereum, which are known for their liquidity and institutional acceptance.

Quantitative and Algorithmic Trading

Many crypto hedge funds employ quantitative and algorithmic trading strategies to capitalize on the extreme volatility and inefficiencies in crypto markets. These funds utilize complex mathematical models, AI, and machine learning (ML) algorithms to identify arbitrage opportunities, execute high-frequency trades, and optimize entry and exit points. By leveraging data-driven insights, these funds aim to achieve consistent returns, even amid highly volatile market conditions.

DeFi Yield Farming and Staking

An increasing number of funds are exploring yield-generating opportunities in the DeFi sector, including yield farming and staking. In yield farming, investors provide liquidity to DEXs and lending platforms in exchange for interest or rewards. In staking, funds lock up assets to help secure PoS networks, earning rewards over time. These strategies enable hedge funds to generate income beyond mere price appreciation.

Multistrategy Funds

Some hedge funds adopt a multistrategy approach, combining long positions in top cryptocurrencies with short positions, derivatives, and options to hedge risks or exploit market dislocations. These funds utilize futures and options markets, which have become more robust in the crypto space, to profit from both bullish and bearish market movements. Multistrategy funds may also allocate capital across various segments of the blockchain ecosystem, such as layer-1 protocols, DeFi projects, or NFT markets.

Venture Capital in Blockchain Start-Ups

In addition to public markets, some crypto hedge funds and asset managers engage in VC investments in blockchain start-ups and early-stage projects. By investing in token sales, seed funding rounds, or equity in blockchain companies, these funds gain exposure to the infrastructure and innovation driving growth in the digital asset market. Notable firms such as Pantera Capital and Andreessen Horowitz (a16z) have made significant investments in key blockchain projects, such as Uniswap, Chainlink, and Filecoin.

Role of Crypto Asset Managers in Market Maturation

As institutional investment in digital assets increases, crypto asset managers and hedge funds are playing a crucial role in the maturation of the cryptocurrency market. Their involvement is helping to build a more robust market infrastructure, enhance liquidity, and promote greater regulatory clarity.

The participation of large hedge funds and asset managers in cryptocurrency markets provides essential liquidity, particularly for major assets such as Bitcoin and Ethereum. This increased liquidity helps reduce volatility and narrow bid–ask spreads, making the markets more appealing to institutional participants. Over time, the presence of these sophisticated investors may contribute to greater market stability.

Additionally, crypto hedge funds and asset managers are influencing the regulatory landscape for digital assets. Many of these firms actively engage with regulators and policy makers to advocate for clearer rules that can facilitate institutional adoption. By participating in industry associations and regulatory working groups, they play a significant role in developing compliant and regulated financial products and services for crypto investors.

The Integration of Digital Assets Into Financial Products

As digital assets such as Bitcoin, Ethereum, and other cryptocurrencies gain prominence, traditional financial institutions and markets are increasingly integrating them into a variety of financial products. This integration is a crucial step toward the mainstream adoption of digital assets, allowing institutional investors, retail investors, and corporations to access this rapidly growing asset class through familiar investment vehicles. Ranging from ETFs and futures contracts to structured products and DeFi yield strategies, digital assets are becoming increasingly embedded in the broader financial ecosystem.

Exchange-Traded Funds and Trusts

One of the most significant advancements in integrating digital assets into traditional finance is the emergence of cryptocurrency ETFs and trusts. These financial products offer investors exposure to digital assets without the need to directly manage or hold the underlying cryptocurrencies, making them more accessible to a wider range of investors, including those who may find the complexities of crypto custody and trading daunting.

Several countries, including Canada and Brazil, have approved Bitcoin and Ethereum ETFs that track the prices of these digital assets. These ETFs trade on regulated stock exchanges, providing a familiar investment vehicle for both institutional and retail investors to gain exposure to the price movements of cryptocurrencies. In the United States, the ProShares Bitcoin Strategy ETF, launched in 2021, offers exposure to Bitcoin through futures contracts, allowing investors to gain indirect exposure to Bitcoin's price without holding the asset itself (Shen and Li 2024). Investors enjoy benefits such as ease of access, liquidity, and regulatory oversight.

Grayscale Investments was an early pioneer in offering institutional-grade exposure to digital assets through its GBTC and other crypto-currency trusts. GBTC enables investors to gain exposure to Bitcoin's price movements via a trust structure that holds Bitcoin on behalf of investors. While it is not an ETF, GBTC is traded over-the-counter and provides a regulated way to invest in Bitcoin. Grayscale has also expanded its offerings to include trusts for other digital assets, including Ethereum, Litecoin, and Chainlink.

There is an ongoing debate in financial markets regarding the differences between spot ETFs (which directly hold the underlying cryptocurrency) and futures-based ETFs (which gain exposure through Bitcoin futures contracts). Spot ETFs provide direct exposure to the asset's price but have faced regulatory challenges in some regions, particularly in the United States, where spot Bitcoin ETFs have yet to be approved. Futures-based ETFs, while offering exposure to Bitcoin price movements, can be influenced by factors such as contango (when futures prices are higher than spot prices) and may incur higher management fees.

Futures, Options, and Derivatives

The integration of digital assets into futures, options, and other derivatives markets has expanded the tools available for institutional and sophisticated investors to gain exposure to cryptocurrencies. Derivatives enable investors to hedge positions, speculate on price movements, and gain leveraged exposure to digital assets without directly owning them.

The launch of Bitcoin futures in 2017 on the CME marked a landmark moment in the institutionalization of digital assets. CME Bitcoin futures allow investors to trade standardized contracts that track Bitcoin's price, providing a regulated environment for speculating on price movements or hedging against market volatility. Ethereum futures were also introduced by CME in 2021, offering similar opportunities for exposure to Ethereum.

In addition to futures, options contracts on cryptocurrencies have further expanded the trading and risk management strategies available to market participants. Options allow investors to buy or sell a digital asset at a predetermined price within a specific time frame, offering flexibility in managing price exposure. Institutional investors can use options to hedge against downside risk or generate income through covered call strategies.

Beyond traditional markets, the rise of DeFi has introduced new types of derivatives, including decentralized options and futures. Platforms such as dYdX and Synthetix offer decentralized derivatives that allow users to trade perpetual futures, options, and synthetic assets in a trustless environment, bypassing traditional financial intermediaries. These DeFi derivatives have become increasingly popular as more investors seek decentralized alternatives to conventional markets.

Structured Products

Structured products that include digital assets provide investors with customizable exposure to cryptocurrencies, along with built-in risk management features. These products are tailored to meet specific investment goals, such as capital protection, enhanced yields, or risk-adjusted returns.

Structured notes linked to the performance of cryptocurrencies are gaining popularity among institutional investors. Typically, these notes combine traditional fixed-income products (like bonds) with exposure to digital assets, allowing investors to benefit from cryptocurrency price appreciation while retaining a degree of capital protection. For instance, a structured note may offer a fixed coupon alongside an additional payout tied to Bitcoin's price performance, providing upside potential while mitigating the risks associated with direct investment.

In some instances, structured products are being tokenized, using blockchain technology to create new types of financial products. Tokenized structured products can be issued on blockchain platforms, enhancing transparency, liquidity, and accessibility for investors. By tokenizing structured notes or other investment vehicles, issuers can reduce settlement times and improve operational efficiency, while also opening new markets for digital asset exposure.

Some investment products are designed to provide downside protection while allowing participation in the upside of digital asset price movements. These capital-protected products are appealing to more conservative investors who want exposure to the growth potential of cryptocurrencies but with reduced risk. For example, a product may guarantee the return of principal (capital protection) at maturity while offering participation in a percentage of the gains from Bitcoin or Ethereum during the investment period.

Yield-Generating Products and DeFi Integration

The growth of DeFi has introduced new yield-generating opportunities for investors, including lending, staking, and liquidity provision in DEXs. These products are being integrated into traditional financial portfolios, providing investors with passive income through digital assets.

Crypto lending platforms allow investors to earn interest on their digital assets by lending them to borrowers. Platforms such as BlockFi, Celsius, and Aave offer interest-bearing accounts for Bitcoin, Ethereum, and stablecoins. Similarly, staking on PoS networks lets investors earn rewards by locking up their digital assets to help secure the network. Both lending and staking present attractive yield opportunities in a low-interest-rate environment.

Yield farming and liquidity mining are key components of DeFi that enable investors to earn rewards by providing liquidity to decentralized exchanges and lending protocols. While these strategies can be highly lucrative, they are also complex and come with risks, such as impermanent loss and smart contract vulnerabilities. Some institutional platforms are now integrating these yield-generating opportunities into structured products, offering a pathway for investors to access DeFi returns with enhanced oversight and risk management.

Digital Asset Custody and Prime Brokerage Services

A significant challenge for institutional investors entering the digital asset space is secure and compliant custody. As more financial products incorporate digital assets, the demand for institutional-grade custodial solutions and prime brokerage services has increased.

Companies such as Fidelity Digital Assets, Coinbase Custody, and BitGo have created secure custody platforms designed for institutional clients. These custodians offer cold storage, multisignature wallets, and insurance coverage to mitigate the risks involved in storing large amounts of digital assets. These solutions are crucial for enabling the launch of financial products such as ETFs, structured notes, and derivatives, which require secure and compliant storage of underlying assets.

In traditional finance, prime brokerage services provide hedge funds and institutional clients with various solutions, including trade execution, financing, and custody. In the digital asset space, prime brokerage services are becoming increasingly important as institutions look for a one-stop solution to manage their crypto investments. Firms like Genesis Trading and Tagomi (now part of Coinbase) offer prime brokerage services, providing clients with access to liquidity, leverage, and integrated custodial services.

Summary

The institutional adoption of digital assets has played a crucial role in legitimizing and stabilizing the cryptocurrency market. Early entrants, such as trusts, ETFs, and corporate treasury allocations, have paved the way for broader acceptance and integration of digital assets into mainstream finance. The participation of crypto asset managers and hedge funds has further advanced market maturation, with sophisticated investment strategies adding liquidity, transparency, and depth to digital asset markets.

As digital assets continue to be incorporated into traditional financial products—such as ETFs, derivatives, and custodial services— their accessibility and appeal to institutional investors are increasing, making cryptocurrencies an essential part of modern portfolio strategies. The growing presence of institutions is likely to continue shaping the future of digital assets, driving innovation while addressing challenges such as regulatory compliance and market volatility.

CHAPTER 10

Final Thoughts

As we conclude our exploration of digital asset investing, it's evident that the landscape is rapidly evolving. This change is driven by technological advancements, increasing institutional adoption, and a growing focus on sustainability and ethical investing. In this chapter, we reflect on the key themes discussed throughout the book, emphasizing the integration of ESG principles into digital asset portfolios. We also highlight the transformative roles of AI and ML in navigating these markets, along with key recommendations for investors.

As digital assets become more prominent, investors must find a balance between the potential for innovation and the necessity of thorough due diligence. This includes staying informed about regulatory developments and maintaining a long-term perspective.

ESG Considerations in Digital Asset Investing

ESG in the Context of Digital Assets

As ESG considerations become increasingly important in investment strategies, digital assets—especially cryptocurrencies like Bitcoin—are facing scrutiny regarding their impact in these areas. Institutional investors, asset managers, and regulators are applying ESG frameworks to assess digital assets and their alignment with sustainable and ethical investment principles. While the decentralized and innovative nature of these assets offers potential benefits, such as financial inclusion and transparency, there are significant challenges, particularly concerning environmental issues, that must be addressed for digital assets to gain broader acceptance in ESG-focused portfolios.

Environmental Impact of Digital Assets

The environmental component of ESG has emerged as a contentious issue in the context of digital assets, notably due to the significant energy consumption associated with blockchain technologies like Bitcoin.

Bitcoin and other cryptocurrencies that utilize the PoW consensus mechanism—such as Ethereum prior to its transition to PoS—require extensive computational power to validate transactions and secure their networks. This process, known as mining, consumes vast amounts of electricity, which raises concerns about the carbon footprint of these digital assets. Bitcoin mining alone is estimated to consume as much energy annually as some small countries, and its environmental impact is influenced by the energy sources used (e.g., coal, natural gas, or renewable energy) (Krause Tolaymat 2018).

Critics, including Mustafa et al. (2024) and Arnone (2024), argue that the carbon emissions generated by Bitcoin mining contribute to climate change, undermining the cryptocurrency's potential as a sustainable financial innovation. This has resulted in increasing pressure on institutional investors—especially those with ESG mandates—to reconsider their exposure to energy-intensive digital assets. Consequently, investors and companies are increasingly focusing on assessing and mitigating the carbon footprint of their cryptocurrency investments.

Mustafa et al. (2024) examined the impact of Bitcoin trading volume on water and sanitation (Sustainable Development Goal [SDG] 6) and climate action (SDG 13). Using ordinary least squares panel data analysis on a sample of 32 countries with available Bitcoin trading volume data from 2013 to 2020, their findings suggest that Bitcoin trading positively impacts progress toward SDG 6, indicating potential benefits for water and sanitation initiatives. However, the study also reveals a significant negative effect of higher Bitcoin trading volume on increased carbon emissions, highlighting the environmental costs associated with cryptocurrency activities.

Some initiatives are focused on making Bitcoin mining more sustainable by utilizing renewable energy sources such as solar, wind, and hydroelectric power. Countries and companies that can access abundant renewable energy have become attractive locations for eco-friendly mining operations. For instance, Iceland and Norway, with their geothermal and hydropower resources, have emerged as hubs for green Bitcoin mining. Additionally, projects such as the Crypto Climate Accord and the development of carbon-neutral mining pools aim to reduce the environmental impact of cryptocurrency networks and align them with global sustainability goals.

Social Considerations in Digital Assets

The social aspect of ESG in digital assets explores how cryptocurrencies and blockchain technologies can advance broader social goals, such as financial inclusion, access to financial services, and the democratization of the financial system.

One of the most significant social benefits of digital assets is their ability to enhance financial inclusion, especially in underserved and underbanked regions worldwide. Cryptocurrencies and DeFi platforms enable individuals to access financial services without relying on traditional banks, which may be unavailable or inaccessible in developing countries. With just a smartphone and an internet connection, individuals can participate in global financial markets, make cross-border payments, and obtain loans or savings products without needing traditional financial intermediaries.

Cryptocurrencies can also reduce the costs and inefficiencies associated with cross-border payments and remittances (Rühmann et al. 2020). Traditional remittance services often charge high fees and can take days to process transactions, particularly in countries with less developed financial infrastructure. In contrast, digital assets facilitate faster, cheaper, and more transparent transactions, benefiting migrant workers and their families who rely on remittances. Stablecoins, such as USDC or DAI, are increasingly used for cross-border transactions, offering a stable, low-cost alternative to volatile cryptocurrencies like Bitcoin.

DeFi platforms create new opportunities for individuals to engage in wealth creation through activities such as lending, borrowing, staking, and yield farming, all without the need for centralized intermediaries. DeFi democratizes access to financial services, allowing people to earn yields on their digital assets and access liquidity through DEXs and lending protocols. However, there are risks associated with DeFi, including the potential for scams, rug pulls, and technological vulnerabilities, which could undermine its social impact if not properly managed.

Despite the promise of financial inclusion, there are concerns that digital assets could worsen wealth inequality. Early adopters of cryptocurrencies, particularly in developed markets, have seen significant financial gains, while many individuals in lower income regions may lack the knowledge, resources, or internet access needed to benefit from digital asset investments. Additionally, the speculative nature of cryptocurrencies has led to high-profile losses for inexperienced investors, potentially creating further disparities if not addressed through proper education and regulation.

Governance in Digital Assets

The governance aspect of ESG in digital assets focuses on decision-making processes, transparency, accountability, and the decentralized nature of blockchain networks.

One of the key features of blockchain technology is its decentralized structure, which means that no single entity controls the network. Instead, decision making is often distributed among participants using consensus mechanisms and governance models. For instance, blockchain networks such as Ethereum and Cardano enable token holders to participate in governance by voting on protocol upgrades, changes to network parameters, and other significant decisions. This decentralized governance model promotes transparency and reduces the risk of centralized control or potential abuse of power.

Blockchain technology also offers transparency by providing a public, immutable ledger of all transactions. This transparency can be a substantial governance benefit, especially in industries where financial reporting, auditability, and traceability are critical. For example, blockchain can enhance supply chain management by maintaining an unalterable record of the origin and journey of goods, thus ensuring ethical sourcing and preventing fraud. Furthermore, decentralized platforms like decentralized autonomous organizations (DAOs) utilize transparent governance models that align with ESG principles, allowing members to democratically vote on important issues.

Additionally, institutional investors are increasingly concerned about the regulatory governance of digital assets. As regulators worldwide develop frameworks for digital assets, compliance with AML laws, KYC procedures, and the prevention of fraud and market manipulation are becoming more vital. Governance frameworks that ensure adherence to these regulations are essential for institutional investors to participate confidently in digital asset markets.

Integrating ESG Into Digital Asset Portfolios

The increasing awareness of climate change, social responsibility, and corporate governance issues has led to a rising demand for ESG-compliant investments across all asset classes, including digital assets. Investors are keen to align their portfolios with their values, making it essential for asset managers to incorporate ESG factors into cryptocurrency portfolios. However, applying ESG frameworks to digital assets is still a relatively new concept due to the evolving nature of cryptocurrencies and the developing standards for assessing their ESG impacts.

Institutional investors, such as pension funds, endowments, and sovereign wealth funds, are bound by strict ESG mandates. As these investors seek exposure to digital assets, they are demanding more sustainable and responsible options. Therefore, asset managers aiming to attract institutional capital must integrate ESG criteria into their digital asset offerings to meet these growing expectations.

Retail investors are also demonstrating an increased interest in ESG investing. Millennials and Gen Z investors, in particular, are more likely to prioritize sustainability and ethical considerations when making investment decisions. As these demographics increasingly invest in digital assets, they expect ESG-aligned options that reflect their values.

Regulators and industry groups are advocating for greater transparency in ESG reporting and the creation of more sustainable financial products. In the realm of digital assets, initiatives like the Crypto Climate Accord and efforts by certain blockchain projects to reduce their environmental impact are addressing these demands. Additionally, governments and regulators are beginning to examine the environmental repercussions of cryptocurrencies, which may lead to future regulations that promote ESG integration. The findings of Mustafa et al. (2024) underscore the necessity to regulate cryptocurrency trading and encourage voluntary sustainable practices, particularly given the disparities in governance frameworks between developed and emerging markets.

Despite the challenges, there are several strategies that investors and asset managers can use to effectively integrate ESG principles into digital asset portfolios. The findings of Mustafa et al. (2024) emphasize the importance of proactive measures to ensure the responsible and sustainable use of cryptocurrencies.

Focus on Energy-Efficient Cryptocurrencies

One of the most direct strategies for achieving this is to concentrate on energy-efficient cryptocurrencies. These digital assets utilize consensus mechanisms that require less computational power and energy compared to traditional PoW systems, such as Bitcoin.

Proof-of-Stake and Energy Efficiency.   There has been growing interest in blockchain networks that employ more energy-efficient mechanisms like PoS. In 2022, Ethereum transitioned from PoW to PoS (a change known as "The Merge"), which significantly reduced the network's energy consumption by over 99 percent. This shift made Ethereum more attractive to ESG-focused investors who had previously avoided the platform due to environmental concerns.

PoS blockchains are specifically designed to address the energy-intensive nature of PoW mechanisms, which require significant computational power and electricity consumption for transaction validation and network security. Unlike Bitcoin, where miners solve complex mathematical puzzles—resulting in immense energy usage

—PoS requires validators to "stake" their cryptocurrency, thereby drastically reducing the need for energy-intensive hardware.

By requiring validators to hold tokens rather than performing energy-hungry calculations, PoS blockchains minimize their carbon footprint, aligning with ESG-conscious strategies, particularly in terms of environmental sustainability.

Ethereum's Transition From PoW to PoS. Ethereum, the second-largest cryptocurrency by market capitalization, made a groundbreaking shift from PoW to PoS with the launch of Ethereum 2.0 in 2022. This transition not only made Ethereum more energy-efficient but also improved its scalability, enabling faster and cheaper transactions. These enhancements improve the user experience and make Ethereum more accessible for DeFi projects and NFTs.

Ethereum's move from PoW to PoS underscores its commitment to sustainability. It demonstrates that high-utility networks can minimize their environmental impact while maintaining security and decentralization. Consequently, Ethereum has become increasingly appealing to ESG-conscious investors, particularly those focused on environmental sustainability in their portfolios.

Polkadot, Cardano, and Tezos as ESG-Friendly Alternatives. Other PoS-based blockchains, such as Polkadot, Cardano, and Tezos, also attract ESG investors due to their energy efficiency and strong governance structures.

- Polkadot is known for its innovative parachain architecture, connecting different blockchains for seamless interoperability. This minimizes energy consumption while supporting the development of diverse blockchain ecosystems. Additionally, Polkadot's decentralized governance model enables token holders to participate in decision making, aligning with ESG governance criteria.
- Cardano is energy-efficient thanks to its Ouroboros PoS protocol and emphasizes social impact. The Cardano Foundation invests

in various global initiatives, particularly in developing countries, aiming to promote financial inclusion, identity verification, and education. This focus aligns with the social components of ESG. Cardano's transparent governance and peer-reviewed scientific approach further strengthen its candidacy for ESG integration.

- Tezos emphasizes energy efficiency and on-chain governance. Its self-amendment capability through on-chain voting allows for network evolution without hard forks, promoting decentralization and democratic governance. This participatory governance structure appeals to investors focused on governance, while its low energy consumption satisfies environmental criteria.

Mustafa et al. (2024) also highlight potential strategies such as directing financial returns from cryptocurrencies toward alternative energy projects and supporting various environmental SDGs. This fosters a positive impact on the overall ecosystem.

Beyond environmental considerations, many PoS blockchains provide better governance structures compared to traditional cryptocurrencies like Bitcoin. Blockchains such as Tezos and Polkadot allow token holders to vote on network upgrades and protocol changes, promoting decentralized governance and transparency. These qualities align with the governance (G) component of ESG, ensuring that investors can actively participate in decision-making processes.

By giving stakeholders a voice in shaping the future of their networks, these blockchains foster a more democratic approach to decision making. This contrasts with Bitcoin, where centralized mining power is concentrated in a few large mining pools that wield significant control over the network.

In addition to existing energy-efficient solutions, blockchain technology is continually advancing with innovations like Layer-2 scaling solutions (e.g., Optimism and Arbitrum). These solutions help reduce energy consumption even further by processing transactions off-chain while maintaining the security of the main chain. This ongoing focus on sustainability, scalability, and governance is likely to increase the number of ESG-compliant digital assets in the future.

New PoS networks, such as Avalanche and Solana, are also implementing energy-efficient models along with governance frameworks that meet ESG criteria. As these networks continue to develop, they provide more options for investors interested in integrating sustainable cryptocurrencies into their portfolios.

Tokenized ESG Investments

Tokenized Green Bonds. Green bonds are financial instruments designed to raise capital for environmentally friendly projects, such as renewable energy initiatives, energy efficiency upgrades, and climate resilience infrastructure. Traditionally, these bonds have been less accessible to retail investors due to high entry barriers, limited liquidity, and complex processes for buying and selling.

By tokenizing green bonds, blockchain technology allows these bonds to be broken into smaller digital units or tokens, making them more accessible to a broader range of investors. This tokenization enables fractional ownership, allowing retail investors and smaller institutional investors to participate in sustainable projects that previously required large capital commitments.

Blockchain's immutable ledger provides real-time tracking of how the funds raised by green bonds are allocated and used. Investors can have greater confidence that their funds are directed toward genuine environmental projects. This level of transparency aligns with the governance aspect of ESG criteria, as it promotes accountability and reduces the risk of greenwashing—misleading claims about environmental benefits.

- Example: A renewable energy company could issue tokenized green bonds on a blockchain to fund the development of a new solar farm. Investors could purchase these tokens, representing fractional ownership in the bond, and track how their investment is used to build clean energy infrastructure, benefiting from both financial returns and a positive environmental impact.

Renewable Energy Credits. Renewable energy credits (RECs) are market-based instruments that represent the environmental benefits of generating electricity from renewable sources, such as wind or solar power. Each REC certifies that 1 megawatt-hour (MWh) of electricity has been produced from a renewable energy resource.

Tokenizing RECs on the blockchain allows for secure, transparent, and efficient trading of these credits. Investors can buy, sell, and trade these tokens to offset their carbon footprint or support renewable energy production. Blockchain ensures that each tokenized REC is unique and cannot be double-counted, addressing concerns about authenticity and legitimacy.

Traditional REC markets can be opaque and fragmented, making it difficult for retail investors or small businesses to participate. Tokenization of RECs creates a more liquid market, allowing for easier access to these credits with lower barriers to entry. Blockchain-based platforms enable faster, more cost-effective transactions, enhancing the efficiency of REC trading.

- Example: An energy company could tokenize its RECs on a blockchain and offer them to institutional and retail investors who wish to invest in and support renewable energy. By holding these tokens, investors indirectly fund clean energy generation and can trade their tokens to balance their energy consumption with renewable energy production.

Social Impact Projects. Tokenizing investments in social impact projects allows investors to support initiatives focused on improving societal outcomes, such as affordable housing, clean water projects, health care access, and education in underserved regions. Blockchain enables the fractionalization and broader distribution of these investments, allowing more people to contribute to impactful social ventures.

Blockchain's inherent transparency allows investors to track how funds are used and measure the success of social impact projects in real time. This accountability ensures that capital is deployed as promised, fostering trust between investors and project leaders.

Investors can be assured that their contributions generate the intended social outcomes.

- Example: A nonprofit organization could tokenize its fundraising for building schools in underserved areas by issuing tokens that represent fractional ownership in the project. Investors can track their contributions through blockchain, ensuring that their money is going directly to building infrastructure and improving education for children in need.

Carbon Credits and Carbon Offsets. Carbon credits and carbon offsets represent the reduction or removal of greenhouse gases from the atmosphere. These instruments are essential for organizations and individuals seeking to reduce their carbon footprint and achieve environmental sustainability goals. By tokenizing carbon credits, we can create a transparent, secure, and efficient market for trading carbon offsets.

Tokenized carbon credits simplify the process for companies and investors who want to purchase carbon offsets and contribute to carbon reduction projects. Blockchain technology provides a transparent ledger that tracks the issuance, sale, and retirement of carbon credits, ensuring the authenticity of these offsets. This helps to prevent issues like double counting, where the same carbon credit is used multiple times by different entities.

Tokenization enhances the liquidity of carbon credits by allowing fractional ownership, making these markets more accessible. Investors can buy small portions of carbon credits rather than needing significant capital to purchase an entire credit. Additionally, blockchain facilitates cross-border carbon trading, enabling organizations worldwide to engage in global carbon markets.

- Example: An organization focused on reforestation could issue tokenized carbon credits on a blockchain. Investors who purchase these tokens would directly fund the planting of trees, and they could track the impact of their investment in real time.

These credits could also be sold or transferred on a marketplace, offering investors flexibility.

ESG-Compliant Tokenized Funds.   Blockchain technology also allows for the creation of ESG-compliant tokenized funds that pool investments into a diversified portfolio of sustainable assets. Such funds could include green bonds, renewable energy investments, or shares in companies with strong ESG performance. By tokenizing the fund, investors can access fractional portions of the overall portfolio, increasing participation and liquidity.

Tokenized funds provide a way to democratize access to institutional-grade ESG investments, allowing retail investors to participate alongside larger investors. The transparency afforded by blockchain grants full visibility into the fund's holdings and performance, making it easier for investors to assess the sustainability impact of their investments.

- Example: An investment manager could create a tokenized ESG fund comprising assets such as renewable energy projects, green bonds, and socially impactful start-ups. Investors could buy tokens representing a share of the fund, benefiting from diversification and gaining exposure to a range of sustainable investments.

Sustainability-Focused Funds and Indexes

Screening Digital Assets for ESG Compliance.   ESG-focused digital asset funds and indexes utilize screening processes to ensure that only projects with positive ESG impacts are included in their portfolios. These screening processes may involve the following:

- Funds typically exclude digital assets that have a high carbon footprint or consume excessive energy. For instance, PoW cryptocurrencies like Bitcoin are often excluded due to the significant energy consumption associated with their mining. In contrast, PoS cryptocurrencies, such as Ethereum (after the

Merge), Cardano, and Tezos, are favored because they are more energy-efficient and consume considerably less power.

- In addition to environmental factors, ESG-focused funds also evaluate the social and governance aspects of digital assets. This assessment may include examining projects that prioritize financial inclusion, promote fair governance structures, and contribute to positive social outcomes, such as enhanced access to financial services or support for decentralized governance.
- For example, a digital asset fund might exclude Bitcoin because of its environmental impact but include Polkadot and Solana, which both utilize energy-efficient consensus mechanisms. Furthermore, the fund may prioritize projects with strong governance protocols, such as Tezos, where community voting on protocol changes ensures that power is distributed among stakeholders.

Diversified Exposure to ESG-Compliant Cryptocurrencies. ESG-focused digital asset funds provide investors with diversified exposure to a range of cryptocurrencies that align with sustainability and ethical standards. These funds aim to distribute risk across multiple ESG-compliant digital assets, thereby minimizing exposure to environmentally harmful or socially irresponsible projects.

Similar to traditional ESG funds, these digital asset funds offer a diversified portfolio that balances risk with potential returns. Investors gain exposure to various blockchain projects, ensuring that they are not overly dependent on any single digital asset while still adhering to their ESG values.

- For example, an ESG digital asset index might track the performance of a basket of PoS cryptocurrencies, such as Ethereum, Cardano, Avalanche, and Polkadot, which are regarded as environmentally friendly and uphold ethical governance. By spreading investments across these assets, investors can reduce their risk while remaining committed to ESG principles.

Excluding High-Carbon Footprint Cryptocurrencies. One of the key strategies employed by ESG-focused digital asset funds is the exclusion of high-carbon-footprint cryptocurrencies, primarily Bitcoin, from their portfolios. Bitcoin's PoW consensus mechanism requires substantial computational power, resulting in high energy consumption and raising concerns about its environmental impact.

Bitcoin mining consumes enormous amounts of electricity, often sourced from nonrenewable energy sources, making it a target for ESG-conscious investors who aim to minimize the carbon footprint of their portfolios. A 2021 study by the Cambridge Centre for Alternative Finance estimated that the Bitcoin network consumes more energy annually than entire countries, such as Argentina or the Netherlands.

In contrast, ESG funds prioritize assets based on PoS mechanisms, such as Polkadot, Tezos, and Algorand, which consume significantly less energy. These projects are designed to be more sustainable while still providing the benefits of decentralization and security.

- For example, an ESG-focused digital asset fund might completely exclude Bitcoin due to its substantial environmental impact and instead concentrate on staking-based cryptocurrencies that achieve similar decentralization and security goals with minimal energy consumption.

Blockchain Projects Promoting Positive Social and Governance Outcomes. Many digital asset funds and indices that focus on ESG criteria go beyond simply screening for environmental factors. They also include projects that promote positive social and governance outcomes. This may involve blockchain initiatives aimed at enhancing financial inclusion, democratic governance, and transparency within their ecosystems.

Projects that target social inclusion are often prioritized in ESG-focused funds. For example, DeFi protocols that provide financial services to unbanked populations or blockchain initiatives that improve access to health care and education align well with the social (S) component of ESG. These projects address global challenges and contribute to societal well-being.

Furthermore, ESG-compliant digital assets emphasize strong governance structures to ensure transparent, decentralized, and accountable decision making. Blockchains with on-chain governance systems—such as Tezos and Cardano—allow token holders to vote on network upgrades and changes, fostering a democratic and transparent process. This aligns with the governance (G) aspect of ESG, which seeks ethical management and accountability.

- For instance, an ESG digital asset index might feature a combination of blockchain projects that support both environmental sustainability and social good. Examples include SolarCoin, which rewards renewable energy producers, and Cardano, which promotes financial inclusion in developing economies.

Simplified ESG Integration for Investors. ESG-focused digital asset funds and indexes offer a straightforward way for investors to integrate cryptocurrencies into their portfolios while adhering to sustainable investment principles. Instead of conducting in-depth analyses of individual blockchain projects, investors can utilize these funds, which feature prevetted, ESG-compliant digital assets.

For both retail investors and institutions seeking exposure to digital assets without the complexity of assessing each asset's ESG impact, these funds provide a convenient solution. By investing in such a fund or index, investors can be confident that their capital supports cryptocurrencies aligned with their ethical and sustainability goals.

- For example, a fund manager offering an ESG-focused cryptocurrency ETF could target institutional investors who want to capitalize on the growth potential of blockchain technology, but are hesitant to support cryptocurrencies with high carbon footprints. This ETF could be positioned as a sustainable alternative to traditional crypto ETFs.

As global demand for sustainable investing continues to grow, the emergence of ESG-focused digital asset funds and indexes may capture a significant portion of the market. Investors are increasingly cognizant of the environmental and ethical implications of their investments, and these products provide a way to engage with the growth of the cryptocurrency space while aligning with socially responsible investing principles.

ESG investing has seen exponential growth in traditional finance, and a similar trend is now emerging in the digital asset realm. Asset managers who launch ESG-compliant cryptocurrency funds stand to benefit from the rising demand for sustainability-driven products among both retail and institutional investors.

By concentrating on sustainable projects with innovative governance structures, these funds may even outperform traditional digital asset indices in the long term, as environmentally and socially responsible projects gain broader acceptance and support from investors.

Use of DeFi and ESG Yield Strategies

As DeFi continues to grow, integrating ESG principles into these strategies is becoming increasingly viable for socially conscious investors. By selecting DeFi projects and protocols that prioritize sustainability, ethical governance, and positive social outcomes, investors can align their portfolios with their ESG values while still benefiting from the lucrative opportunities that DeFi offers.

Yield Farming and ESG Integration.   Yield farming is a popular DeFi strategy that involves providing liquidity to DeFi protocols in exchange for rewards, typically in the form of tokens. Investors can maximize their returns by shifting assets between different liquidity pools. However, incorporating ESG considerations into yield farming requires careful selection of DeFi projects that are both environmentally sustainable and ethically managed.

Some DeFi platforms are forming partnerships with initiatives focused on carbon offsetting and sustainable development. These platforms may allocate a portion of yield farming rewards to fund environmental initiatives or donate a percentage of transaction fees to support renewable energy projects or reforestation efforts.

- Example: A yield farming platform that incorporates carbon offsetting into its operations could automatically use part of the fees or rewards generated to purchase carbon credits, thereby neutralizing its carbon footprint. Investors participating in such platforms can earn passive income while supporting environmentally friendly initiatives.

ESG-conscious investors can seek out DeFi projects operating on energy-efficient blockchains, such as those utilizing PoS or layer-2 scaling solutions. Yield farming on platforms built on Ethereum 2.0, Cardano, or Polygon is aligned with environmental sustainability, as these platforms consume less energy compared to traditional PoW chains (Mendoza Tovar 2022).

Staking and Supporting Governance-Driven Projects.   Staking involves locking up a certain amount of cryptocurrency on a DeFi platform to support the network's operations in exchange for staking rewards. While staking offers passive income opportunities, ESG-conscious investors can enhance this by selecting projects that prioritize sustainable governance and social impact.

Many DeFi platforms enable users to participate in the governance of the protocol through on-chain voting. This allows stakers to influence key decisions, such as protocol upgrades, fee structures, or sustainability initiatives. Engaging in these governance processes ensures that power is distributed among community members, promoting decentralized and transparent decision making—an essential aspect of the governance (G) component of ESG.

- Example: By staking on platforms like Tezos, which incorporates democratic governance mechanisms, investors not only earn staking rewards but also help shape the future direction of the platform. Projects that prioritize transparent decision making and community involvement can be included in ESG-conscious portfolios, as they promote fairness and accountability.

Staking on PoS networks is inherently more energy-efficient than participating in PoW mining, making it a sustainable alternative. Investors can explore staking opportunities on projects such as Cardano, Avalanche, or Algorand, which emphasize both sustainability and strong governance.

Liquidity Provision With ESG Focus.   Liquidity provision involves supplying capital to DeFi exchanges or protocols to facilitate trading. In return, liquidity providers earn fees or governance tokens. For investors who prioritize ESG criteria, selecting liquidity pools associated with platforms or projects that emphasize sustainability and ethical practices can be a method to generate passive income while supporting responsible initiatives.

ESG-Focused Liquidity Pools.   Some DeFi platforms allow investors to choose liquidity pools that specifically support environmental or social causes. These platforms may allocate a portion of the trading fees generated from the pool to sustainability efforts, such as reforestation or renewable energy projects.

- Example: A platform like SolarCoin could establish a liquidity pool where fees earned from transactions are directed toward supporting solar energy development or funding solar projects around the globe. Investors providing liquidity to these pools can earn income while contributing to sustainable energy solutions.

Additionally, DeFi projects can create liquidity pools aimed at financing socially impactful initiatives, such as clean water access, education programs, or health care services in underserved communities. By participating in these pools, liquidity providers can align their investments with projects that produce tangible social benefits.

Sustainable DeFi Protocols and Carbon Offsetting Initiatives.   Some DeFi protocols have integrated carbon offsetting features into their models to reduce the environmental impact of their operations. These protocols enable users to engage in DeFi activities, such as yield farming or staking, while offsetting their carbon footprint, effectively incorporating ESG principles into their investment strategies.

DeFi platforms can collaborate with carbon offsetting providers to ensure that users' activities—whether staking, providing liquidity, or farming yields—automatically contribute to offsetting the carbon emissions associated with blockchain technology. This is especially important for high-volume DeFi participants who wish to mitigate the environmental effects of their investments.

- For example, a protocol like KlimaDAO allows users to purchase carbon credits directly through its platform. By participating in this protocol, DeFi users can support global efforts to reduce greenhouse gas emissions, combining passive income generation with a positive environmental impact.

Additionally, some DeFi platforms are tokenizing green bonds and offering them within liquidity pools. Investors can provide liquidity to these pools, which indirectly funds environmentally sustainable projects, such as renewable energy, energy efficiency, or climate resilience initiatives. These tokenized green bonds generate returns for liquidity providers while directing capital toward sustainability projects.

ESG and Governance in DeFi Protocols.   The governance structures of DeFi platforms play a crucial role in integrating ESG principles. Projects that emphasize decentralized governance, transparency, and community engagement align more closely with ESG values, particularly the Governance (G) pillar. ESG-focused DeFi portfolios often concentrate on projects that empower token holders to participate in governance decisions and influence the ethical direction of the protocol.

DeFi projects that facilitate on-chain voting and maintain transparent decision-making processes provide more inclusive and democratic governance models. These features help ensure that control is distributed among a wide range of stakeholders rather than being concentrated in the hands of a few developers or early investors.

- For example, DeFi platforms such as Uniswap and Aave offer governance tokens that enable users to vote on protocol changes, fee structures, or the implementation of new sustainability initiatives. Including these types of protocols in an ESG-focused DeFi portfolio ensures that governance practices align with ethical investing principles.

Sustainable Development Initiatives in DeFi.   Some DeFi projects are specifically designed to support SDGs, making them appealing to ESG-focused investors. These initiatives may directly invest in renewable energy, sustainable agriculture, or other environmentally beneficial projects.

- For instance, a DeFi platform could create a protocol that funds clean water projects or renewable energy development through liquidity pools or staking mechanisms. By integrating SDGs into their project roadmaps, these platforms provide DeFi users with opportunities to earn rewards while supporting global sustainability efforts.

Active Engagement With Projects

Just as traditional asset managers engage with companies to enhance their ESG performance, investors in digital assets can interact with blockchain projects to promote sustainable practices and improved governance. For instance, investors might encourage these projects to implement more energy-efficient consensus mechanisms, increase transparency in their governance structures, or enhance the social impact of their platforms. By actively participating in governance—such as voting rights in PoS systems—investors can influence the direction of blockchain projects and ensure they align with ESG values.

ESG Metrics and Tools for Digital Asset Evaluation

Traditional financial markets have established frameworks for assessing ESG performance. However, the digital asset space—particularly cryptocurrencies, DeFi projects, and blockchain platforms—is still in the early stages of integrating these evaluation standards. Fortunately, new ESG metrics and tools are emerging to help investors assess the sustainability, ethical practices, and governance structures of digital assets. This makes it easier to incorporate ESG principles into blockchain-related investments.

Environmental Metrics

The environmental aspect of ESG focuses on the sustainability of blockchain projects, especially regarding their energy consumption and carbon footprint. Given the energy-intensive nature of some cryptocurrencies, particularly those that use PoW consensus mechanisms, investors need reliable metrics to evaluate their environmental impact.

Energy Consumption.   One of the most commonly tracked metrics for digital assets is energy usage, especially for PoW-based cryptocurrencies like Bitcoin. Tools such as the Cambridge Bitcoin Electricity Consumption Index provide real-time estimates of the total energy consumption of the Bitcoin network, enabling investors to assess its sustainability. Energy-efficient alternatives like PoS blockchains—such as Cardano, Polkadot, and Ethereum 2.0—are often seen as more environmentally friendly due to their significantly lower energy requirements.

Carbon Footprint.   Carbon footprint calculators for digital assets measure the greenhouse gas emissions generated by mining or validating transactions on blockchain networks (Zhong 2024). Platforms such as the Crypto Carbon Ratings Institute provide carbon footprint data for various cryptocurrencies, helping investors understand the environmental impact of their portfolios.

Some digital assets and blockchain platforms engage in carbon offsetting initiatives or actively support renewable energy projects. Metrics that track the amount of carbon offset per transaction or the investment in green initiatives assist investors in identifying environmentally positive projects.

- One example is KlimaDAO, a decentralized autonomous organization focused on carbon markets. It offers tools for offsetting carbon emissions by enabling investors and companies to purchase carbon credits, ensuring transparency and accountability in efforts to reduce their environmental impact.

Social Metrics

The social dimension of ESG assesses how digital assets contribute to social responsibility, inclusivity, and positive societal outcomes. In the realm of digital assets, social metrics are particularly important for projects that focus on financial inclusion, privacy, education, and health care.

Financial Inclusion. A crucial social metric for blockchain projects is their ability to promote financial inclusion by providing access to financial services for unbanked or underbanked populations. This can be evaluated by tracking the adoption rates of DeFi platforms in underserved regions and measuring how effectively these projects offer affordable and accessible services.

Social Impact Projects. Blockchain-based initiatives that support socially beneficial causes, such as clean water access, education, or health care, can be assessed based on their impact size, the transparency of fund distribution, and the long-term benefits they bring to communities. For example, social impact platforms such as SolarCoin and Empowa, which focus on renewable energy production and affordable housing, respectively, can be evaluated based on the direct social benefits they provide.

User Privacy and Security.   Metrics that evaluate the level of data privacy and security offered by a digital asset project are also vital to the social framework. Projects prioritizing decentralized, secure, and private data management—such as privacy coins like Monero or Zcash—align with social responsibility by safeguarding user rights in the digital age.

- Example Tool: ImpactMetrics is a platform that provides detailed reports on blockchain projects aligned with the UN SDGs. It includes metrics related to poverty reduction, education, and clean energy, allowing investors to screen projects based on their social impact.

Governance Metrics

Governance in ESG evaluates the management structure, transparency, and accountability of digital asset projects. Strong governance is especially important for decentralized platforms, where decision-making processes are often distributed among community members rather than being centralized.

On-Chain Governance.   Many blockchain projects implement on-chain governance mechanisms, allowing token holders to vote on decisions such as protocol upgrades, changes to fee structures, and community initiatives. Governance metrics evaluate the degree of decentralization, voter participation, and transparency of these processes. Projects such as Tezos, Polkadot, and Aave have democratic governance systems that contribute to strong governance scores.

Transparency.   Transparency metrics assess how well a blockchain project discloses information about its development, funding, and team structure. This may include tracking the auditing of smart contracts, public availability of roadmaps, and clarity in how project funds are utilized. Projects with well-documented development processes and regular financial disclosures tend to score higher in governance transparency.

Developer Activity and Community Engagement.   Governance metrics can also track developer activity and community participation. Open-source projects with a high number of contributors and robust developer ecosystems usually exhibit more resilient governance. Projects that engage regularly with their community and seek input from users on major decisions demonstrate a commitment to inclusive governance.

- Example Tool: DeepDAO tracks the governance activities of DAOs, providing insights into voter participation, proposal success rates, and the decentralization of governance. Investors can use this data to assess the governance health of DeFi projects and protocols.

ESG Rating Platforms

Several platforms now provide ESG ratings for digital assets, combining various metrics to offer a comprehensive view of a project's sustainability and ethical performance. These platforms are essential tools for ESG-conscious investors who aim to integrate digital assets into their portfolios while adhering to responsible investment principles.

Crypto ESG Ratings.   These platforms gather data on multiple ESG factors, such as energy efficiency, governance practices, social impact, and carbon offset initiatives. They rank digital assets based on these factors, simplifying the comparison of ESG credentials across different blockchain projects.

- Example Tool: SustAIn Crypto offers an ESG rating system specifically designed for digital assets, providing transparent reports on the environmental footprint, governance structures, and social impact of various cryptocurrencies. This empowers investors to make informed decisions based on a project's overall ESG performance.

Blockchain-Based Tracking and Reporting Tools

Blockchain technology itself provides unique capabilities for ESG reporting and tracking, ensuring real-time transparency and immutability. These tools enable investors to monitor ESG-related data on-chain, thereby guaranteeing the accuracy and accountability of the information.

Blockchain platforms that tokenize carbon credits, renewable energy certificates, or green bonds can supply real-time data on the environmental benefits of an investment. Investors can utilize blockchain-based tools to track how their investments contribute directly to carbon reduction or other environmental objectives.

- Example Tool: Veridium is a blockchain-based platform that tokenizes carbon credits, making it straightforward for investors to track and offset their carbon emissions. Investors can verify that their investments are making a sustainable impact through transparent, blockchain-based records.

Third-Party Audits and Certifications

Another way to ensure ESG compliance in digital assets is through third-party audits and certifications, providing independent verification of a project's ESG claims. These certifications help investors avoid projects that might engage in greenwashing or make misleading claims about their sustainability efforts.

- Example: Blockchain projects can undergo carbon footprint audits by external organizations, such as the Crypto Climate Accord, which certifies projects based on their initiatives to reduce or eliminate carbon emissions. Projects that achieve certifications or meet specific standards can include this information in their ESG metrics, enhancing transparency and credibility.

Artificial Intelligence and Machine Learning in Digital Assets Investing

The integration of AI and ML into digital asset investing has revolutionized how investors analyze the highly volatile and complex cryptocurrency markets. As digital assets continue to grow in scale and sophistication, AI and ML technologies provide powerful tools for enhancing decision making, improving trading strategies, and managing risk. These technologies leverage vast datasets, identify market patterns, and adapt to real-time market changes, making them invaluable in the fast-paced world of cryptocurrencies, DeFi, and tokenized assets. Following are the key ways AI and ML are utilized in digital asset investing.

Predictive Analytics and Market Forecasting

AI-driven models can analyze large amounts of data to forecast future price movements and trends in digital asset markets. ML algorithms are particularly adept at recognizing historical patterns and making predictions based on past behavior.

Sentiment Analysis

AI models can gather and analyze data from news outlets, social media platforms, and forums to gauge market sentiment, indicating whether investors are feeling optimistic (bullish) or pessimistic (bearish). This sentiment analysis can inform trading strategies, helping investors capitalize on shifts in market mood.

Casillo et al. (2022) pointed out that tools based on ML and deep learning techniques can accurately identify market phenomena. Their research demonstrated that an approach utilizing the Recurrent Radial Basis Function Network is effective for predicting a given digital asset by analyzing sentiments expressed in online discussions.

Liu et al. (2024) conducted a case study investigating the correlation between news sentiment and Bitcoin prices. By employing advanced sentiment analysis and financial analysis methods, they showcased the practical application of large language models (LLMs). Their findings revealed a modest but discernible correlation between news sentiment and fluctuations in Bitcoin prices, highlighting that historical news patterns have a more significant impact on Bitcoin's long-term price than immediate news events. This underscores the potential of LLMs in market trend prediction and informed investment decision making.

Price Predictions

AI systems can monitor price movements, trading volume, and market volatility to generate price predictions and identify breakout trends. These systems continuously learn and improve over time, allowing them to adjust their predictions as market conditions change.

- For example, a hedge fund might use AI to forecast price movements in Bitcoin by analyzing historical trading data and trends from social media. If the algorithm detects a pattern reminiscent of previous bull markets, the fund could increase its investment in Bitcoin in anticipation of a price surge.

Mishra et al. (2023) discussed the application of ML algorithms for Bitcoin sentiment analysis to predict market movements and inform financial decisions. They employed a multimethod approach using six techniques: Naïve Bayes, K-Nearest Neighbors, XGBoost, Random Forest, Decision Tree, and SVM. Their findings indicated that Random Forest, Decision Tree, and SVM were the most effective models for predicting Bitcoin movements based on historical price data and sentiment analysis, which included both positive and negative viewpoints. The article concludes that while ML can accurately forecast Bitcoin price shifts and sentiment changes, the interpretability and reliability of these models should also be considered.

Algorithmic Trading and Automation

AI and ML are extensively utilized in algorithmic trading, where trading strategies are automated based on predefined rules and market signals. ML algorithms continuously optimize these strategies by learning from market data and adapting to changing conditions in real-time.

High-Frequency Trading

AI algorithms are crucial in high-frequency trading, allowing trades to be executed at high speeds and capitalizing on minor price fluctuations across exchanges. These AI-driven trades often occur too quickly for human traders to manage, enabling investors to seize arbitrage opportunities in the cryptocurrency market.

AI-Driven Trading Bots

Trading bots powered by AI can automatically execute buy or sell orders based on specific criteria, such as price thresholds, momentum indicators, or technical analysis patterns (e.g., MAs or the RSI). These bots eliminate emotional biases from trading decisions and operate 24/7, making them ideal for digital asset markets, which never close.

- Example: An AI-powered trading bot could be programmed to purchase Ethereum when its RSI indicates oversold conditions and sell it when it reaches overbought levels. The bot executes these trades automatically based on market conditions.

Risk Management and Portfolio Optimization

AI and ML play a critical role in helping investors manage risk and optimize their portfolios in the volatile digital asset space. These technologies assess a portfolio's risk profile in real time and recommend adjustments based on prevailing market conditions.

Risk Prediction Models

AI can develop risk models by analyzing historical data, market correlations, and volatility patterns to forecast potential downside risks. This enables investors to hedge or adjust their portfolios proactively before a significant market downturn occurs.

Dynamic Portfolio Rebalancing

ML algorithms can suggest or execute portfolio rebalancing strategies automatically, considering the investor's risk tolerance, desired asset allocation, and market performance. This is particularly important in cryptocurrency markets, where asset weightings can quickly become unbalanced due to extreme price fluctuations.

- Example: An AI system managing a diversified crypto portfolio might decrease exposure to high-risk altcoins during periods of heightened volatility while increasing allocations to stablecoins or more established assets like Bitcoin to preserve capital..

Fraud Detection

In practice, blockchain and cryptocurrencies are more vulnerable to malfeasance, fraud, and manipulation than many people realize. Castonguay and Smith (2020) argued that the security and trust offered by blockchain technology are only as strong as the underlying code that supports it, and the value of cryptocurrencies is only as dependable as the entity developing them. To address these challenges, AI and ML are being employed to enhance fraud detection and security within the cryptocurrency space. These technologies are essential for identifying fraudulent activities, suspicious transactions, and security breaches on exchanges and blockchain platforms.

Transaction Monitoring

ML algorithms can monitor blockchain transactions in real time, flagging suspicious activities such as wash trading, pump-and-dump schemes, or large transactions that may suggest potential market manipulation. These systems help protect both institutional and retail investors from malicious actors in the digital asset ecosystem.

Smart Contract Audits

AI tools can automatically audit smart contracts for vulnerabilities, identifying potential bugs or security flaws before they are deployed on DeFi platforms. This proactive approach helps prevent costly exploits and reduces the risk of hacks.

- Example: A cryptocurrency exchange might use an AI-powered fraud detection system to identify unusual trading patterns, such as a series of large sell orders placed across multiple accounts within a short time frame, which could indicate an attempt to manipulate prices.

Sentiment Analysis for NFTs and DeFi

AI-driven sentiment analysis is particularly valuable in niche digital asset markets, such as NFTs and DeFi tokens, where social sentiment can significantly influence market trends and investor behavior.

DeFi Sentiment Analysis

AI can track discussions about specific DeFi projects to assess investor sentiment, which helps predict whether a project is likely to gain momentum or face a downturn. This insight is critical in DeFi markets, where trust in a project's development team and community plays a major role in token valuation.

NFT Market Trends

In the NFT space, AI can identify rising artists, popular collections, or emerging trends in digital art, music, and collectibles by monitoring social media channels, NFT platforms, and transaction histories. This capability provides investors with a data-driven advantage when buying and selling NFTs.

- Example: An AI system might analyze sentiment data from Twitter and Discord to detect increasing interest in a specific NFT collection. Investors could leverage this insight to make early purchases before the collection gains broader market attention.

Smart Beta and Factor-Based Investing

AI and ML are being utilized to develop factor-based investing and smart beta strategies for digital assets. These strategies, common in traditional finance, rely on factors such as momentum, volatility, or growth to build portfolios that aim to outperform the market.

AI-Enhanced Factor Investing

ML algorithms can identify and optimize factors particularly relevant to digital assets, including network activity, token utility, developer engagement, and market sentiment. These factors can be used to design portfolios that maximize returns while managing risk.

- Example: A smart beta fund focused on digital assets might use AI to overweight assets with strong momentum and high on-chain activity while underweighting those that show declining developer engagement or poor liquidity.

Enhanced Due Diligence and Research

AI tools are increasingly used by institutional investors to conduct due diligence and research on digital assets, blockchain projects, and token ecosystems.

Data-Driven Insights

AI systems can analyze on-chain data, project roadmaps, whitepapers, and team backgrounds to provide deeper insights into the potential of digital asset projects (Bhumichai et al. 2024). This allows institutional investors to make more informed decisions about investing in or partnering with emerging projects.

- Example: A VC firm looking to invest in a new blockchain start-up might utilize AI tools to analyze the company's on-chain activity, assess developer activity on platforms like GitHub, and review sentiment surrounding the project in online communities.

Recommendations for Investors

As digital assets continue to evolve and play a larger role in the global financial ecosystem, investors face both new opportunities and challenges. The rapid growth of DeFi, the emergence of NFTs, and the increasing involvement of institutional players mean that the digital asset market is constantly changing. To navigate this complex landscape, investors must adopt a thoughtful and informed approach to balance risk and reward while capitalizing on long-term growth opportunities.

Conduct Thorough Research and Due Diligence

The digital asset market is still relatively young, and many projects are speculative in nature. Therefore, it is essential for investors to conduct thorough research on the projects, platforms, and assets they consider investing in.

Understand the Technology

Before investing in digital assets, it's crucial to understand the underlying technology, including how blockchain works and the specific characteristics of each digital asset. For instance, Bitcoin serves as a decentralized store of value, while Ethereum functions as a platform for smart contracts and decentralized applications. Familiarize yourself with the consensus mechanisms, governance models, and use cases of different blockchain networks to make informed decisions.

Evaluate the Team and Project Fundamentals

When investing in altcoins or emerging projects, it is vital to assess the team behind the project, their experience, and their long-term vision. Review the project's whitepaper, roadmaps, and partnerships to gauge its potential for success. Look for projects that address real-world problems, have robust developer communities, and demonstrate a clear path toward adoption and scalability.

Use Trusted Platforms and Custodians

Ensure that you use reputable cryptocurrency exchanges, wallets, and custodians to buy, store, and trade digital assets. Choose platforms with strong security protocols, regulatory compliance, and transparent operations. If managing large sums of capital or having security concerns, consider using institutional-grade custodians.

Stay Informed About Regulatory Developments

The regulatory landscape for digital assets is rapidly evolving, with different jurisdictions adopting various approaches to cryptocurrency regulation. Staying informed about these developments is crucial for investors, as regulations can significantly impact the market.

Monitor Global Regulatory Trends

Governments and regulatory bodies worldwide are increasingly focused on digital assets, particularly concerning AML, taxation, and securities laws. Regulatory changes can affect the legal status of certain assets, exchanges, or decentralized finance platforms. Investors should keep up-to-date with both global and local regulations, as these can influence access to platforms, taxation, and the legality of specific investments.

Prepare for Tax Implications

Cryptocurrencies are subject to tax regulations that vary by country. In many jurisdictions, digital assets are treated as property, and investors are required to report capital gains or losses on their cryptocurrency transactions. Ensure that you understand the tax implications of your investments and consider consulting a tax adviser for compliance.

Focus on Compliance and Regulation

Select exchanges and platforms that adhere to local regulations and prioritize transparency. Regulated platforms generally provide stronger protections for investors and offer the security and assurance necessary for long-term investments.

Teng et al. (2023) outlined several strategies and recommendations for regulators, market participants, and stakeholders based on quantitative analysis and empirical findings. These include:

1. Balancing Innovation and Risk: Formulate regulations that protect consumer and investor interests while fostering an environment conducive to innovation.
2. Promoting Global Regulatory Coordination: Enhance cooperation between regulatory bodies to minimize regulatory arbitrage and improve cross-border collaboration.
3. Utilizing Regulatory Sandboxes: Support the growth of digital asset businesses through innovation hubs that allow for continuous learning and adaptation.

Adopt a Long-Term Perspective

Given the early stage of the digital asset market, adopting a long-term investment perspective is crucial for maximizing returns and navigating periods of volatility.

Focus on the Big Picture

Blockchain technology and digital assets are still developing, and the market is expected to evolve significantly over the next decade. Investors who maintain a long-term view can take advantage of the potential for mass adoption, technological advancements, and the integration of DeFi into traditional financial systems. It is important to avoid getting distracted by short-term price fluctuations and instead concentrate on the broader trends influencing the market.

Be Patient and Avoid Market Timing

Attempting to time the market can be risky, especially in the volatile digital asset arena. Rather than trying to buy at the lowest price or sell at the highest, consider utilizing dollar-cost averaging. This strategy involves regularly investing a fixed amount regardless of the asset's price, which reduces the risk of purchasing at unfavorable prices and helps build your investment over time, thus smoothing out the impacts of volatility.

Adapt as the Market Evolves

The digital asset market is constantly evolving, with new technologies, platforms, and regulations emerging regularly. Investors must be flexible in adapting their strategies as the market matures. Stay informed about new developments, including the rise of DeFi, the influence of central bank digital currencies, and advancements in blockchain scalability and security.

Summary

Digital asset investing is rapidly changing the financial landscape, presenting both unique opportunities and challenges. As this sector evolves, integrating ESG principles will be increasingly important to ensure that digital assets contribute to a more sustainable and ethical future.

The use of AI and ML provides investors with powerful tools to navigate the complexities of these markets, offering deeper insights and enhanced decision-making capabilities. However, achieving success in digital asset investing requires more than just technology; it demands thorough research, staying updated on regulatory developments, and maintaining a long-term perspective.

By embracing these practices, investors can responsibly engage in the growth of digital assets while aligning their portfolios with sustainability and responsibility in mind, positioning themselves for future success in this dynamic market.

Appendix

Glossary of Terms

Altcoins: Refer to all cryptocurrencies other than Bitcoin.

Blockchain: A decentralized and public ledger that records all transactions made on the Bitcoin network.

Bollinger Bands: A widely used TA tool that helps investors and traders assess volatility and potential price movements of assets, including digital assets.

Central bank digital currencies (CBDCs): CBDCs are digital forms of a country's sovereign currency, fully backed and regulated by the central bank.

Correlation breakdown: Correlation breakdowns represent a problem for investors, risk managers, and the financial markets more broadly due to the fact that any risk protection endowed by portfolio diversification is lost.

Cryptography: The practice of securing communication through techniques that ensure data privacy, authenticity, and integrity.

Decentralized applications (dApps): Applications that run on a blockchain rather than centralized servers.

Digital euro: A digital euro would be a digital form of cash, issued by the central bank and available to everyone in the euro area.

Elliptic curve cryptography (ECC): A public-key cryptography algorithm that uses elliptic curves to generate security between key pairs. ECC is used to perform security functions such as encryption, authentication, and digital signatures.

Fibonacci retracement: A popular tool in technical analysis, based on the Fibonacci sequence, which helps traders identify potential levels of support and resistance where price retracements or reversals may occur.

Fundamental analysis: A method used by investors to evaluate the intrinsic value of an asset by examining various economic, financial, and qualitative factors.

Governance tokens: Governance tokens give holders the ability to vote on protocol changes and governance decisions within a decentralized organization or network.

Hedging: A risk management strategy that aims to reduce potential losses by taking offsetting positions in related assets or using specific financial instruments.

Liquidity: Refers to how easily an asset can be converted into cash without significantly affecting its price.

Meme coins: A subcategory of altcoins that are often created as a joke or based on internet culture and memes.

Merkle trees: Data structures that enhance the efficiency of Bitcoin and other cryptocurrencies.

Moving average convergence divergence (MACD): A momentum indicator that helps traders identify trend direction, strength, and potential reversals. It is based on the relationship between two MAs and is displayed as a MACD line and a signal line, along with a histogram showing the difference between the two.

Nodes: Components of a blockchain network, facilitating decentralized transactions. Nodes aim to validate and process transactions without the need for a centralized entity, striving to ensure the integrity and security of the network.

Pair trading: Involves taking opposite positions in correlated assets to hedge risk.

Platform tokens: These tokens are digital assets that power blockchain networks, typically those designed for creating and hosting dApps and smart contracts.

Privacy coins: Cryptocurrencies that are designed to provide greater anonymity and privacy for users by obscuring transaction details such as sender, receiver, and transaction amount.

Proof-of-work (PoW): A process that ensures all participants in the network agree on the state of the blockchain and that transactions are verified and added to the blockchain in a secure manner.

Public-key cryptography: Also known as asymmetric cryptography, public-key cryptography is a method of encryption that uses a pair of keys to protect data from unauthorized access.

Relative strength index (RSI): A key momentum indicator used to assess the speed and magnitude of recent price changes. It helps traders determine whether an asset is overbought or oversold and whether a price reversal is likely to occur.

Risk parity: An asset allocation strategy that aims to distribute risk equally across different asset classes, rather than allocating based solely on capital or expected returns.

Risk tolerance: Refers to an investor's ability and willingness to endure the volatility and potential loss of value in their portfolio.

Security tokens: These tokens represent ownership in real-world assets such as stocks, bonds, real estate, or other investment products.

Sentiment analysis: An essential tool for understanding and predicting price movements in digital asset markets.

Sentiment Indices: These Indices compile various metrics, including social media activity, volatility, and price momentum, to provide a clear picture of the market's emotional state.

Sharpe ratio: The Sharpe ratio compares the return of an investment with its risk. It's a mathematical expression of the insight that excess returns over a period of time may signify more volatility and risk, rather than investing skill.

Sortino ratio: The Sortino ratio is a risk-adjusted performance metric that measures how well an investment or portfolio performs during unfavorable market conditions. It is calculated by dividing an asset's excess returns by the standard deviation of its downside risk.

Smart contracts: Self-executing contracts with terms directly written in code, automatically running when predefined conditions are met.

Stablecoins: Stablecoins are designed to reduce the volatility typically associated with cryptocurrencies by pegging their value to a stable asset like fiat currency (e.g., the U.S. dollar), commodities (e.g., gold), or even other cryptocurrencies.

Strategic asset allocation: This approach focuses on long-term investment goals. It involves setting a target mix of asset classes that aligns with an investor's risk tolerance, financial objectives, and time horizon.

Tactical asset allocation: A short-term, dynamic strategy where investors actively adjust their portfolio weightings to take advantage of market opportunities or to defend against perceived risks

Technical analysis: A method used to predict future price movements based on historical market data, such as price charts, volume, and other market indicators.

Technical indicators: Mathematical calculations based on price, volume, or other market data.

Time horizon: Refers to the length of time an investor intends to hold investments before needing to withdraw funds.

Tokenization: The process of converting ownership of tangible or intangible assets into digital tokens that are recorded and transacted on a blockchain.

Tokenomics: Refers to the economic structure and incentives that govern the digital asset, including the token's supply dynamics, distribution model, and inflation rate.

Trend-following strategies: These strategies use fixed trading mechanism in order to take advantages from the long-term market moves without regard to the past price performance.

Utility tokens: Utility tokens grant users access to specific products or services within a blockchain network. These tokens are used to power dApps and protocols, offering various functionalities such as transaction fees, governance voting, and access to platform services.

Wash sale rules: These rules are designed to prevent investors from claiming a tax loss by selling an asset and then immediately repurchasing the same or a substantially identical asset within a short period.

Whales: Individuals or entities that hold large amounts of cryptocurrency. They may have an influence on the price and liquidity of a cryptocurrency.

References

Abakah, E.J.A., N. Trabelsi, A.K. Tiwari, and S. Nasreen. 2024. "Bitcoin, Fintech Stocks and Asian Pacific Equity Markets: A Dependence Analysis With Implications for Portfolio Management." the *Journal of Risk Finance*.

Abdul. R, M. Irfan, and W.Y. Lau. 2024. "Asset Allocation and Performance." In *Pension at Stake: Issues and Solutions to Defined Benefit Pension Scheme in Malaysia*, 47–71. Singapore: Springer Nature Singapore.

Adhami, S., and D. Guegan. 2020. "Crypto Assets: the Role of ICO Tokens Within a Well-Diversified Portfolio." *Journal of Industrial and Business Economics* 47 (2): 219–41.

Aggarwal, S., M. Santosh, and P. Bedi. 2018. "Bitcoin and Portfolio Diversification: Evidence From India." *Digital India: Reflections and Practice*, 99–115.

Aggarwal, V. 2022 "Optimum Investor Portfolio Allocation in New Age Digital Assets." *International Journal of Innovation Science* 14 (3/4): 648–58.

Ali, M.M., H.W. Cecil, and J.A. Knoblett. 2001. "The Effects of Tax Rates and Enforcement Policies on Taxpayer Compliance: A Study of Self-Employed Taxpayers." *Atlantic Economic Journal* 29: 186–202.

Ali, S., M.S. Ijaz, and I. Yousaf. 2023. "Dynamic Spillovers and Portfolio Risk Management Between Defi and Metals: Empirical Evidence From the Covid-19." *Resources Policy* 83: 103672.

Allen, F., X. Gu, and J. Jagtiani. 2022. "Fintech, Cryptocurrencies, and CBDC: Financial Structural Transformation in China." *Journal of International Money and Finance* 124: 102625.

Alnabulsi, K. 2024. "Asset Tokenization in Real Estate: Theoretical Perspectives and Empirical Approaches." *Blockchain in Real Estate: Theoretical Advances and New Empirical Applications*, 153–68.

Alvarez, F., D. Argente, and D.V. Patten. 2023. "Are Cryptocurrencies Currencies? Bitcoin as Legal Tender in El Salvador." *Science* 382 (6677): eadd2844.

Andrews, W.D., and P.J. 2024. *Wiedenbeck. Basic federal Income Taxation*. Aspen Publishing.

Angwald, A. 2023. "The Illumination of Money: An Ethnography of Bitcoin in El Salvador."

Aponte-Novoa, F.A., A.L.S. Orozco, R. Villanueva-Polanco, and P. Wightman. 2021. "The 51% Attack on Blockchains: A Mining Behavior Study." *IEEE Access* 9: 140549–64.

Arnone, G. "The Social and Environmental Impact of Cryptocurrencies." 2024. in *Navigating the World of Cryptocurrencies: Technology, Economics, Regulations, and Future Trends*, 91–102. Cham: Springer Nature Switzerland.

Arnone, G. 2024. "Popular Cryptocurrencies: Bitcoin and Beyond." In *Navigating the World of Cryptocurrencies: Technology, Economics, Regulations, and Future Trends* 25–33. Cham: Springer Nature Switzerland.

Belguith, R., Y.S. Manzli, A. Bejaoui, and A. Jeribi. 2024. "Can Gold-Backed Cryptocurrencies Have Dynamic Hedging and Safe-Haven Abilities Against DeFi and NFT Assets?." Digital Business 4 (2): 100077.

Benedetti, H., and G.R. Garnica. 2023. "Tokenized Assets and Securities."

Benedetti, H., and S. Labbé. 2023. "A Closer Look Into Decentralized Finance." In the *Emerald Handbook on Cryptoassets: Investment Opportunities and Challenges*, 327–40. Emerald Publishing Limited.

BenMabrouk, H., S. Sassi, F. Soltane, and I. Abid. 2024. "Connectedness and Portfolio Hedging Between NFTs Segments, American Stocks and Cryptocurrencies Nexus." *International Review of Financial Analysis* 91: 102959.

Beyhaghi, M., and J.P. Hawley. 2013. "Modern Portfolio Theory and Risk Management: Assumptions and Unintended Consequences." *Journal of Sustainable Finance & Investment* 3 (1): 17–37.

Bhanu, B.K. 2023. "Behavioral Finance and Stock Market Anomalies: Exploring Psychological Factors Influencing Investment Decisions." *Commerce, Economics & Management* 23.

Bhumichai, D., C. Smiliotopoulos, R. Benton, G. Kambourakis, and D. Damopoulos. 2024. "The Convergence of Artificial Intelligence and Blockchain: the State of Play and the Road Ahead." *Information* 15 (5): 268.

Casillo, M., M. Lombardi, A. Lorusso, F. Marongiu, D. Santaniello, and C. Valentino. 2022. "Sentiment Analysis and Recurrent Radial Basis Function Network For BitcoIn Price Prediction." In *2022 IEEE 21st Mediterranean Electrotechnical Conference (MELECON)*, 1189–93. IEEE. Castonguay, J. 2020. "Jack, and Sean Stein Smith." Digital Assets and Blockchain: Hackable, Fraudulent, or Just Misunderstood?." *Accounting Perspectives* 19 (4): 363–87.

Castro, J.G., E.A.H. Tito, L.E.T. Brandão, and L.L. Gomes.2020. "Crypto-Assets Portfolio Optimization Under the Omega Measure." the *Engineering Economist* 65 (2): 114–34.

Černý, O. 2023. "Bitcoin and the World-Systems Theory: the Case of El Salvador."Che, C., Z. Huang, C. Li, H. Zheng, and X. Tian. 2024. "Integrating Generative AI Into Financial Market Prediction For Improved Decision Making." *arXiv preprint arXiv*: 2404.03523.

Chu, J., S. Chan, and Y. Zhang. 2021. "Bitcoin Versus High-Performance Technology Stocks in Diversifying Against Global Stock Market Indices." *Physica A: Statistical Mechanics and Its Applications* 580: 126161.

Colombo, J., F. Cruz, L. Paese, and R. Cortes. "The Diversification Benefits of Cryptocurrencies in Multi-Asset Portfolios: Cross-Country Evidence." *SSRN* 3776260.

Conlon, T, S. Corbet, and L. Oxley. 2024. "Investor Sentiment, Unexpected Inflation, and Bitcoin Basis Risk." *Journal of Futures Markets.*

Correia, H.C.R.A. 2023. "Investment Policy Statement For Individual Investors: Medium-Low Risk Aversion Client Multi-Asset Balanced Portfolio." PhD diss., Instituto Superior de Economia e Gestão.

Demiralay, S., and S. Bayracı. 2021. "Should Stock Investors Include Cryptocurrencies in Their Portfolios After All? Evidence From a Conditional Diversification Benefits Measure." *International Journal of Finance & Economics* 26 (4): 6188–204.

Dhillon, R., and E. Nikbakht. 2023. "Cryptoassets in a Portfolio Context." In the *Emerald Handbook on Cryptoassets: Investment Opportunities and Challenges*, 185–98. Emerald Publishing Limited.

El Alaoui, A.O., A. Dchieche, and M. Asutay. 2021. "Combining Islamic Equity Portfolios and Digital Currencies: Evidence From Portfolio Diversification." *Fintech, Digital Currency and the Future of Islamic Finance: Strategic, Regulatory and Adoption Issues in the Gulf Cooperation Council*, 31–48.

Farabegoli, F., and N. Fucile. 2023. "Token Valuation: A Systematic Literature Review and Empirical Analysis."Fong, S., and J. Tai. 2009. "The Application of Trend Following Strategies in Stock Market Trading." In *2009 Fifth International Joint Conference on INC, IMS and IDC*, 1971–976. IEEE.

Ghabri, Y., K. Guesmi, and A. Zantour. 2021. "Bitcoin and Liquidity Risk Diversification." *Finance Research Letters* 40: 101679.

Goodell, J.W., M.P. Yadav, J. Ruan, M.Z. Abedin, and N. Malhotra. 2023. "Traditional Assets, Digital Assets and Renewable Energy: Investigating Connectedness During COVID-19 and the Russia-Ukraine War." *Finance Research Letters* 58: 104323.

Gotham, D., L. McKenna, M. Frick, and E. Lessem. 2020. "Public Investments in the Clinical Development of Bedaquiline." *PLoS One* 15 (9): e0239118.

Grossman, M. 2022. "Blockchain in the Middle East and North Africa (MENA): Opportunities For Regional Integration and Economic Growth." *Journal of International Business and Management* 5 (5): 01–19.

Guesmi, K., S. Saadi, I. Abid, and Z. Ftiti. 2019. "Portfolio Diversification With Virtual Currency: Evidence From Bitcoin." *International Review of Financial Analysis* 63: 431–37.

Gunay, S., and S. Muhammed. 2022. "Identifying the Role of Investor Sentiment Proxies in NFT Market: Comparison of Google Trend, Fear-Greed Index and VIX." *Fear-Greed Index and VIX.*

Gurrib, I., and F. Kamalov. 2022. "Predicting Bitcoin Price Movements Using Sentiment Analysis: A Machine Learning Approach." Studies in Economics and Finance 39 (3): 347–64.

Hafishina, A.D.R., J. Abraham, H.L.H.S. Warnars, R.H. Manurung, and T. Nainggolan. 2023. "Disrupting Money: Psychological Factors of Investment Biases in Cryptocurrency." TEM Journal 12 (1).

Han, Z. 2024. "Application of Machine Learning Techniques to Predict Price Trends During Bitcoin Halving Cycles." www.theseus.fi/handle/10024/865388.

Haven, REVISITING BITCOIN'S. SAFE. 2020. "BITCOIN AMID THE COVID-19 PANDEMIC: REVISITING BITCOIN'S SAFE HAVEN AND PORTFOLIO PERFORMANCE-ENHANCING PROPERTIES." Heines, R., C. Dick, C. Pohle, and R. Jung. 2021. "The Tokenization of Everything: Towards a Framework For Understanding the Potentials of Tokenized Assets." PACIS 40.

Hemphill, T.A. 2024. "US Central Bank Digital Currency: Benefits and Challenges to Policy Implementation." Bulletin of Science, Technology & Society: 02704676241285524.

Holovatiuk, O. 2020. "Cryptocurrencies as An Asset Class in Portfolio Optimisation." Central European Economic Journal 7 (54): 33–55.

Honerød-Bentsen, M., and A. Knutli. 2023. "Bitcoin vs. Traditional Indicies Analysing Performance and Risk Metrics for Long-Term Savings." Master's thesis, OsloMet-Storbyuniversitetet.

Huang, X., W. Han, D. Newton, E. Platanakis, D. Stafylas, and C. Sutcliffe. 2023. "The Diversification Benefits of Cryptocurrency Asset Categories and Estimation Risk: Pre and Post Covid-19." the European Journal of Finance 29 (7): 800–25.

Humayun, M. and R. Belk. 2024. "Creating Brand Hive Minds Through Bitcoin and the Blockchain" In Advances in Blockchain Research and Cryptocurrency Behaviour, edited by C. Strong, B. Martin and P. Chrysochou, 229–64. Berlin, Boston: De Gruyter. https://doi.org/10.1515/9783110981551-011.

Ilmanen, A., and J. Kizer. 2012. "The Death of Diversification Has Been Greatlyexaggerated." the Journal of Portfolio Management 38 (3): 15–27.

Irina, C. 2018. "Cryptocurrencies Legal Regulation." BRICS Law Journal 5 (2): 128–53.

Jaatinen, I. 2022. "Global Financial Risks of Cryptocurrencies: A Case Study of El Salvador." Jenweeranon, P. 2023. "Digitalisation in Finance: Regulatory Challenges in Selected ASEAN Countries." Banking & Finance Law Review 39 (3): 507–45.

Jeribi, A., and M. Fakhfekh. 2021. "Portfolio Management and Dependence Structure Between Cryptocurrencies and Traditional Assets: Evidence From FIEGARCH-EVT-Copula." Journal of Asset Management 22 (3): 224–39.

Kanani, P., J. Karasariya, N. Zadafiya, and A. Nayak. 2021. "A Ratiocinative Concept of Algorithmic Trading using MACD Indicator." In *2021 5th International Conference on Electronics, Communication and Aerospace Technology (ICECA)*, 369–76. IEEE.

Kantaphayao, W. 2021. "Cryptocurrencies and Traditional Assets: the Empirical Study in Dynamic Linkages and Portfolio Optimization."Kapengut, E., and B. Mizrach. 2023. "An Event Study of the Ethereum Transition to Proof-of-Stake." *Commodities* 2 (2): 96–110.

Kashyap, R. 2024. "The Blockchain Risk Parity Line: Moving From the Efficient Frontier To the Final Frontier of Investments." *arXiv preprint arXiv*:2407.09536.

Kavaloski, M. 2024. "A Global Crypto Code of Conduct: Crafting and Internationally Centralized Regulatory Body for a Decentralized Asset." *Vanderbilt Journal of Transnational Law* 57: 301.

Kawai, D., K. Soska, B. Routledge, A. Zetlin-Jones, and N. Christin. 2024. "Stranger Danger? Investor Behavior and Incentives on Cryptocurrency Copy-Trading Platforms." In *Proceedings of the CHI Conference on Human Factors in Computing Systems*,1–20.

Kesselman, J.R. 2024. "The Pivotal Role of Capital Gains in Efficient and Progressive Tax Reform." *Canadian Tax Journal/Revue Fiscale Canadienne* 72 (1): 1–32.

Ko, K, T. Jeong, J. Woo, and J. Won-Ki Hong. 2024. "Survey on Blockchain-Based Non-Fungible Tokens: History, Technologies, Standards, and Open Challenges." *International Journal of Network Management* 34 (1): e2245.

Koutsouri, A, F. Poli, E. Alfieri, M. Petch, W. Distaso, and W.J. Knottenbelt. 2020 "Balancing Cryptoassets and Gold: A Weighted-Risk-Contribution Index For the Alternative Asset Space." In *Mathematical Research for Blockchain Economy: 1st International Conference MARBLE 2019, Santorini, Greece*, 217–32. Springer International Publishing.

Kraft, D. 2016. "Difficulty Control for Blockchain-Based Consensus Systems." Peer-to-peer Networking and Applications 9: 397–413.

Krause, M.J., and T. Tolaymat. 2018. "Quantification of Energy and Carbon Costs For Mining Cryptocurrencies." *Nature Sustainability* 1 (11): 711–18.

Kshetri, N. 2023. "Discussion, Conclusion, and Recommendations." In: *Blockchain in the Global South. Palgrave Macmillan, Cham.* https://doi. org/10.1007/978-3-031-33944-8_6.

Le, T.H., and U. Ruthbah. 2023. "Trend-following Strategies for Crypto Investors." SSRN 4551518.

Li, N. 2024. "Research on Tail Risk Hedging in the Digital Asset Market." *Frontiers in Business, Economics and Management* 14 (1): 298–306.

Li, Z., H. Dong, C. Floros, A. Charemis, and P. Failler. 2022. "Re-Examining Bitcoin Volatility: A CAViaR-Based Approach." Emerging Markets Finance and Trade 58 (5): 1320–38.

Liu, C., A. Arulappan, R. Naha, A. Mahanti, J. Kamruzzaman, and R. In-Ho. 2024. "Large Language Models and Sentiment Analysis in Financial Markets: A Review, Datasets and Case Study." *IEEE Access*.

Ma, Y., F. Ahmad, M. Liu, and Z. Wang. 2020. "Portfolio Optimization in the Era of Digital Financialization Using Cryptocurrencies." Technological Forecasting and Social Change 161: 120265.

Maouchi, Y., M. Fakhfekh, L. Charfeddine, and A. Jeribi. 2024. "Is Digital Gold a Hedge, Safe Haven, or Diversifier? An Analysis of Cryptocurrencies, DeFi Tokens, and NFTs." *Applied Economics*, 1–16.

Markowitz, H. 1952. "Portfolio Selection." *the Journal of Finance* 7 (1): 77–91. http://links.jstor.org/sici?sici=0022-1082%28195203%297%3A1%3C77%3APS%3E2.0.CO%3B2-1.

Marthinsen, J.E., and S.R. Gordon. 2024. "Synthetic Central Bank Digital Currencies and Systemic Liquidity Risks." *International Journal of Financial Studies* 12 (1): 19.

Mazanec, J. 2021. "Portfolio Optimalization on Digital Currency Market." *Journal of Risk and Financial Management* 14 (4): 160.

M'bakob, G.B. 2024. "Bubbles in Bitcoin and Ethereum: the Role of Halving in the Formation of Super Cycles." *Sustainable Futures* 7: 100178.

Mendoza Tovar, E. U. T. I. M. I. O. 2022. "Of Thesis: Blockchain for Environmental Sustainability."

Mensi, W., M.U. Rehman, K.H. Al-Yahyaee, I.M.W. Al-Jarrah, and S.H. Kang. 2019. "Time Frequency Analysis of the Commonalities Between Bitcoin and Major Cryptocurrencies: Portfolio Risk Management Implications." *the North American Journal of Economics and Finance* 48: 283–294.

Mishra, R.K, A.R. Ansari, V. Mishra, and A.A. Jothi. 2023. "Machine Learning for Prediction of Emotion Towards Digital Assets." In *International Conference on Advances in Signal Processing And Communication Engineering*, 489–99. Singapore: Springer Nature Singapore.

Mokhtarian, E., and A. Lindgren. 2018. "Rise of the Crypto Hedge Fund: Operational Issues and Best Practices for An Emergent Investment Industry." *Stanford Journal of Law, Business & Finance* 23: 112.

Mustafa, F., C. Mordi, and A.A. Elamer. 2024. "Green Gold or Carbon Beast? Assessing the Environmental Implications of Cryptocurrency Trading on Clean Water Management and Carbon Emission SDGs." *Journal of Environmental Management* 367: 122059.

Nakamoto, S. 2008. "Bitcoin: A Peer-to-Peer Electronic Cash System." doi:10.2139/ssrn.3440802.

Neuby, B.L. 2022. "CENTRAL BANK DIGITAL CURRENCIES AND THE BUSINESS MODEL: REVIEW AND ANALYSIS." *International Journal of Business Research & Information Technology (IJBRIT)* 9 (1).

Olabanji, S.O., T.O. Oladoyinbo, C.U. Asonze, C.S. Adigwe, O.J. Okunleye, and O.O. Olaniyi. "Leveraging Fintech Compliance to Mitigate Cryptocurrency Volatility for Secure Us Employee Retirement Benefits: Bitcoin ETF Case Study." *Asian Journal of Economics, Business and Accounting* 24 (4): 147–67.

Papenbrock, J., P. Schwendner, and P.G. Sandner. "Can Adaptive Seriational Risk Parity Tame Crypto Portfolios?." *SSRN*: 3877143.

Parada, V. 2022. "Remittances to the Moon and Bitcoin to the Land of the Savior: Can El Salvador's Bitcoin Law Effectively Reduce the Cost of International Remittances?." *Houston Journal of International Law* 45: 151.

Parenti, A., and M. Billi. 2023. "Building Trust n Smart Legal Contracts." In *Transparency or Opacity*, 95–114. Nomos Verlagsgesellschaft mbH & Co. KG.

Petukhina, A, and E. Sprünken. 2021. "Evaluation of Multi-Asset Investment Strategies With Digital Assets." *Digital Finance* 3 (1): 45–79.

Petukhina, A, S. Trimborn, W.K. Härdle, and H. Elendner. "Investing With Cryptocurrencies–Evaluating Their Potential For Portfolio Allocation Strategies." *Quantitative Finance* 21 (11): 1825–53.

Platanakis, E., and A. Urquhart. 2020. "Should Investors Include Bitcoin in Their Portfolios? a Portfolio Theory Approach." the *British Accounting Review* 52 (4): 100837.

Pritchard, B.P.A. 2018. "Digital Asset Arbitrage." PhD diss.

Qian, C., N. Mathur, N.H. Zakaria, R. Arora, V. Gupta, and M. Ali. 2022. "Understanding Public Opinions on Social Media for Financial Sentiment Analysis Using AI-Based Techniques." *Information Processing & Management* 59 (6): 103098.

Rashid, A., W. Bakry, and S. Al-Mohamad. 2023. "Are Cryptocurrencies a Future Safe Haven for Investors? the Case of Bitcoin." *Economic research-Ekonomska istraživanja* 36 (2).

Rodríguez, Y.E., J.M. Gómez, and J. Contreras. 2021. "Diversified Behavioral Portfolio as An Alternative to Modern Portfolio Theory." the *North American Journal of Economics and Finance* 58: 101508.

Rossi, A. 2024. "Central Bank Digital Currencies: A New Nexus Between Central and Commercial Banks?." In *Digital Assets and the Law*, 67–82. Routledge.

Rühmann, F., S.A.Konda, P. Horrocks, and N. Taka. 2020. "Can Blockchain Technology Reduce the Cost of Remittances?."

Saef, D., O. Nagy, S. Sizov, and W.K. Härdle. 2024. "Understanding Temporal Dynamics of Jumps in Cryptocurrency Markets: Evidence From Tick-By-Tick Data." *Digital Finance* : 1–34.

Santos-Alborna, A. 2021. *Understanding Cryptocurrencies: Bitcoin, Ethereum, and Altcoins as an Asset Class.* Business Expert Press.

Sapra, N., and I. Shaikh. 2023. "Impact of Bitcoin Mining and Crypto Market Determinants on Bitcoin-Based Energy Consumption." *Managerial Finance* 49 (11): 1828–46.

Sarmini, S., C.R.A. Widiawati, D.R. Febrianti, and D. Yuliana. 2024. "Volatility Analysis of Cryptocurrencies Using Statistical Approach and GARCH Model a Case Study on Daily Percentage Change." *Journal of Applied Data Sciences* 5 (3): 838–48.

Scharfman, J. 2024. "Decentralized Autonomous Organization (DAO) Fraud, Hacks, and Controversies." In the *Cryptocurrency and Digital Asset Fraud Casebook, Volume II: DeFi, NFTs, DAOs, Meme Coins, and Other Digital Asset Hacks*, 65–106. Cham: Springer Nature Switzerland.

Scholz, P. 2012. *Size Matters! How Position Sizing Determines Risk and Return of Technical Timing Strategies.* No. 31. CPQF Working Paper Series.

Serres, J. 2023. "#AfricaToTheWorld: Economic Emancipation and Identity Affirmation in the Age of Global Digital Media." *PhD Thesis*, University of Oxford.

Shen, Y, and X. Li. 2024. "Analysis of Legal Risks of Transactions of Bitcoin Futures in Chinese Mainland." *US-China Law Review* 21 (1): 12–9.

Sheth, D, and M. Shah. 2023. "Predicting Stock Market Using Machine Learning: Best and Accurate Way to Know Future Stock Prices." *International Journal of System Assurance Engineering and Management* 14 (1): 118.

Takei, Y., and K. Shudo. 2024. "FATF Travel Rule's Technical Challenges and Solution Taxonomy." In *2024 IEEE International Conference on Blockchain and Cryptocurrency (ICBC)*, 784–99. IEEE.

Taskinsoy, J. 2021. Bitcoinmania: A Ticking Time Bomb Waiting to Explode. SSRN: https://ssrn.com/abstract=3861836 or http://dx.doi.org/10.2139/ssrn.3861836.

Teng, Huei-Wen, W.K. Härdle, J. Osterrieder, L.J. Baals, V.G. Papavassiliou, K. Bolesta, A. Kabasinskas, et al. 2023. "Mitigating Digital Asset Risks."

Thakur, D.S., R.A. Varma, and D.M. Hake. 2022 "Regulation of Cryptocurrency in India: Issues and Challenges." *Journal of Positive School Psychology* : 8921–29.

Thomadakis, A., K. Lannoo, F. Shamsfakhr, and J.A. Álvarez. 2023 "A Digital Euro Beyond Impulse-Think twice, Act Once."Trotz, E.D. 2021 "Million Dollar Bash: A Nuanced Approach for Calculating Tax Liability for Participants in Decentralized Finance." the *Texas Tech Law Review* 54: 575.

Umar, Z., M. Usman, C. Sun-Yong, and J. Rice. 2023. "Diversification Benefits of NFTs for Conventional Asset Investors: Evidence From CoVaR With

Higher Moments and Optimal Hedge Ratios." Research in International Business and Finance 65: 101957.

Vázquez, E. 2022. "The Technical Fix: Bitcoin in El Salvador." *South Atlantic Quarterly* 121 (3): 600–11.

Volosovych, S., A. Sholoiko, and Shevchenko, L. 2023. "CRYPTOCURRENCY MARKET TRANSFORMATION DURING PANDEMIC COVID-19." *Financial and Credit Activity Problems of Theory and Practice* 1 (48): 114–26. https://doi.org/10.55643/fcaptp.1.48.2023.3949.

Wang, C. 2023. "Trading Securities as Digital Tokens: is a Secondary Market Practicable for Tokenized Exempt Securities?." the *University of New Hampshire Law Review* 22: 39.

Wang, G., Y. Tang, C. Xie, and S. Chen. 2019. "Is Bitcoin a Safe Haven or a Hedging Asset? Evidence From China." *Journal of Management Science and Engineering* 4 (3): 173–88.

Wang, H. 2023 "How to Understand China's Approach to Central Bank Digital Currency?." *Computer Law & Security Review* 50: 105788.

Wang, L., P.K. Sarker, and E. Bouri. 2023. "Short-and Long-Term Interactions Between Bitcoin and Economic Variables: Evidence From the US." *Computational Economics* 61(4) : 1305–30.

Wendl, M., M.H. Doan, and R. Sassen. 2023. "The Environmental Impact of Cryptocurrencies Using Proof of Work and Proof of Stake Consensus Algorithms: A Systematic Review." *Journal of Environmental Management* 326: 116530.

Wronka, C. 2024. "Crypto-Asset Activities and Markets in the European Union: Issues, Challenges and Considerations for Regulation, Supervision and Oversight." *Journal of Banking Regulation* 25 (1): 84–93.

Wu, B., B. Wu. 2023. "Bitcoin: the Future of Money." In: *Blockchain for Teens*. Apress, Berkeley, CA. https://doi.org/10.1007/978-1-4842-8808-5_3.

Wu, X., L. Wu, and S. Chen. "Long Memory and Efficiency of Bitcoin During COVID-19." *Applied Economics* 54 (4) (2022): 375–89.

Xing, F.Z., E. Cambria, and R.E. Welsch. 2018. "Intelligent Asset Allocation Via Market Sentiment Views." *ieee ComputatioNal iNtelligeNCe magaziNe* 13(4): 25–34.

Yang, C., X. Wang, and W. Gao. 2022. "Is Bitcoin a Better Hedging and Safe-Haven Investment Than Traditional Assets Against Currencies? Evidence From the Time-Frequency Domain Approach." the *North American Journal of Economics and Finance* 62: 101747.

Yousaf, I., and L. Yarovaya. 2022. "Static and Dynamic Connectedness Between NFTs, Defi and Other Assets: Portfolio Implication." *Global Finance Journal* 53: 100719.

Youvan, D.C. 2024. "Navigating the Evolution of Ethereum: Vitalik Buterin's Vision for DeFi, Governance, and Scalability."Yuliana, L.E., and M.R. Iswardhana. 2024. "The Geoeconomics Analysis of the Digital Currency Law in El Salvador." *LEGAL BRIEF* 13 (3): 706–19.

Zhong, C. 2013. *Alternatives Thinker: Endowment Investment Philosophy to Active Portfolio Management*. Outskirts Press.

Zhong, C. 2024. *Climate-Conscious Investing: Portfolios Aligned With the Paris Accords*. Business Expert Press.

Zhu, X., P. Singh, J.D. Jayaraman, A.A. Rabaa'i, and A. Mishra. 2022. "Impact of Social Media on Digital Asset Markets." In *Proceedings of the Northeast Business & Economics Association*: 138–41.

About the Author

Dr. Chenjiazi Zhong is the founder of Fundopedia. She is a former portfolio manager (strategy chief investment officer) at BlackRock, the world's largest asset management firm by asset under management (AUM). Before BlackRock, Dr. Zhong was a fund PM at UBS, the world's largest private bank by AUM. She started her career as a Wall Street analyst at Lehman Brothers.

Dr. Zhong has also been a subject-matter expert and consultant in asset management. The institutions she has actively provided expert opinion since 2022 include McKinsey & Company, Boston Consulting Group, Bain & Company, Deloitte, PwC, and Ernst & Young. She is frequently invited to roundtable events and webcasts as a public speaker in the United States and Asia Pacific.

Dr. Zhong is the author of *Alternatives Thinker: Endowment Investment Philosophy to Active Portfolio Management*, *Strategies That Chinese Small and Medium-Sized Enterprises Used to Attract Venture Capital*, and *Climate-Conscious Investing: Portfolios Aligned with the Paris Accords*.

Index

www.ingramcontent.com/pod-product-compliance
Lightning Source LLC
Chambersburg PA
CBHW061145220326
41599CB00025B/4361